FIGURAL CONQUISTADORS

The Bucknell Studies in Latin American Literature and Theory
Series Editor: Aníbal González, Pennsylvania State University

Dealing with far-reaching questions of history and modernity, language and selfhood, and power and ethics, Latin American literature sheds light on the many-faceted nature of Latin American life, as well as on the human condition as a whole. This series of books provides a forum for some of the best criticism on Latin American literature in a wide range of critical approaches, with an emphasis on works that productively combine scholarship with theory. Acknowledging the historical links and cultural affinities between Latin American and Iberian literatures, the series welcomes consideration of Spanish and Portuguese texts and topics, while also providing a space of convergence for scholars working in Romance studies, comparative literature, cultural studies, and literary theory.

Titles in Series

Mario Santana, *Foreigners in the Homeland: The Latin American New Novel in Spain, 1962–1974*

Ronald J. Friis, *José Emilio Pacheco and the Poets of the Shadows*

Robert T. Conn, *The Politics of Philology: Alfonso Reyes and the Invention of the Latin American Literary Tradition*

Andrew Bush, *The Routes of Modernity: Spanish American Poetry from the Early Eighteenth to the Mid-Nineteenth Century*

Santa Arias and Mariselle Meléndez, *Mapping Colonial Spanish America: Places and Commonplaces of Identity, Culture, and Experience*

Alice A. Nelson, *Political Bodies: Gender, History, and the Struggle for Narrative Power in Recent Chilean Literature*

Julia Kushigian, *Reconstructing Childhood: Strategies of Reading for Culture and Gender in the Spanish American Bildungsroman*

Silvia N. Rosman, *Being in Common: Nation, Subjects, and Community in Latin American Literature and Culture*

Patrick Dove, *The Catastrophe of Modernity: Tragedy and the Nation in Latin American Literature*

James J. Pancrazio, *The Logic of Fetishism: Alejo Carpentier and the Cuban Tradition*

Frederick Luciani, *Literary Self-Fashioning in Sor Juana Inés de la Cruz*

Sergio Waisman, *Borges and Translation: The Irreverence of the Periphery*

Stuart Day, *Staging Politics in Mexico: The Road to Neoliberalism*

Amy Nauss Millay, *Voices from the* fuente viva: *The Effect of Orality in Twentieth-Century Spanish American Narrative*

J. Andrew Brown, *Test Tube Envy: Science and Power in Argentine Narrative*

Juan Carlos Ubilluz, *Sacred Eroticism: Georges Bataille and Pierre Klossowski in the Latin American Erotic Novel*

Mark A. Hernández, *Figural Conquistadors: Rewriting the New World's Discovery and Conquest in Mexican and River Plate Novels of the 1980s and 1990s*

Gabriel Riera, *Littoral of the Letter: Saer's Art of Narration*

FIGURAL CONQUISTADORS

Rewriting the New World's Discovery
and Conquest in Mexican and
River Plate Novels of the 1980s and 1990s

Mark A. Hernández

Lewisburg
Bucknell University Press

© 2006 by Rosemont Publishing & Printing Corp.

All rights reserved. Authorization to photocopy items for internal or personal use, or the internal or personal use of specific clients, is granted by the copyright owner, provided that a base fee of $10.00, plus eight cents per page, per copy is paid directly to the Copyright Clearance Center, 222 Rosewood Drive, Danvers, Massachusetts 01923. [0-8387-5645-X/06 $10.00 + 8¢ pp, pc.]

Associated University Presses
2010 Eastpark Boulevard
Cranbury, NJ 08512

The paper used in this publication meets the requirements of the American National Standard for Permanence for Printed Library Materials Z39.48-1984.

Library of Congress Cataloging-in-Publication Data

Hernández, Mark A., 1964–
    Figural conquistadors : rewriting the New World's discovery and conquest in Mexican and River Plate novels of the 1980s and 1990s / Mark A. Hernández.
      p. cm. — (The Bucknell studies in Latin American literature and theory)
    Originally presented as the author's thesis (Ph. D, University of Kansas).
    ISBN-10: 0-8387-5645-X (alk. paper)
    ISBN-13: 978-0-8387-5645-4 (alk. paper)
    1. Spanish American fiction—20th century—History and criticism. 2. Historical fiction, Spanish American—History and criticism. 3. Autobiographical fiction, Spanish American—History and criticism. 4. Geographical discoveries in literature. 5. Latin America—Discovery and exploration—Spanish. 6. Latin America—In literature. 7. Conquerors in literature. 8. National characteristics, Latin American, in literature. I. Title. II. Series.

PQ7082.H57H47   2006
863'.6409358098—dc22

2006042548

PRINTED IN THE UNITED STATES OF AMERICA

Contents

Acknowledgments	7
Introduction: Rereading the Chronicles of the Indies	11
1: Rewriting the *Relación* as Autobiography	23
2: Fictional Marginal Figures and the Rewriting of the New World Historiography	56
3: Rewriting Stories about Vilified Figures from the Conquest of Mexico	83
4: Restaging Columbus	110
Afterword	138
Notes	143
Bibliography	170
Index	185

Acknowledgments

This book originated as my doctoral thesis in the Department of Spanish and Portuguese at the University of Kansas. I would especially like to thank Vicky Unruh, Danny Anderson, and the late Jon Vincent for their encouragement and unwavering support in the formative stages of this project. In addition numerous institutions and individuals provided support, which has enabled its completion: the Consortium for a Strong Minority Presence Scholar-in-Residence Program and Grinnell College for a fellowship, which provided release time and funding to explore preliminary ideas for this book; Tufts University for granting me a one-semester Junior Faculty Research Leave and a Faculty Research Awards Committee grant-in-aid, which allowed me to revise and complete the final editing of the manuscript; and Andy Klatt for translating passages in this book from Spanish into English. I wish to express my gratitude to friends and colleagues who have supported me and this project: Robert Buffington, Elizabeth Coonrod-Martínez, Paul Fallon, Liette Gidlow, Fenfang Hwu, Claudia Kaiser-Lenoir, Edgar Landgraf, Irma López, Kathryn McKnight, Amy Millay, Iani del Rosario Moreno, Laura Podalsky, Douglas Weatherford, and Adriana Zavala. I would like to acknowledge the unconditional support from members of the extended Hernández family: my brother John and his wife Lynda; and my sisters Stephanie and Michelle. I dedicate this book to my mother Mary A. Hernández and in memory of my maternal grandmother, Flora G. Gonzáles. You are pioneering women of strength, courage, wisdom, and kindness.

Finally, I wish to thank the editors of various journals for granting permissions to reprint revised versions of my earlier publications. The following articles have been incorporated into chapters of this book: "The Buffoon and the Voyage of Magellan in Napoleón Baccino Ponce de León's *Maluco*," *Chasqui* 30.1 (May 2001): 3–13; "Restaging the Conquest of Michoacán: Víctor Castillo Bautista's *Nuño de Guzmán o la espada de Dios*," *Latin American Theatre Review* 37.1 (Fall 2003): 25–42.

FIGURAL CONQUISTADORS

Introduction: Rereading the Chronicles of the Indies

> Rereading the New World chronicles, the *cartas, relaciones,* and *historias,* has become a very popular enterprise in the face of the upcoming Quincentennial. While many scholars are straining to hear the voice of the "Other," silenced by the sword of the conquerors and the cross of the missionaries, it is equally important to reevaluate the voices that resounded loud and clear from the New World during the 16th century....
> —Frances Meuser-Blincow, "Rereading the New World Chronicles"

IN THE ABOVE EPIGRAPH FRANCES MEUSER-BLINCOW HIGHLIGHTS A SHIFT in the field of colonial Spanish American literary and cultural studies from an exclusive focus on canonical colonial writings of Spanish conquistadors such as Hernán Cortés's *Cartas de relación* and Alvar Nuñez Cabeza de Vaca's *Los naufragios* to noncanonical writings of indigenous subjects such as Guamán Poma de Ayala's *Nueva coronica y buen gobierno.* Moreover, she alludes to a shift in the methodologies that scholars of colonial Spanish American literary studies have employed to reinterpret the colonial corpus. Indeed, the years leading up to the 1992 quincentennial of Christopher Columbus's first voyage saw an increase in scholarship on early colonial Latin American writings, film, drama, and novels about the discovery, exploration, and conquest of the New World. In the realm of the Latin American novel, the writers hail from numerous countries that share a common colonial past, but their specific social and political circumstances have led them to represent the discovery and conquest in diverse and complex ways.

In this book I analyze a representative selection of Mexican and River Plate novels, published between 1980 and 1992, that rewrite episodes from the discovery and conquest of the New World. I contend that such novels engage in broader cultural conversations about notions of national and cultural identity at the end of the twentieth century. The Spanish chronicles about the discovery and conquest have served as a point of departure for these novelists to explore connections between the colonial past and the present and to interrogate issues of national and cultural identity in the late twentieth century. Their underlying collective project has both legitimating and subversive dimensions. On one level, they privilege the hegemonic voices of the Spanish conquistadors and recertify the canonical standing of the rewritten colonial texts. On another level, however, they radically challenge the univocal visions of the past as rendered by conventional historiographical methods and decenter the official history. All the novels under consideration in this book lay bare the mechanisms and conventions of the Spanish chronicles and challenge a traditional reading of such texts, but, in the end, they ultimately perpetuate the continued transmission of these so-called foundational writings of Latin American literature.

While the number of Latin American novels about the discovery and conquest increased around the quincentennial, interest in rewriting such episodes is not a recent phenomenon. Aníbal González Pérez argues that Latin American writers have returned to the discovery and colonization of the New World at three crucial periods in the nineteenth and twentieth centuries: 1820 to 1898, 1898 to 1968 and 1968 to the present. In each instance, they have not interpreted these periods in their unique sociohistorical context; rather, these periods have served as metaphors for articulating a contemporary discourse about Spanish American social and cultural history.[1] Re-presentations of the discovery and conquest in Latin American literature coincide with and diverge from methodologies that scholars and cultural critics of colonial Latin American studies have employed to read and interpret the Spanish chronicles of the Indies. In the following section I trace the trajectory of key moments when Latin American essayists, literary writers, and colonial scholars and critics have read and reread the Spanish chronicles of the Indies with particular agendas.

The Spanish chronicles of the Indies record the period of discovery, exploration, conquest, evangelization, and colonization of the New World in the sixteenth and seventeenth centuries. This heterogeneous corpus of writings, which encompasses letters, accounts, diaries, histories, and treatises, can be divided into two groups. The first is comprised of works of "original" writers such as Columbus, Hernán Cortés, and Alvar Núñez Cabeza de Vaca, who, as eyewitnesses, provided firsthand accounts of the events they recorded. The second includes the works of the copyists or interpreters such as Bartolomé de las Casas, Gonzalo Fernández de Oviedo, and Francisco López de Gómara, who saw the New World more through reconstructive imagination than through direct contact with the land.[2]

As Walter Mignolo has noted, the Spanish chronicles do not constitute a genre, but rather a discourse type that embraces several subtypes.[3] The development of the chronicles parallels and is marked by the historical events they record. They are by nature a hybrid of historical and literary texts: they are "historical" because of their informative and descriptive intentions and "literary" by virtue of their containing the personal story of an eyewitness informant. The New World chronicles were composed for a variety of reasons, which included informing royal authorities about an expedition of discovery and conquest, settling legal disputes between rival conquistadors over lands, and achieving fame and honor.[4] In the case of chronicles composed by "original" writers, such as Columbus's *Diario de a bordo* (1493), Cortés's *Cartas de relación* (1518–26), and Cabeza de Vaca's *Los naufragios* (1542/1556), the chronicles were conceived as official reports to the crown about the discovery and conquest and were designed to persuade the crown to offer financial compensation for services rendered to the monarchy. These writings, a mixture of historiographical and notarial forms, are represented by the *relación,* a legal document presenting the particular case of a person; it includes incidents of daily life, and does not attempt to reflect a transcendental truth.[5] In the case of chronicles composed by copyists, such as Las Casas's *Historia de las Indias* (1552) and his *Brevísima relación de la destrucción de las Indias* (1552), Oviedo's *Historia general y moral de las Indias* (1535), and Gómara's *Historia de la conquista de México* (1552), the chronicles conformed to the rhetorical conventions of Spanish Renaissance humanist historiography, which included a medieval providentialist scheme (which sees all events as part of a divine plan), a lofty tone, the presence of moral and theological dilemmas of the period, and elegant rhetorical prose.[6]

The first retrospective look at colonial writings and the chronicles was part of a vast enterprise of cultural self-definition within which the category "colonial literature" began to take shape in nineteenth-century Spanish America. As part of their movement for independence from Spain, Creole elites from Latin American countries required a beginning for their emerging literature. Between 1820 and 1898, Spanish American writers re-created imaginatively and polemically the colonial period and inflected their narratives with a marked anti-Spaniard/anticlerical streak and, at times, a nostalgia for the old order. In accordance with the tenets of the emerging liberal/ romantic historiography, these writers viewed the colonial period as Latin America's medieval period and emphasized the *Volk* aspects of national culture.[7]

At this same time, a change in the concept of historiography led to the excision of the founding texts of the New World from the historiographical canon. Critics incorporated chronicles such as Bernal Díaz del Castillo's *Historia verdadera de la conquista de la Nueva España* (1568) into Spanish American literature because of a change in the historiographical concept of truth and the literary-political need to posit a beginning for Spanish American literature, then in the process of identifying itself vis-à-vis Spanish and

European literature.[8] In the colonial period, historical truth was understood in relation to the predominant ideology of Christian providentialism—that is, how events occurred as part of a divine plan. Under the influence of eighteenth-century rationalism and nineteenth-century positivism, historiography underwent a change that recognized the true as "what is verifiable."[9] With this change, writings that did not fit the positivist concept were relegated to literature.[10]

Although the Spanish chronicles formed part of the literary canon and became topics for novels in the nineteenth century, they occupied a marginal position in the study of Spanish American literature between 1898 and the early 1980s.[11] However, one noteworthy exception to this overall indifference was Alfonso Reyes's collection of essays titled *Letras de la Nueva España* (1948), in which Reyes redirected attention to the chronicles by designating colonial texts as a "homemade" literature whose nascent genres were the chronicle and the missionary theater.[12] Nonetheless, most scholars continued to ignore studying the chronicles, and even those who incorporated them into literary histories of Latin American literature viewed them as aesthetically inferior to literature from the Spanish Renaissance. Enrique Anderson Imbert typifies this attitude in the introduction to his *Historia de la literatura hispanoamericana, vol. 1: La Colonia: Cien años de la República* (1967):

> [Las crónicas son] sin arquitectura, fluidas, sueltas, complejas, libres, desproporcionadas, donde las anécdotas realistas andan por un lado y los símbolos cristianos por otro. No tienen esas crónicas la composición, la unidad, la congruencia, el orgullo artístico e intelectual de las creaciones del Renacimiento. . . .[13]

> [The chronicles are formless and variable, lacking structure, proportion, and coherence. Anecdotal accounts compete with Christian symbolism. . . . They don't have the unity, the coherence, the artistic and intellectual pride of Renaissance works. . . .]

As René Jara points out, literary critics as late as the 1970s continued to display indifference and contempt toward the study of Latin American colonial writings in general and the chronicles in particular. Speaking of the colonial texts, he notes that

> Muchos de nuestros críticos han confinado a estos discursos a los subterráneos de los archivos, condenándolos a la espera de algún historiador inclinado a desempolvar documentos exóticos, o algún anticuario aficionado a las curiosidades, venga a desenterrarlos. . . .[14]

[Many of our critics have relegated these discourses to basement archives, awaiting exhumation by some historian inclined to dust off exotic documents or an antiquarian enamored of such curiosities. . . .]

Many chronicles remained buried in the archives and the footnotes of literary histories until a new generation of literary scholars rediscovered them in the early 1980s, a topic to which I will return shortly.

Unlike most scholars and literary critics, Spanish American Boom writers in the 1960s turned their eyes to the chronicles and discovered, from their twentieth-century vantage point, affinities between those writings and the contemporary Spanish American novel. They read the chronicles as the foundations of Latin American literature, in which the seeds of incipient literary strategies would later blossom in the writings of contemporary poets and novelists, and underscored their magical and fantastic characteristics. In his article "Fantasía y creación artística en América Latina y el Caribe" (1979), Gabriel García Márquez posits a connection between contemporary narrative and the chronicles in the context of the literary evolution of the continent:

> En América Latina y el Caribe, los artistas han tenido que inventar muy poco, y tal vez su problema ha sido el contrario: hacer creíble su realidad. Siempre fue así desde nuestros orígenes históricos, hasta el punto de que no hay en nuestra literatura escritores menos creíbles y al mismo tiempo más apegados a la realidad que nuestros cronistas de Indias. También ellos—para decirlo con un lugar irremplazable—se encontraron con que la realidad iba más lejos que la imaginación. . . . Un problema muy serio que nuestra realidad desmesurada plantea a la literatura, es el de la insuficiencia de las palabras. . . . De modo que sería necesario crear todo un sistema de palabras nuevas para el tamaño de nuestra realidad.[15]

[Latin America and Caribbean writers haven't had to invent very much. In fact, their challenge since the beginning of our history may have been just the opposite: to make our reality believable. The chroniclers of the Indies are both our least believable writers and those most faithful to our historical reality. To use an unavoidable cliché, they too found that reality was stranger than fiction. . . . The challenge posed to literature by our extravagant reality is the insufficiency of words. . . . To do it justice one would require an entirely new lexicon.]

Such Boom novelists as García Márquez, aware of the insufficiency of language to describe a complex Latin American reality, identified and selected passages in which the chroniclers grappled with words that communicated the incommensurability of the New World and that resonated with their own contemporary situation.

By the early 1980s, literary scholars of the colonial period also had renewed interest in the chronicles. A new paradigm in Spanish American colonial studies began to emerge, as suggested by the proliferation of monographs, articles, and special issues journals devoted to colonial Spanish American literature and culture.[16] The dominant paradigm of reading the chronicles, with an attentive eye for evidence of an American essence, dramatically shifted when a new generation of colonial scholars rediscovered them and brought to bear a new set of methodological concerns.[17] Mignolo attributes this renewed attention to the chronicles to an effort to locate the origin of Spanish American literature in the sixteenth century, as the Boom writers had proposed,[18] while Birgit Scharlau cites the crisis of Western rationalism and the ensuing reconceptualization of relations between European and non-European cultures to account for this shift in paradigm.[19] Scharlau further notes that since scholars no longer viewed the chronicles as a reflection of distant realities but as a site of European projections of the "other," they problematize the figure of the chronicler and observer of foreign cultures and seek to address for what purposes and for whom the chronicles were written.[20]

Monographs by Enrique Pupo-Walker on the Inca Garcilaso de la Vega (1982) and the literary vocation of historical thought in America (1982), by Noé Jitrik on Columbus's *Diario de a bordo* (1983), and by Beatriz Pastor on narrative discourse of the conquest (1988) focused on the literary qualities of the chronicles and applied the techniques of literary analysis to nonliterary discourses.[21] This different approach to the chronicles must be seen not only as a move toward the emergence of a new paradigm (to use Mignolo's term) in colonial Spanish American literary studies but also, I may add, as evidence of the legitimization of colonial Latin American studies as a discipline in its own right, a discipline seeking to carve out a space for itself in the North American academy. Pupo-Walker's, Jitrik's, and Pastor's studies sought to demonstrate that early colonial Spanish American writings possessed the same degree of literary and rhetorical sophistication as did twentieth-century Spanish American narratives of the Boom. The departure from the conventional approach of reading the chronicles as a storehouse of facts also created the conditions for other critics to situate both Spanish and Amerindian chronicles within the sociohistorical context of the sixteenth and seventeenth centuries and to analyze the rhetorical strategies by which writers communicated their messages. Exemplifying this latter trend are studies by Margarita Zamora on the *Comentarios Reales* (1988) and Columbus (1992), by Rolena Adorno on Guaman Poma de Ayala's *Nueva corónica y buen gobierno* (1986), by Walter Mignolo on the typology of the chronicles (1982), and by Kathleen Ross on the narrative of Sigüenza y Góngora (1994), and the critical collections of essays edited by Alvaro Félix Bolaños and Gustavo Verdesio (2002) and by Santa Arias and Mariselle Meléndez (2002). The shift in paradigm in colonial Latin American literary studies—from the concept of colonial literature to colonial discourse, and most recently, to colonial semiosis—is evidenced by the literary history of the colonial period, edited by Ana Pizarro (1993), which reflects the pluricultural nature of Latin American writings.[22]

In the Spanish American novel of the 1980s and 1990s, writers have shared many of the same concerns as literary scholars in identifying alternative enunciative positions from which to retell episodes from the discovery and conquest. For instance, post-Boom novelists such as Abel Posse have been rereading the chronicles, seeking not to identify aesthetic connections between the Boom novels and the chronicles but to use the latter as a point of departure for articulating a counterdiscourse to the "official history" about the conquest and for questioning the notion of a Spanish American cultural essence that denies the heterogeneity of Spanish American society and culture. According to Posse, literary writers are obligated to pose a direct challenge to the received notion of history and to reposition the chronicles of the Indies as the beginning of the tale of Latin America's cultural heterogeneity:

> Fueron los poetas y novelistas quienes lanzarían sus carabelas de papel para descubrir la versión justa.
> Había que recuperar una conciencia sepultada del hombre americano.
> Era necesario *legitimar* nuestro *imaginaire*. Poner en valor la idiosincrasia de nuestros pueblos; valorizar nuestra sensibilidad que, aunque de raíz cultural europea, está modificada por la realidad del mestizaje y la superposición de culturas de las sucesivas corrientes de inmigración.
> Nuestro trabajo necesariamente tenía que usar la historiografía, para a veces negarla, modificarla, reinterpretarla.
> La literatura latinoamericana, más allá de lo estrictamente estético, cumplió una función *desmitificadora*.
> [E]se trabajo tiende en América Latina a crear un campo de reflexión y conciencia de nuestro ser y de nuestro Continente. . . .
> Nos toca descubrir. Descubrirnos.[23]

[It was the poets and novelists who would launch their literary caravels to discover a truthful accounting. . . .
It was imperative to recover the buried conscience of the American people.
We had to *validate* our *imaginaire,* our idiosyncrasy, the sensibilities of our peoples, with cultural roots in Europe but modified by the reality of *mestizaje* and by the cultures superimposed in successive waves of immigration.

> Our task necessarily required us to draw from historiography, but also to deny it, to modify it, to reinterpret it.
>
> Beyond the purely aesthetic, the function of Latin American literature was to *demythify*. . . .
>
> This work . . . tends to create in Latin America a space to reflect on our nature and that of our Continent. . . .
>
> Our task is to discover, to discover ourselves. . . .]

As Posse notes, the chronicles of the Indies are inscribed within the context of early Spanish imperialism and narrated from the vantage point of the dominant voices. Latin American writers in the 1980s and 1990s tried to rewrite tales from the chronicles to tell the story of Latin America's rediscovery of itself in a supposedly postcolonial, yet still neoimperial, age.[24] Posse's trilogy concerning the discovery and conquest—*Daimón* (1978), *Los perros del paraíso* (1982), and *El largo atardecer del caminante* (1992)—re-creates from a twentieth-century Latin American perspective and in modern-day Peru the legend about the rebellion of Lope de Aguirre, Columbus's arrival in the New World, and the adventures of Cabeza de Vaca in the southwestern United States, northern Mexico, and modern-day Paraguay. These tales underscore parallels between historical circumstances from the fifteenth and sixteenth centuries in Spain and those in twentieth-century Latin America.

The resurgence in the 1980s and 1990s of Spanish American novels dealing with the discovery and conquest also coincides with the reemergence of the historical novel as a dominant trend in Latin American literature and forms part of a broader process in which Latin American writers have reexamined the meaning of the colonial period.[25] In the third period of his schema (1969 to the present), which encompasses the period under consideration in this book, González Pérez argues that Spanish American writers have questioned the previous tendency to emplot history as a "figural allegory." By figural allegory, González Pérez means a narrative form for visualizing history and interpreting historical events, a form consisting of a beginning, middle, and end and presupposing that it is possible to have a global, totalizing, almost divine vision of the historical process. He cites as representative of this trend in narrative Reinaldo Arenas's *El mundo alucinante* (1969), Antonio Benítez Rojo's *El mar de las lentejas* (1979), Abel Posse's *Daimón* and *Los perros del paraíso,* and Edgardo Rodríguez Juliá's *La noche oscura del Niño Avilés* (1984). These novels question the adequacy of figural allegory and the linear notion of time to account for the historical process, and the images from the colonial period are openly textual, mediated, and noticeably elaborated on the basis of documents and language.²⁶ Writers from this third period no longer try to reconstruct imaginatively events from the colonial period but instead show how any reconstruction depends on the interpretation of the residual texts generated by writers from that period. Focusing on the past as a text, as a construction of language, these writers reveal the specific temporality of literature, which is not easily domesticated to historical periodizations.²⁷

Since the publication of González Pérez's article, individual works in the corpus of historical novels that rewrite the discovery and conquest have attracted critical attention, in the form of book-length scholarly monographs, critical anthologies, dissertations, and articles. In her monograph *Latin American Novels of the Conquest: Reinventing the New World* (2002), Kimberle S. López employs the concepts of "anxiety of identification" in Harold Bloom's *The Anxiety of Influence* and "colonial desire" in Robert Young's *Colonial Desire.* She analyzes five recent Spanish American historical novels dealing with the early period of conquest, narrated with a focus on fictional and fictionalized conquistadors and would-be conquistadors.²⁸ Spanish American authors, argues López, rewrite the moment of crisis that originated transculturation from the perspective of the conqueror, but, through the representation of colonial desire and the anxiety of identification, make manifest the gaps in the rhetoric of conquest. All these novels deconstruct the conquistadors' perspective in order to point to the gaps and contradictions in the rhetoric of empire.²⁹

The present book analyzes the fictional rewriting of historiographical discourse embedded in eight novels of this subcorpus published in Mexico or the River Plate (Argentina, Paraguay, and Uruguay) during the 1980s and 1990s. It pays particular attention to the use of fictional autobiographies and testimonials in rewriting historiographical discourses about the conquest and their relationship to contemporary politics in Latin America. I have organized my book around novels in which renowned Spanish conquistadors from the conquest rewrite their original *relaciones,* fictional marginal figures contest the official historiography about the conquest, vilified figures from the conquest of Mexico rewrite the diffuse cultural myths about *mestizaje* and the black legend of Spanish colonialism, and the figure of Columbus used to meditate on the legacy of the discovery and conquest for modern Spanish America. Moreover, my book situates the issue of textual production and the rewriting of history within the tradition of Spanish American literature and combines "traditional" as well as "postmodern" historical novels within each chapter.

With the exceptions of *Maluco, Gonzalo Guerrero, El largo atardecer del caminante,* and *Vigilia del Almirante,* the novels I analyze in this book have received limited critical attention.³⁰ While I cite their pertinence to the topic, I do not examine in great depth other novels, such as Alejo Carpentier's *El arpa y la sombra,* Posse's *Los perros del paraíso,* and Juan José Saer's *El entenado,* because they have already been the subject of other studies.[31] By examining this corpus of novels, I show how Mexican and River Plate novelists use major and marginal figures both to reflect upon the ways that institutional powers have invoked episodes from the discovery and conquest to explain and legitimate the present. They also revisit this period to critique the recent historical past, especially in the case of the River Plate nations of Uruguay and Argentina, which endured military dictatorships in the 1970s and 1980s.

Chapter 1 focuses on major historical conquistadors—Hernán Cortés and Alvar Núñez Cabeza de Vaca—who remember their ordeals and rewrite their official reports to the crown. Armando Ayala Anguiano's *Cómo conquisté a los aztecas* and Abel Posse's *El largo atardecer del caminante* recast Cortés's *Cartas de relación* and Cabeza de Vaca's *Los naufragios,* respectively, as confessional autobiographies that restore the human dimension of the conquest excluded from the *relaciones.* In *Cómo conquisté* the interventions of a twentieth-century editor, whose presence is felt through the inclusion of a prologue, footnotes, and graphics related to the conquest of Mexico, challenge the fictional Cortés's reinterpretation of events and oblige the reader to take into account the ideological contexts in which Cortés's image as a hero or villain in Mexico has emerged. In *El largo atardecer,* a twentieth-century editor frames the fictional Cabeza de Vaca's autobiography as a tale of survival in the midst of hardship and injustice and establishes analogies between the fictional Cabeza de Vaca's plight in the sixteenth century and that of Argentines during the Dirty War (1976–82).

Chapter 2 examines the tales of apocryphal marginal figures who retell famous voyages of discovery and colonization of the River Plate and parody the conventions of the *relación* and *arbitrista* writing to discredit the truth value established in the official historiography. Napoleón Baccino Ponce de León's *Maluco: La novela de los descubridores* and Antonio Elio Brailovsky's *Esta maldita lujuria* present, respectively, Ferdinand Magellan's voyage to circumnavigate the globe (1519–22) and the Spaniards' establishment of an outpost at Viedma, Patagonia, in 1779. In *Maluco* Juanillo de Ponce, the buffoon of the expedition, submits a *relación de servicio* to Philip II and requests financial compensation for his service to the crown. *Maluco* inserts the figure of the buffoon from Golden Age literature into a contemporary novelistic discourse to parody the conventions of the *relación de servicio* and to transform the latent aesthetic dimensions of the chronicles about Magellan's voyage into a postmodern novel in which the bounds between fiction and history are blurred. Similarly, in *Esta maldita lujuria,* the sword-maker Ambrosio de Lara, a peripheral figure from Patagonia, submits a letter to the viceroy of Buenos Aires in 1810 and attempts to persuade him to send an expeditionary force to conquer, once and for all, the elusive Ciudad de los Césares, the mythical El Dorado of the River Plate. In the course of his letter, Lara incorporates an irreverent retelling of the sexual escapades of explorers and conquistadors such as Columbus, Cabeza de Vaca, and Vasco da Gama to communicate the transformation of the New World from a utopia into a dystopia. In retelling the history of the colony in Patagonia as well as that of the New World itself, the novel obliquely alludes to and critiques the repressive policies of the military junta during the Proceso in Argentina, especially with regard to its policy toward sexual expression. Invented marginal figures in these River Plate novels function as catalysts to destabilize the monological truth espoused by the official historiography and to render a humorous account of famous historical episodes from the discovery and conquest.

Chapter 3 further explores the issue of rewriting history from the margins through vilified Spanish figures who implicitly rewrite diffuse cultural myths in the retelling of the conquest of Mexico. Eugenio Aguirre's *Gonzalo Guerrero* re-creates the life of the Spaniard-gone-native in the Yucatán Peninsula, from his capture by indigenous forces in 1511 through his eventual death at the hands of Spaniards in 1536. By proposing the Gonzalo Guerrero/Ix Chel Can dyad, instead of Cortés/La Malinche, as the origin of Mexican *mestizaje,* the novel reinvents the cultural myth of Mexican *mestizaje* without challenging the underlying ideological paradigm of the superiority of the Spaniards over the indigenes. On the other hand, the *Diario maldito* retells the life of the conquistador Nuño de Guzmán during his tenure in New Spain (1526–38). Cast as a travel diary, the novel records Guzmán's thoughts and deeds in the New World and reveals the complex humanity of this vilified historical figure, regarded as the embodiment of the black legend of Spanish colonialism. This novel explores the ideological contexts in which Guzmán's image as a cruel and bloodthirsty tyrant was forged.

Whereas chapters 2 and 3 examine marginal figures who question the official historiography about the discovery and conquest, chapter 4 returns to the major figure of Columbus and analyzes the retelling of his life and voyages, as well as the divergent responses to the commemoration of the quincentennial of the first voyage in Augusto Roa Bastos's *Vigilia del Almirante* and Herminio Martínez's *Las puertas del mundo: Una autobiografía del Almirante. Vigilia* rehumanizes the historical Columbus and reveals the shortcomings of ideological interpretations of Columbus and his enterprise, which traditionally have sought to portray him as a genius solely responsible for Christianizing the New World or as a criminal who initiated the genocide of Amerindian populations. The novel employs a complex narrative structure that alternates between the fictional Columbus's remembering his life as he lies on his deathbed in Valladolid in 1506 and the meditations of an intellectual who in 1992 revisits the legacy of Columbus for Spanish American history. *Las puertas* rewrites Columbus's writings about the voyages of discovery and offers an iconoclastic portrait to trivialize the whole controversy and to parody the rhetorical conventions through which the historical Columbus endowed his account with authority.

Indeed, as Frances Meuser-Blincow points out, rewriting the New World chronicles became a popular enterprise in the years surrounding the Quincentennial. Spanish American novelists during the 1980s and 1990s produced historical novels that reimagined the discovery and conquest and decentered the official history with a focus on major historical figures as well as marginal and fictitious ones. It is to these novels that I will turn in the following chapters.

1
Rewriting the *Relación* as Autobiography

Hernán Cortés, el conquistador de México, fue hábil estratega, gran político, cronista, fundador de hospitales, explorador, poblador y estadista; pero también aparece como codicioso y cruel; gestionó la venida de religiosos humanos e importó plantas y animales que mejoraron la industria y la economía de Nueva España; mas otras faltas, como el herrar a los esclavos indios y la muerte de Cuauhtémoc, opacan esas cualidades.
—Manuel Orozco y Berra, *Historia antigua de las culturas aborígenes de México, Tomo segundo* (1880)

[Hernán Cortés, the conqueror of Mexico, was an able strategist and a great politician, chronicler, founder of hospitals, explorer, colonizer, and statesman. However, he also comes off as greedy and cruel. While he arranged for the arrival of many well-meaning religious workers and imported plants and animals that improved New Spain industrially and economically, these qualities are tarnished by other faults such as the branding of enslaved Indians and the death of Cuauhtémoc.]

Los naufragios han retenido una condición provisional, casi de borrador.... [Es] en su configuración inconclusa... donde acaso residen algunas de las instancias más punzantes de zozobra.
—Enrique Pupo-Walker

[*Los naufragios* has maintained a provisional quality; it is something of a first draft.... Some of its most anguishing moments may be attributable to this inconclusive form....]

SINCE THE PUBLICATION OF CARPENTIER'S *EL ARPA Y LA SOMBRA* IN 1979, Spanish American novels that rewrite the discovery and conquest have proliferated. Two such novels, which constitute the focus of this chapter, are Armando Ayala Anguiano's *Cómo conquisté a los aztecas* (Mexico, 1990) and Abel Posse's *El largo atardecer del caminante* (Argentina, 1992). Armando Ayala Anguiano (b. León, Guanajuato, 1928), a historian and novelist, has published six novels—*Las ganas de creer* (1958), *El paso de la nada* (1960), *Unos cuantos días* (1965), *Cómo conquisté a los aztecas* (1990), *Juárez: Biografía novelada* (1991), and *El día que perdió el PRI: Ficción política* (1994). He has also published eight collections of essays—*La aventura de México* (1967), *México antes de los aztecas* (1967), *México de carne y hueso* (1967), *Conquistados y conquistadores* (1971), *México en crisis: El fin del sistema* (1982), *JLP: Secretos de un sexenio* (1984), *Zapata y las grandes mentiras de la Revolución Mexicana* (1985), and *Salinas y su México* (1995). Abel Posse (b. Córdoba, Argentina, 1934) is a novelist, literary critic, and career diplomat who has worked at the Argentine embassies in Moscow, Venice, Paris, Israel, and Prague. He has published twelve novels—*Los bogavantes* (1968), *La boca del tigre* (1971), *Daimón* (1978), *Momento de morir* (1979), *Los perros del paraíso* (1982), *Los demonios ocultos* (1987), *La reina del Plata* (1988), *El viajero del Agartha* (1989), *El largo atardecer del caminante* (1992), *La pasión según Eva* (1994), *Los cuadernos de Praga* (1998), and *El inquietante día de la vida* (2001)—and in 1987 he received the prestigious Premio Internacional Rómulo Gallegos for *Los perros del paraíso*.[1]

Armando Ayala Anguiano's *Cómo conquisté a los aztecas* re-creates Hernán Cortés's conquest of Mexico from the *Cartas de relación* (1518–26) and other accounts such as Bernal Díaz del Castillo's *Historia verdadera de la conquista de la Nueva España* (1568) and Francisco López de Gómara's *Historia de la conquista de México* (1555). In this novel a twentieth-century editor frames the autobiography of the fictional Cortés through a preface, footnotes, and graphics dealing with Cortés and the conquest of Mexico. Alongside José Luis Martínez's monograph *Hernán Cortés* (1990) and Vicente Leñero's play *La noche de Hernán Cortés* (1992), *Cómo conquisté a los aztecas* participates in an ongoing cultural conversation about Cortés as the origin of Mexico's modern cultural and national identity. Similarly, *El largo atardecer del caminante* re-creates Alvar Núñez Cabeza de Vaca's experiences in the New World based on *Los naufragios* (1542/1555) and other accounts such as Fernando González de Oviedo's *Historia natural de las Indias* (1535). As in *Cómo conquisté a los aztecas,* a twentieth-century editor frames a confessional autobiography; here it is of Cabeza de Vaca with a preface and occasional footnotes.

Both exemplify recent Spanish American novels in which major historical figures from the discovery and conquest rewrite their official reports to the crown and gloss later commentaries of their accounts as fictional autobiographies that critique the official historiography and clear a space from which alternative beginnings may be narrated. They tease out and exploit the latent autobiographical potential of the *relación* (a personal petition that soldiers submitted to the king seeking recompense for services rendered) and sanction the location of the origins of contemporary Spanish American narrative in the Spanish chronicles of the Indies. In the process, they perform an act of literary decolonization and Latin Americanize the first European images of the New World. In other words, contemporary Spanish American novelists are discovering the autobiographical elements of the chronicles and transforming them into modern autobiographical narratives. They are refashioning sixteenth-century historiographic texts into modern literary texts that tell the discovery and conquest from a Latin American rather than a Eurocentric vantage point.

As of this writing, *Cómo conquisté a los aztecas* has received scant critical attention. In his dissertation on the historical novel in Mexico (1980–93), Manuel F. Medina argues that *Cómo conquisté a los aztecas* presents a modern-day defense of Cortés as a hero of the Mexican nation. By employing Hayden White's theory of historical writing, he further asserts that while the Cortés in the *Cartas de relación* emplots his story as a comedy, Ayala Anguiano in *Cómo conquisté a los aztecas* emplots the same story as a tragedy, without any intent of challenging or subverting the authority of the *Cartas de relación*.[2] My own reading differs substantively from Medina's. I will argue that the fictional Cortés and the twentieth-century editor subtly undermine the heroic image of Cortés in the *Cartas de relación:* they humanize him and invite the reader to assume a more reflective stance toward the legacy of Cortés in the formation of a Mexican national and cultural identity. While *Cómo conquisté a los aztecas* does not denigrate the heroic image of Cortés, it obligates the reader to reflect critically about the received notions of truth as recorded in the official history about the conquest of Mexico.

By contrast, *El largo atardecer del caminante* has been the subject of numerous scholarly studies. Kimberle S. López focuses on the fictionalized Cabeza de Vaca, the representation of the liminal figure of the converso, and his anxiety of identification both toward the indigenous inhabitants of the New World and toward the Judaic inhabitants of the Old World. The fictionalized Cabeza de Vaca, López argues, fashions a new self between the competing impulse to identify with the Amerindians, with whom he shares many common characteristics, and to distinguish himself from them, because they lack many elements of Spanish Catholic culture.[3] Richard A. Young argues that *El largo atardecer* is a New Historical novel that meditates on the process of writing and reveals the textual nature of all narratives, while it constructs another version of reality.[4] Kerstin Bowsher interprets the novel as an attempt to rediscover the roots of Latin American identity, which for Posse have been distorted and obscured by traditional historical accounts of the discovery and conquest of the New World. Moreover, she interprets the novel as an account of the shipwreck of modernity conceived as a project of liberation, and believes that through its rewriting of the narrative discourse of the conquest, *El largo atardecer* provides a critique of European colonialism, as experienced by Latin America, and of modernity itself.[5] Likewise, both David Bost and Lola Colomina-Garrigós argue that the novel explores the forms of power that have shaped and distorted Latin American reality and that Posse uses earlier historical works (primarily the *Naufragios* and *Comentarios)* as palimpsests upon which to reinscribe a contemporary interpretation.[6] Seymour Menton focuses on the dialogical and metafictional dimensions of the novel and underscores how the novel amplifies Cabeza de Vaca's original writings and humanizes this historical figure,[7] while Angel García Ronda praises this novel for its humanization of Cabeza de Vaca, the interpolation of Argentine expressions, and the presence of melancholy in this fictional sixteenth-century autobiography.[8]

Building upon the insights of the above-mentioned critics, I will further argue that *El largo atardecer del caminante,* by rewriting Cabeza de Vaca's *Naufragios* as an editor-mediated autobiography, obligates the reader to establish parallels between sixteenth-century Spanish and twentieth-century Latin American society and culture. After considering the pertinence of Sylvia Molloy's theory of Spanish American autobiography to the analysis of these two novels' autobiographical dimensions, I will examine the strategies by which the works transform the canonical *Cartas de relación* and the *Naufragios* into contemporary autobiographies that contest the official historiography of the New World and recuperate what has been lost or forgotten.

According to Molloy, Spanish American autobiography is defined as self-writing that purports to narrate the story of a first-person narrator who exists only in the present of his or her enunciation.[9] She further proposes that such a narrative is a way of reading and writing, filtered through the dominant discourses of the day; it is hybrid in nature, and tends to illuminate what has been repressed, denied, or forgotten.[10] Her theory about autobiography, however, excludes colonial writings such as Cabeza de Vaca's *Naufragios,* because their primary concern is not marked by the textual self-confrontation that constitutes her principal focus:

> [T]he circumstances in which these texts were written preclude, or at least considerably modify the textual self-confrontation that marks autobiographical writing. The fact that the abovementioned texts are concerned primarily for a privileged reader (the King of Spain, the Bishop of Puebla, an ecclesiastical tribunal) who has power over writer and text; the fact, too, that the narration of self is more a means to achieve a goal than the goal itself; the fact, finally, that

there is rarely a crisis in this self-writing (or a self in crisis), make these texts, in my view, only tangentially autobiographical.[11]

In other words, colonial writings are unautobiographical by Molloy's standards, since they were written at the request of an institutional authority, and institutional discourses circumscribed their presentation of self.

The work of many scholars of colonial Spanish American literature, however, suggests that they would probably take exception to Molloy's assertion regarding the absence of autobiography in the colonial period. Stephanie Merrim, for example, analyzes the autobiographical elements in the *Segunda carta de relación* of Cortés in the context of autobiography in sixteenth-century Spain, while other scholars of colonial convent writing such as Kathleen Myers and Kathryn McKnight focus on the spiritual autobiographies of nuns written at the request of their confessors.[12] The current generation of colonial scholars seeks to recuperate the experiences of women in the New World and redefine the concept of autobiography, which they claim has been based primarily on male writings.

Although scholars disagree as to the existence of autobiography in colonial writings, most agree that the *relación (probanza de mérito)* contains what Molloy would call "distant forms of the autobiographical mode."[13] According to Roberto González Echevarría, the term *relación* in the sixteenth century referred to a legal document in which the petitioner told his life story and the pertinent facts related to his case, based on his authority as an eyewitness.[14] Historians such as B. Sánchez Alonso classify both the *Cartas de relación* and the *Naufragios* in his *Historia de la historiografía española* (1941) as "relaciones autobiográficas," legal accounts written without any aesthetic purpose on the part of the original author.[15]

Recent Spanish American novels about the discovery and conquest, such as *Cómo conquisté a los aztecas* and *El largo atardecer del caminante*, then, tease out and develop the autobiographical potential of the *Cartas de relación* and the *Naufraugios*. As Molloy claims about Spanish American autobiography, both novels illuminate what has been repressed, denied, or forgotten. They artistically transform the chronicles from legal petitions to the king, where the representation of the I is in the background, to modern autobiographies where the I is in the foreground. Both the fictional Cortés and the fictional Cabeza de Vaca of the novels write retrospective accounts of their experiences in the New World and, in the spirit of Bernal Díaz del Castillo, address posterity and engage the commentaries that have been written about their own original accounts. Although they retain some of the legalistic discourse of the *Cartas de relación* and the *Naufragios*, both novels are marked by textual self-confrontations.

In Ayala Anguiano's *Cómo conquisté a los aztecas,* this textual self-confrontation manifests itself at two levels. First, an "editor/collaborator" employs paratextual devices such as graphics (photographs, paintings, and illustrations), footnotes, and a preface to Cortés's fictional autobiography to establish a critical dialogue among the discussants about Cortés and the conquest of Mexico. At the second level, the Cortés of the novel confronts his earlier self from the *Cartas de relación* as the basis for telling his intimate life story from the days of the conquest. Essentially, the fictional Cortés fills in the silences from the *Cartas de relación* and demythifies his public image without discrediting his contention that the conquest was just. The editor/collaborator, however, undermines this viewpoint.

Similarly, in Abel Posse's *El largo atardecer del caminante,* textual self-confrontation occurs at two levels. At the first level, an anonymous twentieth-century editor includes an introduction and footnotes to Cabeza de Vaca's autobiography. At the second level, the fictional protagonist Cabeza de Vaca rereads his *Naufragios* and the state-sponsored version of his story, which he emends by including what had been denied, repressed, or forgotten in his official report to the crown. In both novels, then, the autobiographical potential is elaborated upon and comes to the forefront as a fundamental strategy for reinterpreting the *crónicas* from a late twentieth-century Latin American critical vantage point.

The original *Cartas de relación,* written at different times and places between 1519 and 1526, are official reports from Cortés to the Emperor Carlos V.[16] Each *relación* records different phases and circumstances related to the conquest of Mexico as well as Cortés's participation as leader of this conquest. The *Primera relación,* dated July 20, 1519, was signed by Cortés and members of the town council of the Villa Rica de la Vera Cruz. In this *relación* Cortés discusses two previous expeditions by explorers to the Yucatán Peninsula, preparations for his own expedition, and the political and military events that led to his decision to break ranks with Diego Velázquez, the governor of Cuba, and to establish the town of Vera Cruz under the jurisdiction of the crown. The *Primera relación* closes with an inventory of indigenous objects that Cortés sent as gifts to the emperor. The *Segunda relación,* dated October 30, 1520, is a long report that can be divided into three parts. The first narrates events dealing with the march through the interior of Mexico and culminates in the Spaniards entering the Aztec city of Tenochtitlán. The second part describes in detail the city, its peoples, and its customs, including everything related to the court of Moctezuma. The third part begins with the arrival of Cortés's enemy Pánfilo de Narváez in Vera Cruz and narrates the confrontation between the two, Cortés's return to Tenochtitlán, the rebellion of the Aztecs and the expulsion of the Spaniards (popularly known as the "Sad Night"), and the Spaniards' retreat to Tlaxcala, where they regroup and found the city of Segura de la Frontera. The *Tercera relación,* signed on May 15, 1522, in Coyoacán, consists of two parts. In the first part, Cortés narrates the siege of Tenochtitlán, which ends with the capture of Cuauhtémoc. Cortés depicts himself as an astute, valiant, and well-organized military strategist responsible for the success of the Spanish forces against the Aztecs. In the second part, Cortés seeks to demonstrate that the conquest and his leadership are not over but have only just begun, because, according to him, many indigenous groups in the region still pose a threat to Spain's control of the territory. He also details his plans for reconstructing the destroyed cities, repopulating the countryside, organizing the mines and agriculture for the economic benefit of the crown, and, finally, launching new expeditions of discovery and conquest in other areas. The *Cuarta relación,* dated October 15, 1524, and signed in Temixtitán, continues the dominant themes from the *Tercera relación* in which Cortés outlines his plans to govern the new territories. It also emphasizes the financial expenses that Cortés had assumed in order to carry out the conquest and to defend himself against attacks from his enemies about squandering the wealth of Mexico. The *Quinta relación,* signed in Tenuxtitán on September 3, 1526, consists of two parts. The first is a long, detailed account of the land expedition to Hibueras (modern-day Honduras), the goal of which was to punish the rebellion of Cristóbal de Olid. It also recounts Cortés's return to Mexico, where, a few days after his return, he was stripped of his title as governor and subjected to an inquiry (*juicio de residencia*). The second part consists of Cortés's defense against accusations that his enemies in the court had leveled against him. Although what we regard today as the *Cartas de relación* was not originally conceived as an organic unity, the fact that each *relación* deals with a different phase of the conquest of Mexico and the role of Cortés in that enterprise enables a reading, as Angel Delgado Gómez notes, as if they were individual chapters from a single text.[17]

The *Cartas de relación* is, first and foremost, a legal document that justifies Cortés's rebellion against Diego Velázquez, the governor of Cuba, Cortés's usurpation of power, and his conquests of Mexico, Guatemala, and Honduras. In the sixteenth century the *relación* as a genre combined the epistle (*la epístola*) and the legal document.[18] As an epistle it narrated and informed about multiple aspects of an expedition, and it described and commented on actions and behaviors, including reactions of the author to what surrounded him. As a legal document, the *relación* implicitly guaranteed the veracity of the narrative.[19] The framework of the *relación,* then, served as a vehicle for guaranteeing the impartiality of the message inscribed within this discourse. Regarding its style, scholars such as Marcelino Menéndez y Pelayo, F. A. MacNutt, and Ramón Iglesia have noted the "calm and distant" tone of the *Cartas de relación,* and, according to Delgado Gómez, these characteristics are consistent with those of a *relación,* which required the writer to adopt a dispassionate tone to be credible and convincing.[20]

Unlike most *relaciones* that are still slumbering in the archives, Cortés's second, third, and fourth *relaciones* were widely circulated and read as early as 1524. Printing houses in Europe published the second, third, and fourth *relaciones* at an early date, and by the mid-sixteenth century, entire or summarized editions were available in Latin, Italian, German, French, and Flemish.[21] In Spain, after the publication of the *Cuarta relación* in Toledo in 1525, a royal decree from March 1527 prohibited the publication or sale of the *relaciones* Cortés had written in the Indies. The *relaciones* were not reissued until 1749, when González Barcia prepared his edition, and finally, with the discovery of the *Carta de Vera Cruz* and the *Quinta relación* in the nineteenth century, the five *relaciones* were published as what today we know as the *Cartas de relación.*[22]

From the preceding summary of the history of the publication of the *Cartas de relación,* it is evident that the historical Cortés lost sole authorship over his writings. Printers and editors for centuries have assumed the status of coauthors in that they have shaped what we know today as the *Cartas de relación.* Thus, the novel *Cómo conquisté a los aztecas* inscribes itself within a long-standing historical tradition of revising the *Cartas de relación.* It focuses on a well-known historical figure from the conquest—Cortés—who writes his autobiography and presents a demythified version of himself and his exploits as recorded in his *Cartas de relación.* This autobiography, however, comprises only one layer of the narrative structure, for an editor, in turn, frames the novel with a preface, divides it into three parts, and employs an array of paraxtextual devices to corroborate and question the version of the conquest of Mexico as presented in the *Cartas de relación* and in the fictionalized autobiography. At both narrative levels, the text focuses on the process of rewriting a historical or autobiographical account, beyond the scrutiny of an institution of power. Both revised versions amend the official history and invite readers to reconsider the meaning of the conquest of Mexico in the late-twentieth century.

Cómo conquisté a los aztecas, then, represents one more episode in the continual process of rewriting the story of the conquest. This process is dramatized at two levels. First, the fictional Cortés rereads his *Cartas* and Bernal Díaz del Castillo's *Historia verdadera de la conquista de la Nueva España* as the textual basis for his autobiography. Unlike the original *Cartas,* in which, as Stephanie Merrim has noted, the autobiographical dimensions are at the service of history, the Cortés of this novel places history at the service of autobiography. That is, the main focus of the novel is to make the reader privy to Cortés's actual state of mind during the conquest, to ideas and thoughts that could not be expressed in the formulaic *carta de relación,* which was of a public nature and might be signed by other authorities to guarantee its veracity.[23] Cortés's autobiography, then, demythifies his public image without fundamentally challenging the underlying premises of the official history.

In the process of writing his autobiography, the fictional Cortés resembles the editor of the novel, for both autobiographer and editor frame, annotate, comment, and appropriate the written authority of others to tell their own stories. Cortés recasts his heroic self from the original *Cartas de relación,* in which, as a picaresque character who reveled in reminiscing and retelling episodes from the conquest of New Spain to future generations of readers, he had defended his actions before Carlos V. The fictional Cortés of the novel is well aware of what others have said about him, so his autobiography serves as a forum to respond to his commentators and detractors, and to remember his glory days.

In the first chapter, Cortés defines his public persona by adapting a passage from the final chapter of Francisco López de Gómara's *Conquista de México* (1555):

Era Cortés de buena estatura y cuerpo, bien proporcionado y membrado. El color de su cara tiraba a ceniciento, y si hubiera tenido el rostro más largo, mejor hubiese parecido. Sus ojos eran de mirar apacible y por otras partes grave. Las barbas las tenía prietas, pocas y ralas. . . . Oí decir que cuando mancebo en Santo Domingo fue algo travieso sobre mujeres, y que se acuchilló algunas veces con hombres esforzados y siempre salió con victoria; de cuando anduvo en aquellas cuestiones le quedó una señal de cuchillada cerca del labio de abajo, la cual señal se le veía si alguien miraba bien en ello, más él cubríasela con las barbas. . . .[24]

[Cortés was tall and formidable, well proportioned and strong-limbed. His was fair-skinned and would have been more handsome had his face been longer. His eyes were placid if not solemn. His whiskers were sparse and black. . . . I heard it said that as a young man in Santo Domingo he was somewhat adventurous with the women, that he engaged in knife-play with offended men on several occasions, always emerging victorious, and that as a result of one such incident he had scar on his lower lip that was visible if one looked for it but that he ordinarily kept it hidden with his whiskers. . . .]

Cortés's presentation of self via the comments of López de Gómara offers a demystified and critical portrait of his physical stature. While the real

Cortés and his troops may have defeated the Aztecs, his encounters with rival Spaniards did not always yield similar results. The fictional Cortés's critical portrait of his heroic self is intensified as a result of the editor's insertion of portraits of Cortés throughout the novel.

The first portrait (see fig. 1), initially completed by an anonymous Spanish painter in the nineteenth-century, invites readers to compare the visual and verbal representations of Cortés, as set forth in the public space of the museum and the private sphere of the fictional autobiography.[25] Since this portrait focuses on the facial features of the youthful Cortés, readers cannot help but laugh, because the beard and mustache remind them of Cortés's battle scars from those unsuccessful amorous conquests.

The second portrait (see fig. 2), painted in Toledo in 1530 by an anonymous artist, hangs today in the Hospital de Jesús in Mexico City and depicts the historical Cortés as a military genius at the height of his glory.[26] Both verbal and visual texts of Cortés as a youth and adult engage in dialogue with the mythical stature of Cortés in the official history and invite a more dispassionate discussion about the legacy of Cortés as to the founding and formation of present-day Mexico.

The levity with which the fictional Cortés pokes fun at episodes from his personal life also extends to key moments in his public life. As Molloy argues, autobiographical writing addresses what has been omitted or repressed from the official record. Such is the case when the fictional Cortés explains the acceptance of twenty maidens (*doncellas*) in the city of Tabasco. Before engaging in sexual relations with them, Cortés emphasizes the importance of their baptism:

> [E]s pecado muy grande tener comercio carnal con paganos, y luego escogí una para mí y las otras las repartí entre los principales españoles para que usaran de ellas. Bien sabía que lo que hacíamos seguía siendo pecado, pero el hombre es débil y no quedaba otra cosa que pedir perdón a Nuestro Señor por aquellos pecados que cometíamos para tener más ánimo de propagar nuestra santa fe. . . .[27]

> [It is a grave sin to engage in carnal intercourse with pagans. I later chose one for myself and apportioned the others among the most important Spaniards for their own use. I well knew that what we were doing was still sinful, but man is weak and I could only ask the forgiveness of Our Lord for those sins that we were committing in order to give us the strength to propagate our Holy Faith. . . .]

The irreverence of such comments serves to desacralize the historical Cortés of the *Cartas de relación,* for they undermine the image of a devout and faithful servant of God and the king. Cortés's cavalier attitude about his behavior in the New World obligates readers to reexamine the intensity

Figure 1. *Retrato de Hernán Cortés* (Portrait of Hernán Cortés) by José Aparicio Quintana. Image courtesy of the Town Hall of Medellín (Badajoz).

with which intellectuals have either deified him for having brought "civilization" to the Aztecs or demonized him for his extermination and destruction of the Aztecs.[28]

As the editor of the novel undermines Cortés's authority, so does the fictitious Cortés, who frequently contradicts himself or attempts to manipulate

Figure 2. *Retrato de Hernán Cortés* (Portrait of Hernán Cortés) by an unknown artist. Image courtesy of El Hospital de Jesús, Mexico City.

the reader with feigned concern. When he remembers his visit with Ixtlixóchitl, the ruler of Texcoco, he decides to baptize him "con el nombre de don Fernando, con el que lo llamaré en adelante para no complicar más esta relación con tantos nombres de indios [. . .]"[29] [with the name don Fernando, the name by which I shall refer to him henceforth, so as not to complicate this *relación* with so many Indian names . . .]. This comment underscores his inconsistency in the use of indigenous names, for up to this point these names have littered the narrative. At another moment, Cortés strategically invokes his concern for the reader to justify his decision to shorten the narration. He carefully responds to his detractors by alluding to but glossing over the criticisms directed at him regarding the treatment of the Aztecs. In recalling strategies for defeating the Aztecs, Cortés remains vague about the specifics and justifies his actions: "[P]or no dar cuenta de todas las particularidades que nos acaecieron, que sería prolijidad, no diré sino que los desbaratamos y matamos muchos sin que me matasen ni hiriesen ningún español. [. . .]"[30] [So as not to relate all the particularities that befell us, which would be a prolixity, suffice it to say that we overwhelmed them and killed many, while I did not suffer a single Spanish death or injury. . . .] Cortés invokes his concern for the reader to justify his strategic omission of "las particularidades,"—that is, the details of the slaughter of the Indians. This glossing over the story's details intensifies the dramatic effect when the editor includes reproductions of paintings and photographs related to the defeat of the Aztecs, as evidenced in the scene of Moctezuma's death (see fig. 3).[31] The historical Cortés and his troops killed not only an anonymous mass of Aztecs but also their leader Moctezuma. The expressions of grief and pain on the faces of the Aztecs at the sight of their dead leader illustrate the conquest's human toll on those populations. The fame and glory of Cortés, the text suggests, were achieved at the expense of the indigenous populations. Such visual texts graphically display the devastating consequences of Cortés's military conquest of the indigenous cultures and serve to interrogate the authority of prior written accounts.

Beyond contradicting Cortés's fictional autobiography, the editor seeks to enhance his own authority and stature. In the preface to the novel, he attempts to establish himself as committed to the principles of objectivity and to the faithful transcription of the historical account. He acknowledges his indebtedness to an array of sources in reconstructing the circumstances surrounding the conquest. Among the sixteenth-century historiographical sources he names are Bernal Díaz del Castillo, whose *Historia verdadera de la conquista de la Nueva España* narrates the conquest of Mexico from the soldier's point of view; Bernardino de Sahagún, a friar who collected

Figure 3. *La muerte de Moctezuma* (The Death of Moctezuma) by José Ximena. Image courtesy of Princeton University Library.

and compiled ethnographic reports on Aztec culture; and Francisco López de Gómara, Cortés's official biographer, who glorifies him as a hero. Among the twentieth-century anthropological studies about pre-Columbian civilization and culture he mentions those of Angel María Garibay K. and of Miguel de León Portilla, who compiled indigenous versions of the conquest in his *Visión de los vencidos* (1957). The consultation of a vast array of sources sympathetic to both Cortés and the Aztecs leads the reader to conclude that the editor will offer a balanced and impartial account of the conquest. He further reinforces this impression when he explicitly states that his role has been minimal in modifying Cortés's autobiography: "El texto sólo ha sido retocado para facilitar la lectura y algunas veces reacomodado por convenir al seguimiento del hilo dramático...".[32] [The text has merely been touched up to make it more readable and in some places reordered to make it easier to follow the dramatic thread....]

Nevertheless, the editor understates his other role in commenting on the autobiography, for his "touch-ups" and modernizations of the "original" text highlight the inclusion of the present moment of writing in the representation of the past. The editor does not maintain a neutral role, but inflects Cortés's autobiography with his own accent and agenda of demythifying Cortés in order to reexamine his role in the formation of a national identity. The editor seeks to underscore the complexity and contradictions of Cortés and to redefine the debate, which traditionally has centered on viewing him either as a brilliant military strategist who brought Christianity to Mexico or as a murderer and rapist who destroyed the indigenous populations.

His claims to the contrary, precision and objectivity are not among this editor's virtues. Later in the preface, he erodes his own authority when he is imprecise as to the percentage of the autobiography based on the *Cartas*. He thus loses the stature of an editor in the strictest sense of the term, and, as he states on the following pages, he assumes the role of "collaborator" in writing the autobiography. He explains this change of status as follows:

> [P]or haber sido Hernán Cortés un escritor tan lúcido y vigoroso, que además dejó una amplísima producción literaria, las ocasiones en que se hizo necesario rellenar algunas lagunas fueron muy pocas. Por tal motivo aparece como principal autor del libro y yo sólo reclamo el crédito de colaborador. [...][33]

> [Since Hernán Cortés was such a lucid and vigorous writer who additionally left us an extensive body of literature, there were very few occasions when it was necessary to fill in lacunae in his accounts. Consequently, he appears as the principal author, and I ask only to be acknowledged as a collaborator....]

With this statement the fictional Cortés loses sole authorship of his autobiography, and the editor assumes a spectral authority over the narrative. His presence inherently destabilizes the authority of Cortés's own account, as the editor assumes a critical stance toward the material he edits. Throughout the novel, the reader is aware of reading a modernized version of the conquest of Mexico, translated from sixteenth-century to twentieth-century discourse.

The editor also influences our reading of Cortés's narrative through the use of footnotes. Although only seven notes appear in the novel, they perform numerous functions. First, they serve to correct alleged factual errors. At the beginning of the novel, the editor intervenes to point out remaining factual inaccuracies in Cortés's autobiography. He claims that Cortés should not have addressed his official reports to Carlos I and Juana, for "[Juana] había sido declarada loca y cesada en sus funciones. La conquista de México se realizó bajo el reinado de Carlos I de España (V de Alemania)."[34] [Juana had been declared insane and removed from the throne. The conquest of Mexico was accomplished under the reign of Charles I of Spain (Charles V of Germany).] Such editorial comments deflate the elevated rhetoric of the *Cartas de relación* and depict the fictional Cortés as ridiculous for not having realized, years after the fact, that the queen was insane. Such a move draws attention to the purported authority of the editor and his motives for serving as a mediator between the autobiography and the twentieth-century reader. Later, in the chapter on the Sad Night, the editor questions the veracity of Cortés's report about the number of casualties that the Spaniards suffered. He remarks, "[O]tras fuentes menos interesadas en disminuir el monto de los daños aseguran que los españoles muertos sumaban cerca de medio millar."[35] [Other parties less interested in minimizing Spanish casualties report that their dead numbered almost five hundred.] The text thus suggests that recuperation of a pristine account of history is impossible, for the interpretation of past events is always situated between events that happened prior to and after the discussed event. Historical representation of a past event, then, is always anachronistic.

In addition to correcting factual errors and calling attention to the mediated nature of historical writing, the editor uses footnotes to challenge the official history's representation of the Aztecs as barbarians. After Cortés describes Moctezuma's palace, the editor intervenes in order to justify Cortés's astonishment: "En la Europa de principio del siglo XVI no había jardines botánicos ni zoológicos. De allí el asombro de Cortés al ver estas instalaciones. [. . .]"[36] [There were no zoological or botanical gardens in Europe at the beginning of the sixteenth century. This explains the astonishment of Cortés upon seeing such establishments. . . .] Extrapolating from this footnote, the reader may speculate that the editor highlights the "civilization" of the Aztecs to critique their alleged "cultural barbarism" as depicted in the original *Cartas de relación*. Moreover, the association of the indigenous populations with civilization and the conquerors with barbarism inverts their roles as presented in the story about the conquest. In the same chapter, the editor offers examples of the sophistication of Aztec culture. He showcases their technological advances—for example, their system of aqueducts—to counter allegations of their purported barbarism. And by showing the sophistication of Aztec civilization, the editor challenges the premise upon which the conquest was justified and legitimated.

At other strategic moments, the editor includes photographs and paintings dealing with the historical Cortés and the conquest in order to contradict the official history and unmask the violence behind the written word. At the end of the first chapter, the fictional Cortés claims that he accepted the lead role of the expedition to New Spain because "prefería ser rico de fama más que de dinero [. . .]"[37] [I would prefer to be well known rather than possessed of riches . . .]. Immediately following the written text is a photograph of the ruins at Cempoala, a city of the Totonaca Indians (see fig. 4).[38] This modern-day photograph of a tourist site suggests the extent of the devastation that the Spaniards wrought on this indigenous group; the ruins of a single temple are all that remain. The juxtaposition of verbal and visual texts graphically demonstrates the costs inflicted on the indigenous culture for Cortés to achieve his fame and reputation as a conquistador. The intrusion of the present via the photograph once again fills in the gaps of the official historiography about the genocide of the indigenous populations.

The final footnote on the last page of the novel reiterates the polemical nature of Cortés and his writings and their effect on the course of Mexican history. In the first paragraph, the editor recapitulates the fate of Cortés's remains from his burial in 1547 through their rediscovery in Mexico City in 1946. This summary dramatizes how the corpus of Cortés's writings has stimulated heated debate about his legacy for both historians and literary writers alike, from the sixteenth century through the present. The physical corpse of Cortés has been transferred from site to site, and so has his textual corpus. Its significance has been subjected to constant recontextualization and reinterpretation. In *Cómo conquisté a los aztecas* neither the editor nor the fictional Cortés endows his version with indisputable authority about the conquest of Mexico and the character of the historical Cortés. Both the editor and the fictional Cortés function, nonetheless, to create a new site of discussion in the ongoing polemic that portrays Cortés either as the villain responsible for all the problems of modern Mexico or as a hero whose exploits merit comparison with those of the Roman emperor Caesar. Together they invite the reader to assume a more dispassionate stance toward Cortés, to challenge the authority of the written word as the truth, and to reread the *Cartas de relación*—a foundational text of modern Mexico—with a more critical eye.

Ayala Anguiano's *Cómo conquisté a los aztecas* transforms the *Cartas*

Figure 4. *Ruinas de Cempoala* (Ruins at Cempoala) by Armando Ayala Anguiano. Image courtesy of Armando Ayala Anguiano.

de relación from a sixteenth-century nonliterary discourse, the *relación,* into a twentieth-century autobiography marked by textual self-confrontations. These confrontations emerge as the fictional Cortés shows how the conventions of the *relación* shaped his presentation of self and as the twentieth-century editor contradicts the autobiography of Cortés with footnotes and photographs. Both the fictitious Cortés and the editor collaborate to demythify the official history and to invite readers to reexamine the legacy of Cortés in the formation of modern Mexico.

Unlike the historical Cortés of the *Cartas de relación* and the fictional Cortés of *Cómo conquisté a los aztecas,* both of whom achieve fame and recognition for their heroic military exploits in New Spain, the historical Cabeza de Vaca of the *Naufragios* (1542) and *Comentarios* (1555) achieved recognition for surviving trials and tribulations in regions that correspond today to the southwestern United States, northern Mexico, and the River Plate region. This antiheroic conquistador and his narratives about the New World are the subject of Abel Posse's *El largo atardecer del caminante,* winner of the 1992 Extremadura-América Prize of la Comisión española del quincentenario. A fictional seventy-year-old Cabeza de Vaca remembers his experiences in the New World and writes his autobiography as a means of critiquing his own *Naufragios* and *Comentarios,* the official record about his experiences in the southwestern United States (1528–37) and his subsequent expedition to the River Plate region to rescue the survivors of the Mendoza expedition (1540–42). The fictional Cabeza de Vaca addresses his narrative not to the king of Spain but rather to future generations of readers that he hopes will discover the manuscript of his autobiography. Indeed, his wishes are ostensibly realized, for an anonymous twentieth-century editor prepares the manuscript for publication as *El largo atardecer del caminante* and adds a preface and footnotes. Unlike the editor of *Cómo conquisté a los aztecas,* who subverts the authority of Cortés in both the *Cartas de relación* and the novel, the editor of *El largo atardecer del caminante* limits his interventions to facilitate the reading of the autobiography and to obligate the reader to establish parallels between sixteenth-century Spanish society and twentieth-century Latin America. The rewriting of the *Naufragios* and the *Comentarios* as an autobiography purportedly written in the sixteenth century and the editor's annotation of this autobiography in the twentieth century converge on the issue of rewriting the past to discuss the present.

Naufragios, first published in Zamora, Spain, in 1542 and subsequently revised and printed with the *Comentarios* in Valladolid in 1555, records Cabeza de Vaca's experiences from the departure of the disastrous Pánfilo de Narváez expedition to Florida in 1528 to his wanderings through the present-day southwestern United States (Texas, New Mexico, and Arizona) and northern Mexico (the states of Chihuahua and Sonora). His report is addressed to the King Carlos V as a petition in order to receive recognition and remuneration for his service to the crown.[39] This narrative consists of thirty-nine chapters and can be divided into five sections. The first section (chapters 1 and 2) records the departure of the Pánfilo de Narváez expedition from Sanlúcar de Barrameda on June 17, 1527, its arrival in Hispaniola (the modern-day Dominican Republic), and its stay in Cuba, where the expedition spent the winter of 1527–28 but experienced setbacks. The second section (chapters 3–7) deals with the arrival of the expedition in Florida (near Tampa Bay) and the exploration of the coastal and interior lands. The third section (chapters 8–15) narrates calamities that befell the expedition. Of the three hundred men who had landed in Florida, only four would survive: Andrés Dorantes, Alonso del Castillo Maldonado, the Moroccan slave Estevanico, and Cabeza de Vaca. The fourth section (chapters 16–33) chronicles the hardship of Cabeza de Vaca and his companions among indigenous tribes in modern-day Texas and describes the behavior and customs of such tribes. The fifth section (chapters 34–39) begins with Cabeza de Vaca and his companions meeting a group of Spanish soldiers laying siege to native communities in northern New Spain and ends with Cabeza de Vaca's stay in Mexico and eventual return to Castile in 1538.

Stylistically speaking, *Naufragios* is notable for its differences from other early New World chronicles such as Columbus's *Diario de a bordo,* Cortés's *Cartas de relación,* and Oviedo's *Historia natural de las Indias.* It is renowned for the absence of the rhetorical framework of erudite theologians and historians trained in the classic tradition of scholarship, the virtual absence of the interpolated stories characteristic of many sixteenth- and seventeenth-century chronicles, and its emphasis on the differences instead of the similarities between the New World and Spain.[40] *Los naufragios* displays features found in travel literature, medieval hagiography, Byzantine narrative, and picaresque narrative. However, according to Enrique Pupo-Walker, the pronounced autobiographical projections, reminiscent of Bernal Díaz del Castillo's *Historia verdadera de la conquista de la Nueva España,* el Inca Garcilaso de la Vega's *Comentarios reales,* and Carlos Sigüenza y Góngora's *Los infortunios de Alonso Ramírez,* significantly distinguish *Los naufragios.*[41] He further argues that the autobiographical projections intensify throughout the narrative: in chapters 1–6, the "legal" I of the testimonial witness predominates; in chapters 7–15 it is the "meditative" I who reflects on his suffering and hardship; and finally, in chapters 16–39 the "pious" and "sermonizing" I comes to the forefront. As Cabeza

1/REWRITING THE *RELACIÓN* AS AUTOBIOGRAPHY

de Vaca becomes more distant from Spanish institutions of authority, the need to tell his own story supersedes the need to provide an official, "objective" report about his discoveries.[42]

Cabeza de Vaca's *Los naufragios* is a classic of Spanish American colonial historiography and literature and has received extensive attention from historians and literary critics alike.[43] Only the writings of Columbus, the *Cartas de relación* of Cortés, several writings of Las Casas, and the *Comentarios reales* by el Inca Garcilaso de la Vega have surpassed the level of international distribution that the *Naufragios* has achieved since the sixteenth century.[44] In the realm of literature, Cabeza de Vaca and his experiences in the New World have become the focus of several novels, including most recently Abel Posse's *El largo atardecer del caminante,* the only Latin American novel about the life and experiences of Cabeza de Vaca.[45] This work presents the life story of Cabeza de Vaca from his childhood years in Jerez de la Frontera through the final years of his life in Seville. A penniless former explorer, he writes his memoirs about the New World and his recent failure at seducing a young woman named Lucinda. The novel concludes with the imminent death of Cabeza de Vaca and a plea that his memoirs find their way into the hands of future generations of readers.

El largo atardecer del caminante showcases the fictional autobiography of the seventy-four-year-old Cabeza de Vaca, who comments on the official historiography about the conquest and divulges previously untold secrets about his New World experiences. Unlike the Cabeza de Vaca of *Los naufragios,* in which the legal nature of the *relación* circumscribes his life story and governs the presentation of his public persona, the Cabeza de Vaca of *El largo atardecer del caminante* addresses his autobiography to posterity and remembers his experience in a lyric, confessional mode. He describes this change in attitude as follows:

> [C]uando me puse a escribir, comencé con el tono de siempre, el estilo del señor que a través de solemne notario se comunica con su rey. . . . No sin trabajo fui rompiendo las frases y los silencios convencionales. Mi brazo y mi mano se resistían. Por fin, ya seguro de que el mío podría ser un libro absolutamente secreto . . . empecé a lograr que la punta de la pluma más o menos calcase la voz interior. Empecé a caer en mí mismo. . . . Continuamente tuve que repetirme que ese libro sería como para ciegos: no había ojos que amenazasen la libertad de expresarme; porque los ojos del otro son el fin de nuestro yo, de nuestra espontaneidad. Así pude ir convenciéndome de que el otro no existiría, al menos hasta mucho tiempo después de mi muerte. Y desemboqué el lujo de la libertad. Una libertad de papel. Una nueva forma de caminar, de aventurarme por los desiertos, adecuada para el viejo que ya soy. . . .[46]

[When I sat down to write, I began in my customary tone, in the style of a lord communicating with his king by means of dictation to a solemn scribe. . . . Though I struggled against the resistance of my hand and arm, neither my conventional phrasing nor my conventional reticence were easily violated. Finally, convinced that my book could remain absolutely secret . . . I began to prevail upon the point of my quill to more or less heed my inner voice. I retreated into my thoughts. . . . I had to tell myself repeatedly that the world would be as a blind man to this book: no prying eyes would threaten my freedom of expression, because the eyes of the other limit us and fetter our spontaneity. Thus was I able to convince myself that the other would not exist, not at least until long after my death. And I experienced the luxury of freedom on the page. A new way to walk, to venture forth in the deserts, suited to the old man that I now am. . . .]

What the reader witnesses is the transformation of Cabeza de Vaca from a public figure in the *Naufragios* to a private self in an autobiography, from a conscientious and law-abiding servant of the crown to a critic of Spain's colonial enterprise in the New World. By surpassing the convention of the *relación,* where the autobiographical element (the personal story) is subordinate to the act of informing, the fictitious Cabeza de Vaca achieves the freedom to narrate an introspective story about his experiences. He verbally articulates them as freely as he was able to wander and participate in an alien culture. He feels compelled to write this testament, he explains, in order to discuss, without fear of persecution from the Inquisition, his allegedly heretical behavior, especially his adoption of indigenous modes of viewing the world.

El largo atardecer del caminante does not, however, present the manuscript of Cabeza de Vaca's autobiography in a straightforward manner. As in Ayala Anguiano's novel, an anonymous twentieth-century editor adapts the autobiography by inserting a preface titled "Noticia de Cabeza de Vaca" and two footnotes. The framing of the autobiography with an editorial voice dispels the illusion that readers have unmediated access to the protagonist's private life and invites them to read the novel against the backdrop of Latin American testimonial narrative, which is defined by John Beverly in *Against Literature* (1993). According to Beverly, testimonial narrative includes a novel-length narrative in book form, told in the first person by a narrator who is also the real protagonist or witness of the events recounted. The unit of narration is usually a significant life experience, and in many cases the narrator is someone who, if literate, is not a professional writer. The production of a testimonial often entails the tape recording and transcription of an oral account by an interlocutor who is an intellectual, a journalist, or a writer.[47] In many respects *El largo atardecer del caminante* can be read as a testimonial, since the Cabeza de Vaca of the novel occupies a subaltern position in relation to the colonial enterprise, the story that he tells incorporates a silenced voice that contests and contradicts the official record about the conquest, and the editor collaborates with the informant to issue a collective history of marginalized groups and members demanding just treatment before institutions of authority.

El largo atardecer del caminante re-creates the Cabeza de Vaca episode of Spanish American historiography and literature in order to denounce repression and censorship under dictatorship. The novel blends sociopolitical and aesthetic commentary to reveal the mechanisms by which the institutions of history and literature establish a sanctioned interpretation of the past. It revisits the inherited cultural legacy of the colonial past with Spanish American eyes cognizant of the needs of modern society. The anonymous twentieth-century editor of *El largo atardecer del caminante* assumes a position of authority over Cabeza de Vaca's fictional autobiography just as historiographers and literary historians of Spanish America have assumed interpretative power over Cabeza de Vaca's *Naufragios*. Such power over the text serves to dramatize how re-creating the past for historians and novelists provides a vehicle for criticizing the present.

In the preface the editor devises a dual strategy in establishing the master code for reading the secret autobiography as a subversive critique of the official history of Cabeza de Vaca's life and experiences in the New World. First, in accordance with the sanctioned interpretation of the episode, the editor gestures toward the uniqueness of the conquistador's experience, thereby preparing the reader for the retelling of the story from a Spanish American perspective. The editor remarks,

> Por elegancia o por una extraña pasión subversiva, se separó [Cabeza de Vaca] del tipo humano del «Conquistador». A pie, desnudo como un indio, desarmado y sin cruces ni evangelios (visibles), se lanzó a la caminata más descomunal de la historia....[48]

> [Whether motivated by elegance or an unusual and subversive passion, Cabeza de Vaca separated himself from the human type known as "Conquistador." Barefoot and naked as an Indian, unarmed with weapon, cross, or bible, he set out on the most extraordinary peregrination in history....]

Clearly the editor detects the latent, subversive elements of Cabeza de Vaca's story. That this conquistador not only failed in his mission but also adopted indigenous cultural practices and modes of thought prompts readers to interpret the autobiography as the development of such potential. Cabeza de Vaca occupies a marginal position, analogous to that of the indigenous populations, in relation to Spanish imperial authorities as he offers a critique of the colonial enterprise. In other words, the editor proposes that the twentieth-century reader view Cabeza de Vaca sympathetically as a humanized conquistador instead of the mythic conquistador from institutionally sanctioned history.

After humanizing the Cabeza de Vaca in the novel, the editor defamiliarizes the Cabeza de Vaca from the official history by juxtaposing literary writers and texts from the past and present. The comparison of Cabeza de Vaca's stay with the Tarahumara Indians of northern Mexico in the sixteenth century to that of Antonin Artaud's visit with this same tribe in the twentieth century cues readers to identify and contemplate other historical parallels between sixteenth-century Spain and twentieth-century Latin America and to note the theatrical dimensions of the official history and the autobiography of Cabeza de Vaca. Throughout the novel, theatrical metaphors serve as an organizing principle for emplotting history and autobiography in that both are portrayed as following formulaic scripts to produce meanings.

Besides juxtaposing historical characters and literary writers from disparate epochs, the editor invites readers to approach Cabeza de Vaca's life through that of other literary characters, especially Don Quixote. Neither Cabeza de Vaca nor Don Quixote adhered to the dominant codes of conduct of their day, and, according to the editor, Cabeza de Vaca manifested idealism in exploring the New World:

> Todo hombre tiene sus molinos de viento personales. Los de Cabeza de Vaca fueron la selva paraguaya, los desiertos a los que se hizo buscando más iniciaciones espirituales que tesoros [. . .] y sobre todo el mar: cada uno de sus embarques terminó en naufragio.[49]

> [Every man has his own personal windmills. Those of Cabeza de Vaca were the Paraguayan forest, the deserts where he sought not treasure but spiritual initiation, . . . and above all the sea: every one of his journeys led to a shipwreck.]

Essentially, Cabeza de Vaca displayed naïveté regarding his decision to curtail the authority of the Spaniards in Paraguay, while advocating humane treatment for the indigenous populations.

Both Cabeza de Vaca and Don Quixote upheld personal codes of ethics that did not enable them to function effectively in changing historical and social contexts. The parallels between Cabeza de Vaca and Don Quixote also extends to their physical appearance, for Cabeza de Vaca is described as having "[una] barba valleinclanesca y aquijotada"[50] [a Valle-Inclanesque, quixotified beard]. The juxtaposition in the preface of Cabeza de Vaca and Ramón Valle Inclán as writers prepares readers for the subsequent cameo appearance of the Marqués de Bradomín from Valle Inclán's *Sonatas* (1902) and the nostalgic tone in which Cabeza de Vaca recounts the seduction of the young Lucinda. Thus, the editor inscribes his preface within the parameters of the conventional interpretation of the Cabeza de Vaca story as a tale of failure, but then proceeds to erase boundaries between the sixteenth and the twentieth century and between the historical and the literary in order to dismantle history and reconfigure a cultural narrative of the colonial past that presents Cabeza de Vaca as a precursor of the twentieth-century struggles in Latin America for freedom from state-sponsored repression and terrorism as evidenced during the Argentine Dirty War (1976–82).

Toward the end of the novel, the senseless death of Cabeza de Vaca's daughter Amaría at the hands of the Spanish military parallels the disappearance of political dissidents in twentieth-century Argentina at the hands of the military junta. Cabeza de Vaca learns from his mestizo son Amadís, who was enslaved and transported to Spain, that Amaría met a violent death in the New World at the hands of a sergeant "Videla." As Amaría's death is senseless, cruel and random, so were the disappearances of many innocent Argentine citizens whom the government had labeled as subversive and worthy of elimination, as part of a campaign to extirpate "un-Christian" elements from Argentine society. By inserting the name of an infamous Argentine military dictator in a sixteenth-century fictionalized autobiography, the editor invokes the remote past to establish parallels between the climate of oppression and violence perpetrated by the conquistadors in the sixteenth century and the military junta of the twentieth.

The strategy of inserting literary and historical anachronisms in the period of the Spanish conquest of the New World in order to criticize the twentieth-century sociopolitical situation in Latin America also infiltrates Cabeza de Vaca's autobiography. In recalling his literary friendship with the Marqués de Bradomín, the protagonist of Ramón Valle Inclán's *Sonatas* (1902), the fictional Cabeza de Vaca points out how censors from the Inquisition consistently thwarted the literary endeavors of his friend and also affected his own secret autobiography. He notes: "Estos son tiempos en que por un adjetivo se puede perder la vida, y él [el marqués] preferirá siempre un buen adjetivo. [. . .]"[51] [These are times in which one may lose one's life for using the wrong adjective, and the marqués will always prefer a good adjective. . . .] Writing under the eyes of the Inquisition in the sixteenth century or of a military dictatorship in the twentieth leads writers to attain a higher level of awareness about their relationship to language and to the process of writing. The marqués's writings are censored not only for his scandalous use of language but also for the overtly political nature of his plots. This fictionalized Marqués de Bradomín has moved beyond writing a Don Juanesque autobiography of the *Sonatas* and is drafting a book of "aventuras imaginarias en México" [imaginary adventures in Mexico],[52] an allusion to Valle Inclán's *Tirano banderas* (1926), renowned for its indictment of Latin American dictatorships. The situation of the Marqués de Bradomín in *El largo atardecer del caminante* is suggestive of the precarious situation of Argentine writers under the military dictatorship. Cabeza de Vaca further laments, "[T]oda verdad íntima y auténtica se transforma en un hecho penal. [. . .]"[53] [Every intimate and authentic truth becomes a criminal act. . . .] At one level, he is referring to the Inquisition's practice of censorship in the sixteenth century; at another, he is alluding to the imprisonment and torture of dissident writers in contemporary Latin America. Once again, the insertion of literary anachronisms into a sixteenth-century fictional autobiography serves as a strategy for re-creating the past in order to criticize the present.

Clearly, the editor views history as a cyclical process that reenacts a story about violence, the abuse of power, and repression. A similar attitude emerges in Cabeza de Vaca's fictional account and is expressed with a theatrical metaphor. According to Cabeza de Vaca, the Spanish imperial enterprise has produced a hierarchy of abuses in which the king exercises power over the conquistadors, while they in turn exercise power over the indigenous populations of the New World. In the end, both conquistadors and indigenous populations are assigned secondary roles in a drama in which Carlos V assumes the role of protagonist. For the novel's Cabeza de Vaca, Carlos V was

> el gran protagonista de esta eterna comedia que representamos los cómicos de la lengua. En cada generación estamos hermanados por haber pisado las mismas tablas, pese a la diferencia y la oposición de los roles: Cortés, el conquistador feliz, el torvo Pizarro y sus hermanos y los Almagro; Orellana, Alvarado; Ponce de León que salió a buscar la magia de la eterna juventud y encontró la punta de una flecha envenenada. Y Atahualpa y Moctezuma, los desdichados y perplejos emperadores que comprendieron el sentido de la civilización cuando los degollaban o los llevaban al suplicio. Protagonistas en una interminable representación.[54]

> [the great protagonist of this eternal comedy in which we linguistic comedians perform. In each generation we are united by having strutted the same boards, despite the variety and opposition of our roles: Cortés, the satisfied conqueror, the baleful Pizarro and his brothers, Almagro, Orellana, Alvarado, and Ponce de León, who set out in search of eternal youth and was met with a poisoned

arrowhead. And Atahualpa and Moctezuma, those unfortunate, baffled emperors who understood the meaning of civilization when their throats were slit or when they were led to their executions. Protagonists in an eternal drama.]

The script of history has assigned roles to the conquistadors and the indigenous populations to perform in the drama about the conquest of the New World and in the hidden tale about the abuse of power.

In the act of writing his autobiography, the fictional Cabeza de Vaca realizes that the creation of a conquistador prototype and a pattern of conquest that met the needs of the imperial enterprise have influenced the conquistadors' dreams about the New World. He makes this observation when he recalls the unfulfilled dreams of Pánfilo de Narváez, who modeled his visions of discovery and conquest after the experience of Cortés in New Spain: "Su México sería la Florida con sus secretas ciudades de oro. El también vencería a un gran emperador, tendría sus malinches, aboliría ídolos demoníacos y sería recibido por el gran César Carlos I."[55] [His Mexico would be Florida, with its secret cities of gold. He too would vanquish a great emperor, he would have his Malinches, he would abolish demonic idols and would be received by the great caesar, Charles I. . . .] As the conquistadors attempt to conquer the indigenous populations, the desire for wealth and fame conquer them in turn. When Spaniards assume the identity of the conquistador as scripted in institutional histories, they forfeit the possibility of deviating from the norm. In many respects, the fictional Cabeza de Vaca views the official history as a mirror that reflects not the individual stories of the conquistadors but the crown's configuration of reality:

> [E]stos espejos que sin indigestarse devoran nuestras figuras y las escenas de nuestra vida. [. . .] Extraño objeto lleno de conocimientos pero condenado a la desmemoria. Nada puede sacarse de él: es como un lago quieto en el que todos nos ahogamos y desaparecemos.[56]

> [These mirrors that devour our figures and the scenes of our lives, that do so and suffer no indigestion. . . . [They are] strange objects condemned to know these things but disremember them. Nothing can be retrieved; they are like a quiet lake in which we all drown and disappear.]

His autobiography seeks to recover private memories of his public self and to legitimate the heterogeneity of experiences in the New World. History empties the *petite histoire* of its immediate significance and resignifies it with a monolithic meaning in accordance with the agenda of an institutional authority. To reclaim ownership of his story and recode it as a tale denouncing the conquest as an imperialist enterprise that abused the indigenous population as well as the conquistadors, Cabeza de Vaca writes his secret autobiography as an act of defiance and resistance.

Since the fictional Cabeza de Vaca rewrites *Los naufragios* as autobiography in order to reclaim authority over his own story and challenge the official history of the conquest, he inevitably engages Fernando González de Oviedo's version of his experiences as recorded in the *Historia general y natural de Indias* (1535). According to the fictional Cabeza de Vaca, historical truths are manufactured by institutions of authority. He comments that González de Oviedo has exercised supreme interpretative power over the version of his story that will be transmitted from generation to generation:

> [Oviedo] está convencido de que la Conquista y el Descubrimiento existen sólo en la medida en que él supo recuperar, organizar y relatar los hechos. Es el dueño de lo que se suele llamar ahora «la Historia». Lo que él no registre en su chismosa relación, o no existió o es falso. . . .[57]

> [Oviedo is convinced that the discovery and the conquest exist only insofar as he was able to recover, organize, and recount their particulars. He owns what is now called "history." Whatever has no place in his gossipmongering *relación* either did not happen or is false. . . .]

Instead of openly and directly contesting the official history, however, he does so obliquely by writing his autobiography for posterity. The historian's power over the written word supersedes the power of military conquest. The fictional Cabeza de Vaca notes this as follows:

> Oviedo [. . .] será el conquistador de los conquistadores, el depósito de la verdad. [. . .] Hará con la pluma mucho más de lo que efectivamente hicimos nosotros con la espada. [. . .] Para bien o para mal, la única realidad que queda es la de la historia escrita. El mismo Rey termina por creer lo que dice el historiador en vez de lo que le cuenta quien conquistó el mundo a punta de espada. Todo termina en un libro o en un olvido.[58]

> [Oviedo . . . will conquer the conquerors. He will be the repository of truth. . . . He will accomplish much more with the pen than we have done with the sword. . . . For better or worse, the only reality that remains is what is written as history. In the end, the king himself believes more in what he is told by the historian than by the very man whose sword conquered the world. All that is not written is forgotten.]

In order for his story to escape oblivion, Cabeza de Vaca is compelled to record his personal experiences in writing as a counternarrative to the history promulgated by institutional authorities. The subordination of Cabeza de Vaca's eyewitness experiences in the New World to the grand design of telling the imperial story of discovery and conquest demands rectification.

As the official history of a people sets the stage and assigns the scripts to the protagonists, Cabeza de Vaca views the process of writing his autobiography as an act of dismantling that historical stage and constructing his own, from which he will perform his self-created script. His meditations on the process of writing extend to the preparatory "prewriting" moments, for to write about his past self the fictional Cabeza de Vaca dons clothing from that historical moment. He remarks,

> Es en este papel que divago al atardecer. Es sobre este regalo de Lucinda donde escribo con eso nuevo y extraño que llamaría libertad. [. . .] Me pongo al atardecer en mi escritorio. [. . .] Pero antes me visto con medias finas y alguno de los viejos trajes que exhumé. Me visto como para visitarme a mí mismo y dialogar con los otros Alvar Núñez Cabeza de Vaca, los que ya murieron o merodean dentro de mí como almas en pena. [. . .][59]

> [I assume this role as the day fades, writing on this gift from Lucinda with a strange new sensation that I might call freedom. . . . I sit down at my desk in the evening. . . . , but first I put on a fine pair of stockings and one of the old ensembles that I have exhumed. I am attired as though to visit myself and converse with the other Alvar Núñez Cabeza de Vacas, those who have already died or who lurk within me like tormented souls. . . .]

As historians establish a dialogue and interpret written documents with the past from the vantage point of the present, the fictional Cabeza de Vaca reexamines the multiple historical Cabeza de Vacas—those recorded in the official history as well as those unedited in his soul—to understand his immediate historical circumstances.

The divergence in explanations between historical and autobiographical accounts is most evident at the moment when the historical Cabeza de Vaca reenters Spanish "civilization" and attempts to wear shoes after having gone barefoot for eight years. According to the editor of the autobiography, Cabeza de Vaca's inability to wear shoes is emblematic of his transformation from a conquistador to a cultural outsider: "[Y]a tenía pie de indio: no le entraban las botas. . . .]"[60] [Now his feet were as an Indian's: they received no boots. . . .] However, in his autobiography, the fictional Cabeza de Vaca views this scene as a moment to acknowledge his estrangement from Spanish culture and to play the role of a Spaniard. He remembers:

> Las botas son como coturnos. Coturnos de esos de madera, que hacen caminar como muñecos a los actores que retumban fuerte sobre el tablado de escena. O son como zancos también. Y uno se mueve oscilando en lo alto, como zancudo

de feria. Uno se bambolea y hay que disimular. En México-Tenochtitlán fui recibido con mis botas-coturnos, creo que me los había prestado el Gobernador. Cortés me miraba con sorna. Yo ya había perdido la costumbre de ser soldado español (tal vez, incluso de ser español) y me bamboleaba un poco como si entrase en zancos en el salón donde se me homenajeaba.[61]

[Boots are like cothurni, those wooden cothurni that constrain actors to walk like oversized marionettes, each footfall resounding against the boards. Or they are like stilts. And one teeters on high, like a stilt-walker at a fair. One staggers along and dissimulates his distress. In Mexico-Tenochtitlán I was received in my cothurni-boots; I think that the governor had lent them to me. Cortés eyed me derisively, for I had lost the bearing of a Spanish soldier, or perhaps the very manner of being Spanish, as I lurched as though on stilts into the hall where I was to be honored.]

The theatrical rendition of Cabeza de Vaca's triumphant reentry into Spanish culture undercuts the seriousness with which imperial authorities attempt to reclaim him as unchanged by the New World experience, though the fictional Cabeza de Vaca himself no longer views himself as institutional authorities defined a Spaniard. Thus, cultural identity is constructed as a theatrical role.

The fictional Cabeza de Vaca's challenge to the official history moves beyond the representation of his personal story to encompass a comprehensive critique of the "discovery" as a manifestation of imperial colonialism. According to his account, the rhetoric of discovery and conquest concealed the Spaniards' deep-seated desire to project their own psychological anxieties onto the New World and to legitimize its destruction. In the novel, the explorer and conquistador Pedro de Cieza explains this circumstance as follows:

[N]osotros [los conquistadores] no hemos descubierto ni conquistado. Sólo habíamos pasado por arriba. Habíamos más bien cubierto, negado sin conocer amordazado. Nos mandaron a imperar. Eso hicimos, nada más. No fuimos a descubrir, que es conocer; sino a desconocer. Depredar, sepultar lo que hubiese. Avasallar silenciando, transformando a todos los otros en ninguno. Señoreando, por fin, en un pueblo de fantasmas, de *ningunos*. . . .[62]

[We conquistadors have neither discovered nor conquered. We have but passed through unknowingly—concealing, silencing, declining to see. We were sent to rule and did no more. We came not to discover, which is to know, but to disregard, to plunder, to entomb that which was. To subjugate by silencing, transforming all others into nobody. To be lords, after all, of a city of ghosts, of nobodies. . . .]

In part the fictional Cabeza de Vaca's autobiography participates in filling in the moments of silence and saying what would have been unthinkable in his original *relación* to the king, in recuperating those silenced voices buried in the volumes of recorded history.

The absence of reprisals from a higher authority for divulging a private truth contrary to the public truth bestows on the fictional Cabeza de Vaca a sense of freedom. As he transforms himself from a conquerer in history into an adventurer, he recaptures a more authentic sense of self, which he states as follows:

> No hice otra cosa sino tratar de desembarazarme de él buscando más la aventura que la conquista y el poder. Fui un peatón, un caminante de reinos perdidos, de nuevos misterios. Para consolarme, más de una vez, cuando me tenían detenido, conjeturé que el castigo no era absurdo pues en lo profundo de mí nunca había cumplido con propósitos del Imperio.[63]

> [I tried only to unburden myself of him, seeking adventure rather than conquest or power. I was a rambler, a wanderer in lost kingdoms and new mysteries. More than once when I was held against my will, I consoled myself with the thought that my punishment was not unreasonable, since deep down I had never adequately deferred to the goals of the empire.]

The fictional Cabeza de Vaca makes a radical break with his historical self, for as José Rabasa notes, the historical Cabeza de Vaca of *Los naufragios,* though he advocated a more humane treatment of the indigenous populations, never denounced the Spanish colonial enterprise:

> Cabeza de Vaca could never have assumed the position Las Casas takes in the 1550s (a unique one indeed) of total condemnation of the Spanish enterprise in the New World.... We should not, however, project an anti-imperialist position or be seduced by his heroic, colorful narratives of colonial adventures....[64]

Posse, however, in his contemporary rendition suggests otherwise. The fictional Cabeza de Vaca's defiance of the project of imperialism manifests itself most explicitly in his mission to the Río de la Plata region, where he attempts to reestablish order in modern-day Paraguay. He designs his own flag as the authority under which he will attempt to establish order: "Hice estampar un nuevo escudo de familia en las grandes velas: una cabeza de vaca tan imponente como la del cíbolo que decapitaron los guerreros del cacique Duljàn al borde del «camino de las vacas»."[65] [I had a new Cabeza de Vaca coat of arms displayed on the largest sails: a cow's head as imposing as that of the bison decapitated by Duljàn's warriors along the *camino de las vacas.*] In the process of rewriting *Los naufragios* as autobiography, Cabeza de Vaca transforms his public self from an obedient and loyal servant seeking recognition and favors from the crown to a renegade at odds with the objectives and tactics of colonial imperialism.

Posse's *El largo atardecer del caminante* presents the first Spanish American novelistic re-creation of Cabeza de Vaca and his experiences in the New World. It revisits Cabeza de Vaca's odyssey in order to tease out and develop the latent potential of the *Naufragios* and relate it to contemporary sociopolitical and aesthetic preoccupations in modern Spanish American culture and society. As to sociopolitical concerns, the novel extends Cabeza de Vaca's critical stance toward the conquistadors' abuse of the indigenous populations in the sixteenth century to include human rights violations that military dictatorships perpetrated against civilian populations throughout twentieth-century Latin America. The insertion of anachronisms in Cabeza de Vaca's fictional autobiography obliges readers to interpret it against the backdrop of both the *Naufragios* and the editor's preface of the novel. History becomes the weapon by which institutional authorities consolidate and legitimate their power, so in order to counteract the official history, Cabeza de Vaca appropriates the discourse and strategies of the crown to make way for authorizing silenced voices to speak.

These novels rewrite the *Cartas de relación* and the *Naufragios,* respectively, as editor-mediated autobiographies. The first undermines the official history about the conquest of Mexico; the second undermines Gonzalo Fernández de Oviedo's interpretation of Cabeza de Vaca's experiences in the New World. They develop unrealized possibilities from the original canonical colonial writings. In *Cómo conquisté a los aztecas,* the fictional Cortés provides a retrospective account of his conquest of New Spain and provides an intimate confessional perspective on his life as a conquistador. While poking fun at his indiscretions as a youth and adult, the fictional Cortés undermines his own heroic standing, and the twentieth-century editor extends this demythification process through paratextual devices such as photographs and footnotes that contradict both the original *Cartas de relación* and the fictional autobiography in the novel. The historical Cortés is portrayed as neither villain nor hero but as a human being whose legacy for modern Mexico should be reexamined in an attempt to come to terms with the legacy of the conquest on the formation of Mexican national identity.

On the other hand, *El largo atardecer del caminante* presents the editor-mediated story of Cabeza de Vaca, who rewrites the *Naufragios* as an introspective autobiography that re-creates his wanderings in the New World as a means to critique the standard interpretation of his account as that of a loyal servant of the crown who returned unchanged by his experiences.

Through the interventions of the editor in the preface combined with the fictional Cabeza de Vaca's remarks in his autobiography, readers establish historical parallels between sixteenth-century Spanish and twentieth-century Latin American societies, where intolerance and oppression predominate. Retelling the Cabeza de Vaca episode from colonial Spanish American history transforms the fictional Cabeza de Vaca into a prophet and enables the editor to explore the past to better understand twentieth-century Latin American society and culture. While scholars such as Enrique Pupo-Walker and Beatriz Pastor approached the chronicles as if they were literary texts from their inception, Armando Ayala Anguiano and Abel Posse transform those same historiographic writings into fictional autobiographies and highlight the enduring importance of the chronicles of the Indies for modern Spanish American narrative and culture.

2
Fictional Marginal Figures and the Rewriting of the New World Historiography

> Vencido por vosotros, os ha vencido, a su vez, el Nuevo Mundo y ha agotado o debilitado vuestro antiguo vigor. Nunca han llevado otro fruto las riquezas. [. . .]
> —"Carta 88" from Flemish scholar Justus Lipsus to his Spanish friend Bartolomé Leonardo de Argensola (1603)

> [Once you conquered it, the New World then vanquished you, debilitating and depleting your former vigor. Wealth has never borne any other fruit. . . .]

> The episodes of moral decay always coincide with the progression of effeminacy, lewdness and luxuriance of the nations. These phenomena can only be ascribed to higher and more stringent demands which circumstances make upon the nervous system. . . .
> —Richard von Krafft-Ebing, in *Psychopathia Sexualis* (1881)

IN CHAPTER 1, I EXPLORED HOW AYALA ANGUIANO'S *CÓMO CONQUISTÉ A los aztecas* and Posse's *El largo atardecer* employ famous conquistadors to revise episodes from the early New World historiography and to transform sixteenth-century *relaciones* into twentieth-century confessional autobiographies that enter into dialogue with the official historiography on Cortés and Cabeza de Vaca. In this chapter I will shift the focus to invented marginal figures that retell episodes from the discovery and conquest of the River Plate in the sixteenth and eighteenth centuries and put forth versions of events excluded from the official history about the colonial period.[1]

Contemporary novelists in the River Plate are reinterpreting the New World historiography about the exploration, discovery, and conquest with socially marginal figures that narrate historical events from a subversive and distinctly humorous viewpoint. Such is the case with Napoleón Baccino Ponce de León's *Maluco: La novela de los descubridores* (Uruguay, 1990) and Antonio Elio Brailovsky's *Esta maldita lujuria* (Argentina, 1990). *Maluco* retells the famous voyage of Ferdinand Magellan (1519–21) from the perspective of the expedition's buffoon, who, years later, submits a *relación de servicio* to King Charles V in hopes that the monarch will recognize his contributions and compensate him for service rendered to the crown. *Esta maldita lujuria,* cast in the form of a lengthy letter from a sword-maker in Patagonia to the viceroy of Buenos Aires in 1810, narrates the founding and settlement of the town of Carmen de Patagones in 1779 and retells the colonial history of the New World as a tale of unrealized and frustrated dreams of finding the Ciudad de los Césares, the River Plate version of the myth of El Dorado. In both novels, invented marginal figures—a buffoon in *Maluco* and a sword-maker in *Esta maldita lujuria*—challenge the official history of a particular historical event from the colonial period and establish parallels with the recent sociopolitical history of Uruguay and Argentina during the 1970s and 1980s.

Both narrators employ epistolary modes of narration to correct, emend, and overturn the official historical record in order to tell their own stories that reveal the underside of the New World. While Juanillo the buffoon submits his petition to Charles V as a mock *relación de servicio* and appropriates its conventions in order to denounce injustices, Ambrosio de Lara, the sword-maker, casts his narrative as a personal communiqué that exhorts the viceroy from Buenos Aires to disavow the myth of the Ciudad de los Césares. Through his letter, Lara reveals himself as a disillusioned colonist whose scandalous vignettes about the sexual adventures of famous explorers and conquistadors implicitly critique for the twentieth-century reader the military junta's censorship of sexually explicit references during the Proceso. Juanillo and Lara bring to the forefront the act of storytelling and their marginal social positions as fundamental strategies for undermining the conventional historical record.

On September 8, 1519, the Portuguese explorer Ferdinand Magellan and his fleet of five ships—the *Trinidad, San Antonio, Concepción, Victoria,* and *Santiago*—set sail from Seville and headed westward, around the southern tip of South America, in search of the Moluccas Islands. Almost three years later, on September 6, 1522, only the *Victoria* and 18 of the original 270 members of the expedition returned to Sanlúcar, Spain.[2] Magellan was not among those survivors, for he lost his life at the hands of indigenous populations in the Philippines in April 1521.

Magellan never achieved a level of attention and recognition compared to that of other famous sixteenth-century explorers and discoverers such as Columbus and Vasco da Gama. As recently as 1967, the historian William F. E. Morley noted that "For every volume on Magellan published since the World War, five have appeared on Columbus. . . ."[3] Historians have attributed this lack of interest in the life and accomplishments of Magellan to the fact that Portuguese historians have viewed him as a traitor, while Spanish historians have been disinclined to glorify a hero who was not Spanish by birth.[4] Since Magellan himself left no written account of the voyage, the task of recording it fell to Peter Martyr of Anglería, an Italian at the Spanish court, who prepared the official history of Magellan's voyage based on personal interviews with surviving crew members. Martyr's account of the voyage constitutes the focus of the seventh chapter of the fifth *Decades* (1526). Another surviving crew member, Antonio Pigafetta, refused to hand over his notes to Martyr and offered them as a report in personal homage to King Charles V of Spain. He subsequently drafted a fuller report that was first printed in an abridged translation in French in 1525.[5]

While most professional historians have ignored Magellan's voyage, a handful of Southern Cone and Mexican novelists have shown renewed interest in retelling that voyage as recorded in Pigafetta's *Relación del primer viaje en torno del mundo* (1527). During the 1960s, writers from the Spanish American Boom hailed Pigafetta as a precursor of their fiction. For instance, García Márquez alluded to Pigafetta in his acceptance speech of the Nobel Prize for Literataure in 1982:

> Antonio Pigafetta, un navegante florentino que acompañó a Magallanes en su primer viaje alrededor del mundo, escribió a su paso por nuestra América Meridional una crónica rigurosa que sin embargo parece una aventura de imaginación. Contó que había visto cerdos con el ombligo en el lomo, unos pájaros sin patas cuyas hembras empollaban en las espaldas del macho, y como otros alcatraces sin lengua cuyos picos parecían una cuchara. [. . .] Contó que al primer nativo que encontraron en la Patagonia le pusieron enfrente un espejo, y que aquel gigante enardecido perdió el uso de la razón por el pavor de su propia imagen.
>
> Este libro breve y fascinante, en el cual ya se vislumbran los gérmenes de nuestras novelas de hoy, no es ni mucho menos el testimonio más asombroso de nuestra realidad de aquellos tiempos. Los cronistas de Indias nos legaron otros incontables. [. . .][6]

> [Antonio Pigafetta, a Florentine navigator who went with Magellan on the first voyage around the world, wrote, upon his passage through our southern lands of America, a strictly accurate account that nonetheless resembles a venture into fantasy. In it he recorded that he had seen hogs with navels on their haunches, clawless birds who hens laid eggs on the backs of their mates, and others still, resembling tongueless pelicans, with beaks like spoons. . . . He described how the first native encountered in Patagonia was confronted with a mirror, whereupon that impassioned giant lost his senses to the terror of his own image.
>
> This short and fascinating book, which even then contained the seeds of our present-day novels, is by no means the most staggering account of our reality in that age. The chroniclers of the Indies left us countless others. . . .][7]

Evidently, García Márquez's remarks have inspired later writers to retell Pigafetta's account. These rewritings include a short narrative entitled "La historia de historias de Antonio Pigafetta" by the Argentine critic and short-fiction writer Héctor Libertella, from his collection of short stories *¡Carvernícolas!* (1985); *El viaje más largo* (1993) by the Mexican novelist Mario Huacuja; *El regreso* (1999) by the Mexican novelist, short-story writer, and poet Herminio Martínez; and *Maluco: La novela de los descubridores* (1990) by Napoleón Baccino Ponce de León.

Napoleón Baccino Ponce de León (b. Montevideo, 1947) is a novelist, short-story writer, and critic of Spanish American literature. By 1992 he had dedicated himself exclusively to becoming a professional writer.[8] To date he has published three novels—*Maluco: La novela de los descubridores* (1990), *Un amor en Bangkok* (1994), and *El arte de perder* (1995)—and a biography of Aaron de Anchorena, an Argentine, titled *Aaron de Anchorena: Una vida privilegiada* (1998). His *Maluco: La novela de los descubridores* has gone through eleven printings, been translated into twelve languages (including an English edition called *Five Black Ships: A Novel of the Discoverers*), and been awarded numerous literary prizes. These prizes include the 1990 Premio Blanes de Oro (Montevideo), awarded annually for an Uruguayan book that has achieved national and international recognition; the 1990 Premio Latinoamericano de Narrativa (Mexico), awarded annually for the best novel published in Latin America; a second-place finish in the 1991 "Rómulo Gallegos" Premio de Novela competition; and the prestigious 1990 Casa de las Américas Premio de Novela (Cuba), whose jury lauded the novel for its "tratamiento de un tema universal resuelto con notable profesionalismo en el que destaca la estilización del lenguaje de las crónicas del descubrimiento, el agudo sentido del humor, el alto vuelo imaginativo, con los que logra trascender la recreación de una época para convertirse en un texto de honda significación contemporánea [...]"[9] [treatment of a universal theme, accomplished with notable professionalism, particularly reflected in a literary style reminiscent of the chronicles of discovery, a sharp sense of humor, and a soaring imagination, with which he has managed to transcend the re-creation of an era and produce a text of profound contemporary significance ...].

Although *Maluco* follows the accounts of Magellan's voyage as recorded in Martyr's *Decades* and Pigafetta's *Relación del primer viaje,* it adds humorous glosses in order to change our modern interpretation of those accounts. In the novel the buffoon Juanillo, who submits his own version of the voyage to Charles V, is encloistered at the monastery in Yuste, in order to receive the pension that Philip II had suspended after the king discovered that Juanillo was criticizing the official version. The novel consists of nine chapters and an appendix, in which the king's advisor Juan de

Sepúlveda unequivocally concludes that, although he cannot ascertain the veracity of Juanillo's account, he regards it as at least entertaining. Modeled after Pigafetta's *Relación,* the novel recounts in a chronological fashion the voyage from its departure in 1519 through the return of the *Victoria* in 1522. Each chapter interweaves stories within stories that tell the lives of other crew members and incorporates Juanillo's parenthetical, digressive comments to the king. The narrative, at moments, is expressed with lyrical language, manifests the markings of orality, and communicates the pervasive monotony of life aboard the ship.

Critics of the novel have focused on the marginal status of the buffoon and the appropriation of discursive forms from the sixteenth century. In her dissertation on the rewriting of the discovery and conquest of the New World in a selection of Spanish American novels, Viviana Plotnik argues that marginal figures are the key element of a strategy to contest discourses of power as embodied in the chronicles of the Indies. Moreover, she posits that such figures critique the practices of Spanish Renaissance historiography that produced a truth value favorable to the designs of the crown and transform the chronicles into contemporary Spanish American narratives that bring to the forefront the imprecise boundaries between literature and history, or "fiction" and "fact," in the Spanish Renaissance.[10] Other critics have focused on the discursive composition of the novel and its role in altering our understanding of the past. Malva Filer argues that *Maluco* is different from other 1980s River Plate narratives such as Juan José Saer's *El entenado* (Argentina, 1982), Eduardo Galeano's *Memorias del fuego* (Uruguay, 1984), and Abel Posse's *Los perros del paraíso* (Argentina, 1983), because it appropriates discursive forms from the sixteenth century (the *relación de servicio,* the *crónica,* and the picaresque novel) and subverts them through the anachronistic vision of the narrative voice.[11] She further postulates that the text's transgressiveness results not from the occasional exaggerations and fictitious details but rather from the reproduction of old discursive forms that negate attitudes toward the life, hierarchies, and values of the society in which such forms originated. For Filer, retelling Magellan's voyage from the viewpoint of a *pícaro* is the fundamental element in challenging the veracity produced by the practices of the official historiography.[12]

As Filer notes, picaresque elements are undeniably present in *Maluco*. Indeed, Juanillo invokes the classical picaresque topoi of "la necesidad" (need) and "el hambre" (hunger) as reasons for writing his letter to the king in the first place, and he refers to himself as a "truhán," a Renaissance term commonly referring to a *pícaro.* Furthermore, prior to joining Magellan's expedition, Juanillo served numerous masters in a manner reminiscent of Lazarillo de Tormes, and he even draws attention to the fact that he is the illegitimate son of a prostitute and unknown father, a converso Jew, an element that, according to Filer, underscores Juanillo's social inferiority.[13] What Filer overlooks, however, is the literary and cultural sophistication of this so-called *pícaro*. Juanillo displays a remarkable breadth and depth of knowledge of classical and medieval history and literature as well as a skill with lyrical language. He incorporates interpolated stories and digressive anecdotes in a manner reminiscent of Cervantes's *Don Quixote* (1605/1615) and New World chronicles such as el Inca Garcilaso de la Vega's *Comentarios reales* (1605/1615). And he directly insults and denounces his addressee, Charles V, just as the infamous Lope de Aguirre insulted Philip II in his letter in 1556. None of these elements is common in picaresque literature and points the reader to the Spanish buffonesque literary tradition.[14] Juanillo is a buffoon (not a *pícaro*) who enacts the role of the *pícaro* and the chronicler.[15]

Although *Maluco* toys with the conventions of the *relación de servicio* from the period of the conquest and the conventions of picaresque and buffonesque literature from the Spanish Renaissance, I will argue that the buffonesque tradition is the base from which the novel launches its assault on the truth values of the chronicles of the Indies in general and the official history about the voyage of Magellan in particular. After situating the novel within the Spanish buffonesque literary tradition, I will show how the novel taps the subversive potential of the buffonesque tradition to critique the truth values manufactured by the official history about the discovery and conquest. In the process of retelling the story of the voyage, Juanillo calls attention to and critiques the conventions of sixteenth-century humanist historiography and uses the rhetorical conventions of the *relación de servicio* to fashion his own life story and to denounce the abuses of imperial power. Proposing an alternative model for narrating the period of exploration and discovery, *Maluco* (which means "crazy" in Portuguese) reveals the mechanisms through which this historiography established its authority and reinscribes the voyage within the medieval and Renaissance literary tradition of "la literatura de los bufones," which Francisco Márquez Villanueva defines as a body of court buffoon writings from the medieval and Renaissance periods that entertained the king in exchange for modest financial compensation that enabled the buffoon to survive.[16]

Early in the novel, Juanillo makes a passing reference to "los Francesillos" and "los pericos."[17] The name "Francesillos" alludes to sixteenth-century imperial court buffoons, specifically to Francesillo de Zúñiga (1502–31), court buffoon to Charles V and author of a scandalous chronicle on the king's reign titled *Crónica burlesca del emperador Carlos V* (1527). (I will discuss both text and writer in greater detail in the next segment of the chapter.)[18] The term *los pericos* evokes for the reader the picaresque literary tradition in general and more specifically the Mexican picaresque novel *El periquillo sarniento* (1816) by Joaquín Fernández de Lizardi. *Maluco,* therefore, rewrites the voyage of Magellan and subverts the discursive formation that comprises the chronicles of the Indies not only by mimicking the authoritativeness of legal discourses but also by inscribing the *relación de servicio* in the sixteenth-century tradition of buffoonesque literature, untapped for its subversive qualities prior to its insertion into this late twentieth-century narrative. Thus, the novel questions the reliability of any historical account, scrutinizes the accuracy of such accounts, and exploits the subversive possibilities of the medieval and Renaissance Spanish literary tradition of the buffonesque.

The key to subverting the official history and questioning the existence of a noncontingent historical truth lies in relocating the speaking position of the narrative voice from that of a cultured imperial chronicler (such as Peter Martyr or Francisco López de Gómara, or even a soldier such as Bernal Díaz del Castillo), to that of an equally cultured buffoon named Juanillo de Ponce, and I would argue *Maluco* uses this strategy to present a parallel history of Magellan's voyage and a parody of the repertoire of techniques from the early New World historiography. The net effect of this strategy is to encourage the reader to examine the text creatively and critically and to establish parallels between the sociohistorical circumstance of a fictional marginal figure in the sixteenth century and a modern-day figure in Latin American society. The buffoon, not the *pícaro,* is the hub from which *Maluco* launches its assault on the official history and levels criticism at the declining state of the Spanish empire, at the behavior of imperial officials, and at the king himself. The point is not so much that *Maluco* reweaves diverse genres from the past to create a postmodern historiographic metafiction. Plotnik, Cordones-Cook, and Verani have hailed *Maluco* as a paradigmatic example of historiographic metafiction (as defined by Linda Hutcheon in *The Poetics of Postmodernism*), citing to support their assertion its incorporation of diverse literary genres, the self-interrogation of the narrator, and the presence of a narrator from a marginalized group. Approaching *Maluco* as a Spanish American manifestation of international historiographic metafiction, however, overlooks much of the work's significance. As Jean Franco reminds us, "postmodernism cannot adequately describe those texts that use pastiche and citation not simply as style but as correlatives of the continent's uneasy and unfinished relationship to modernity."[19] As with many New Historical novels, the novel obliges the uninitiated contemporary reader to become more familiar with Spanish Renaissance and baroque historical and literary traditions and to contemplate the continuities and ruptures between Peninsular and Spanish American writings. The novel, in short, resurrects a marginalized figure from the Spanish medieval and Renaissance literary tradition in order to eliminate the aura of authority traditionally attributed to the chronicles or to other historical writing.

As *Maluco* reworks Francesillo de Zúñiga's *Crónica burlesca del Emperador Carlos V*, a cursory overview of Zúñiga's life and career as a buffoon as well of the primary features of his text will deepen the reader's understanding of the novel. Zúñiga was born in the last decade of the fifteenth century in the town of Béjar, Salamanca. A *judío converso* of humble origins, he was a tailor by profession and subsequently entered, as an *hombre de placer,* the personal service of the Duque de Béjar, one of the most prominent noblemen and a member of the Spanish court.[20] He then accompanied the Duque de Béjar to the Spanish royal court, and, in 1522, Charles V appointed him imperial buffoon to the court. Francesillo served the king until 1529, when he lost royal favor, retired from the court, and returned to his place of origin. There he was placed under the protection of the Duque de Béjar. In September 1531, about five months before his death at the hands of assassins, Francesillo was named *alguacil mayor de la villa de Béjar* (the town sheriff of Béjar). By the end of his life, he had attained the status of a *caballero.*

Most likely "Zúñiga" was not his original family name, since, as was the case with most *conversos,* Francesillo's true identity would have been discarded in favor of the adopted name of his protector or patron. Similarly, the title "conde," which he often used when referring to himself, exemplified the common practice of court clowns who adopted the title or even the complete name of the highest members of the nobility. According to George Mariscal, both these strategies led to the assimilation of the nonaristocractic individual and, in a figurative sense, re-created him or her as a living parody of the dominant groups. At the same time, Francesillo's claim of being a *cristiano viejo* caused a great deal of laughter in courtly circles, and underlying such laughter was a profound uneasiness, since many of those seeking royal favor laid claim to similarly bogus genealogies.[21]

As with many court buffoons, Francesillo is ironically positioned within the hierarchy of the court by names that do not signify a real identity but point instead to the privileged class of which he is the distorted reflection. This kind of renaming, however, was merely one part of a context in which all language had a powerful exchange value. The buffoon's primary activity of linguistically transforming court reality by nicknaming it, then, was both a service by which he earned his livelihood and a means to gain special favors from his superiors. According to Mariscal, such a practice must not be read as the potentially subversive introduction of free play into the power dynamics of the court nor as the liberating force of the carnivalesque, since in fact it worked to reinforce rigid social categories and conventions.[22] By putting the language of daily life at the service of the privileged classes for their entertainment and his own self-deprecation, the buffoon revealed his complete identification with the official ideologies.[23] Practical concerns determined by everyday life thus produced the buffoon's behavior and text. His self-deprecation and subservient posture were the necessary and reasonable consequences of the desire to escape the insecurity of living outside the court and to survive within what was often a hostile environment.

As is the case for *Maluco,* the original *Crónica burlesca* is a text founded on orality, a kind of spoken representation that reproduces the structures of conversation.[24] The possible subject positions articulated by such a communicative situation, founded upon the opposition master/servant, were severely limited. While the potential for manipulating language was very real, the system itself was jealously maintained by the ruling elites.[25] In the final analysis, Francesillo in the *Crónica burlesca* was less interested in re-creating the past than in influencing the present in the most limited of terms—that is, to entertain his public and earn sufficient money to survive. The slightest wrong move might have decided his social status and identity. Thus, the buffoon is less an individual than a necessary function of the overall ensemble of social relations at a court whose center is the king. Yet it is precisely because the jester is so closely associated with the source of courtly power (often having direct access to the king when others did not) that he must be taken seriously.[26]

The buffoon in *Maluco,* however, finds himself in different circumstances from those of Francesillo de Zúñiga. Juanillo is not actually the imperial buffoon of Charles the V, but mimics the authority of one. In his letter to Charles V, the physically deformed *converso* Juanillo rewrites the history of Magellan's voyage on the pretext that the official chronicles falsified the true history, that their stories did not take into account the suffering of the crew members, and that the buffoon wants his pension reinstated. Juanillo's motivations for writing his letter echo the reasons of Bernal Díaz del Castillo for having written the *Historia verdadera de la conquista de la Nueva España,* but with a focus on the crew's sufferings, he reveals the deeper purpose to undermine rather than uphold the sociopolitical order.

In the novel, the end of Juanillo's career as a *pícaro* serving a master on shore sets the stage for him to assume the role of buffoon aboard the expedition to the Moluccas Islands. When Philip II later deprives him of his pension, Juanillo returns to the pangs of hunger, "los perros de la necesidad,"[27] that characterized his youth as a *pícaro*. From the opening of the novel, Juanillo incorporates the rhetorical conventions of the *relación de servicio,* intermingled with topoi reminiscent of the picaresque:

> En el año de la Encarnación de Nuestro Señor Jesucristo de 1519, yo, Juanillo Ponce, natural de Bustillo del Páramo, en reino de León, me vine con mi señor, el conde don Juan, a su señorío. [. . .] Y como quiso la suerte que aquel gran señor, el más generoso y amable de los amos, a quien Dios tenga en el Purgatorio [. . .] muriese a pocas semanas en los brazos de Eros [. . .] determiné venir a Sevilla a ejercer mi profesión de truhán y tener así ocasión de probar suerte en las Nuevas Indias descobiertas. [. . .]
>
> En mala hora me dirigí a la Casa de Contratación y exhibí mi gracia y mi donaire ante los oficiales encargados del reclutamiento de la gente, que luego de reírse ruidosamente el relato de mis muchas vicisitudes, decidieron aceptarme como el hombre de placer de la flota. [. . .]²⁸

> [In the year of the Lord Jesus Christ fifteen hundred and nineteen, I, Juanillo Ponce, native of Bustillo del Páramo in the kingdom of León, accompanied my master Don Juan to his estates. . . . And since fate decreed that this noble lord, the most kind and generous master imaginable, whom God grant a place in purgatory . . . should die a few weeks later in the arms of love . . . I resolved to press on to Seville to ply my trade as a jester and to try my luck in the New Indies. . . .
>
> To my misfortune, I presented myself at the Colonial Office, where I demonstrated my wit and skill to the officials charged with taking on men for the expedition. After much laughter and boisterous merriment at my recounting of past exploits, they agreed to hire me as jester of the fleet. . . .]²⁹

Like Alvar Núñez Cabeza de Vaca in *Los naufragios* (1542/1555) and Bernal Díaz del Castillo in the *Historia verdadera de la conquista de la Nueva España* (1568), here Juanillo invokes the formulaic conventions of the *relaciones* in that he states the beginning date of his service to the crown and his place of origin. He further casts his life story as a *relación de servicio* when, as in the case of Cabeza de Vaca, he promises to recount his travails and hardships endured during the expedition:

> [D]eterminé, antes de morir, dar cuenta a Vuestra Alteza de los muchos prodigios y privaciones que en aquel viaje vimos y sufrimos, junto a las muchas maravillas y placeres que tuvimos; para que Su Majestad sepa y medite en su noble retiro de cómo las ambiciones y caprichos de los príncipes afectan a la vida de quienes andan por el mundo a ciegas, siempre sujetos al arbitrio de los poderosos. [. . .]³⁰

> [I made up my mind that before I died I would acquaint Your Majesty with the many wonders and hardships we saw and suffered throughout that journey, the

great amount of pain and hunger we had to endure, as well as the myriad marvels and joys we experienced, so that in your noble retreat Your Highness might learn of and reflect on the ways our princes' ambitions and caprices affect the destinies of those of us who stumble blindly through life at the whim of powerful men. . . .][31]

In other words, Juanillo's narrative will address the consequences for the common man resulting from an abuse of power. His narrative will parody the conventions of the *relación de servicio,* because he will assume the role of the court jester (*el bufón*), who at times plays the part of the rogue (*el pícaro*) and at others that of the loyal Spanish soldier requesting financial compensation from the crown.

As the protagonist of *Maluco,* Juanillo consciously and deliberately inscribes his *relación de servicio* in this sixteenth-century buffonesque tradition. At the end of the first chapter, he calls attention to his obligation as a professional buffoon to "hacer reír olvidando nuestros dolores para mitigar las penas ajenas"[32] [make people laugh, forgetting our own sorrows in order to help soothe those of others].[33] In the buffonesque tradition, Juanillo renders an account of Magellan's expedition that subverts the reader's expectations for a *relación de servicio*. The numerous digressions in which he tells, in a burlesque tone presumably intended to eliminate boredom, the life stories of fellow crew members goes against the traditional historical tendency to showcase Magellan's heroic and glorious exploits. At one point in the novel, Juanillo himself explicitly acknowledges that his *crónica* is at variance with those of Antonio de Pigafetta and Peter Martyr:

[B]ien sabe Juanillo que estás harto e impaciente, maldiciendo esta crónica de locos parlachines, y al loco de su autor. Tú quieres ver acción. Quieres ver a tus hombres trepar por los obenques, lanzarse a las vergas, tensar las jarcias y arrojarse a la aventura. [. . .] [S]igo chinchando con tanto bablablá como si aún no hubieras tenido bastante. Además, Pedro Mártyr, y el otro, Pigateta o como se llamase, ¿no despacharon ellos en dos párrafos todo este asunto que me lleva a mí tantas páginas? [. . .] ¿Para qué tanto rodeo [. . .] ?[34]

[Juanillo is well aware that you are bored and impatient, and are cursing this chronicle of crazy chatterboxes and its even crazier author. You want to see action. You want to see your men climbing the rigging, flinging themselves from the spars, tightening the ropes, and dashing forward to adventure. . . . Yet I go on bothering you with all this blah-blah-blah, as if you hadn't already had more than enough of it. Besides, didn't Peter Martyr and that other fellow, Pigateta or whatever his name was, deal with this part of the journey, which is taking me so many pages, in a couple of paragraphs? . . . Why all this beating around the bush . . . ?][35]

Unlike the soldier who formulaically chronicles his exploits in a *relación de servicio* and addresses the king in the elevated legalistic rhetoric of the sixteenth century, the buffoon in *Maluco* re-creates the behind-the-scenes preparations for the voyage and, as an actor preparing to raise the curtain of a theatrical performance, addresses the king. Juanillo asks the king to prepare his sensory modalities for a narrative that will resemble a live performance: "[P]urifique sus narices del muelle aroma de las sedas y terciopelos de su corte, y aspire el aroma incomparable del aire marino saturándolo todo. [. . .] Deje que lo penetre el escozor de la sal y el estruendo de las olas, sienta en tus imperiales tripas el incomparable sabor de las nauseas."[36] [Let Your Majesty now cleanse his nostrils of the gentle perfumes of the silks and velvets of his court, and breathe instead the incomparable tang of the overpowering salt sea air that seeps into everything. . . . Let the smarting salt and the roar of the waves fill his ears; may he even experience in his own guts the unforgettable sensation of seasickness.][37] Juanillo's remarks suggest that the conquest, for all accounts of it, was a performance for the king, and thereby he undermines the immutable truth claims of dominant accounts.

Juanillo submits his petition to Charles V, moreover, not only to receive remuneration for his service to the crown but also to amplify the official history about the voyage of Magellan. For Juanillo the official history embodied in Martyr's *Decades* and the *Relación* of Pigafetta provides only a limited view of the enterprise and is based on the formulaic legal rhetoric. His posture toward the written historical record, as I have noted, is similar to that of Bernal Díaz in the *Historia verdadera de la conquista de la Nueva España*:

> ¿[D]ebía aceptar yo sin más, las paparruchas y embustes de vuestros cronistas? Para ellos es tan simple como cocinar un guisado a partir de cuatro o cinco ingredientes. Pero ¿qué saben ellos, Alteza, de lo que en verdad sentíamos cada uno de nosotros ante estos cuatro o cinco grandes hechos a lo que se limita su historia? Pues os digo que es allí donde está la verdad, muy dentro de cada uno de quienes fuimos partícipes de esa empresa y en nadie más, ni siquiera en Vos, Majestad. [. . .][38]

[Should I simply accept all the nonsense and lies invented by your chroniclers? For them it's as simple as cooking a stew, once they have prepared its four or five ingredients. But what do they know, Sire, of how each of us really felt as we lived through the four or five historic events they base their accounts on?

I would say that the truth lies in the feelings with those of us who took part in the expedition experienced, and which no one else can know, not even Your Majesty.][39]

Juanillo's account provides humorous seasoning to a conventional tale and incorporates the heterogeneous voices and stories of the crew members to question the dominant version of these experiences.

In the tradition of previous chroniclers such as Bernal Díaz, Juanillo comments and corrects other accounts, with the added flair of exaggeration and absurdity. When he remembers his experience in Brazil, for example, he parodies the common analogy made between the topography of the land and the contours of a woman. Like Columbus in his *Diario de a bordo,* Juanillo eroticizes the landscape in graphic detail:

> [L]a bahía enmarcada por una espesa vegetación semejaba al sexo de una mujer con su entrada estrecha y su interior cálido. [. . .] [E]ra como el vientre de mi madre del que yo no quería salir por no ejercer esta esforzada profesión de nos; que si el Paraíso era el premio a una vida virtuosa, por fuerza debía parecerse al vientre de mi madre, de donde venía a ser cierto que nacer es morir y reventar un día, volver a la verdadera vida; que si en realidad había regresado al vientre de mi madre qué diablos hacían en él los capitanes, cómo se atrevía don Hernando a entrar en él cubierto de hierros. [. . .][40]

> [The bay, surrounded by its thick vegetation was like a woman's sex, with its narrow entrance and warm insides. . . . that it was like my mother's womb, which I had not wanted to leave so that I would not have to start out on this wretched profession of mine; that if paradise were the reward for a virtuous life, then it would necessarily be like my mother's womb, and then it was only natural to think that to be born is to die, and that when we give up the ghost we are returning to true life. But, at the same time, if it were true that I had gone back to my mother's womb, then what the devil were all the captains doing in there with me, and how did Don Fernando dare come in all dressed in armor . . . ?][41]

As the buffoon of the expedition, Juanillo hyperbolically relates his own life experiences to his descriptions of the landscape. Shortly thereafter, he mocks Columbus's idea that the world assumed the shape of a woman's breast, with paradise located on the nipple[42] and makes ludicrous the issue about the earth's shape by overpersonalizing Columbus's remarks. Juanillo considers whether the contour of the landscape

> se trataba del pezón de la teta de su madre o de la mía, aunque pienso que sería de la suya, ya que menguados bienes depararía el Paraíso de estar situado en la magra teta de mi madre, que de no ser por una nodriza que, según mi tío mío,

era fabulosa lechera, no estaría yo aquí escribiéndote estas cosas. ¿Habría conocido por ventura el Almirante a mi nodriza? [. . .]⁴³

[means the breast of the mother of the great Admiral or my mother's breast. I think it must have been his mother's, because if paradise were part of my mother's scrawny teat, it would have little bounty to offer—if it had not been for a wet nurse who, according to an uncle of mine, was a fountain of milk, I would not be here writing these lines for you. Could the Admiral have met my wet nurse, I wonder?]⁴⁴

He mockingly partakes in the tendency among the chroniclers of responding to their predecessors. His humorous chronicle derives its authority from exposing the underside of Columbus's diary and making fun of other chroniclers who take the official version too seriously.

The incorporation of intertextual references is not limited to the Spanish chronicles.⁴⁵ Plotnik and Filer have also noted connections between *Maluco* and *Don Quixote;* the priest from Don Quixote's village becomes the chaplain of the Magellan expedition,⁴⁶ for instance, and the relationship between Magellan and Juanillo de Ponce is similar to that between Don Quixote and Sancho Panza. Plotnik further notes the presence of interpolated stories in *Maluco* but fails to examine their relationship to the main narrative. I would argue, however, that these interpolated stories reinforce the principal theme of disillusionment in Juanillo's life story and highlight the vital importance of the creative imagination in overcoming a threatening situation or enduring a banal existence.

Juanillo's recollection of his deletion from the official roster provides a point of departure for retelling Blas's loss of a childhood friend named Francisco to a phantom ship during the voyage. According to Blas, the town regarded Francisco as the village idiot, whom all the children would tease because he was uncomfortable around them and because his mother was big-breasted. When Francisco learns about the imminent departure of Magellan's expedition for the Spice Islands, he decides to recruit Blas to accompany him. By leaving La Almunia and earning a fortune, Blas would escape his marginal position within the local community and start a new life elsewhere. So Francisco has dreams for his friend, but the expedition fails to fulfill them. As in the case of Juanillo, the dream turns into a nightmare. Under these circumstances, telling stories becomes a way of life and a strategy for survival aboard Magellan's expedition: "[H]ablábamos mucho entonces, pero como no había mucho de que hablar, la gente no sólo se prestaba o se robaba las historias, sino que también se las intercambiaban a falta de otros objetos de trueque."⁴⁷ [We certainly talked a lot during those days, Your Highness, but since there wasn't much to talk about, we not only borrowed or stole other people's stories, but traded them, since they were the last things we had left to barter with.]⁴⁸

In his capacity of professional buffoon, Juanillo tells stories to other crew members to alleviate the boredom and monotony of daily life aboard the ship, and his doing so reiterates the novel's theme of disillusionment. A tale about the Duchess Rosinalda and King Cacavus of Hungary, dealing with seduction and betrayal, provides a case in point.⁴⁹ According to this story, the Duchess Rosinalda, under siege by King Cacavus and seeking to ensure her own safety and the marriage of her daughter to the future king of France and Hungary, decides to offer Cacavus her body in exchange for a treaty that would end the fighting and secure her interests. She gradually convinces the king and his troops to consider the deal by making her tactics more provocative each day. On the first day, she walks along the battlefield naked, in full view of the Hungarian army; on another day, she exposes her breasts, which distracts enemy troops so much that they abandon their posts and disobey their commanders. Rosinalda's lifting of her red velvet skirt and showing her genitalia to the enemies, however, is the decisive act of seduction. King Cacavus calls off the siege, with the understanding that he will possess her body.

His dream of sexual conquest is frustrated, however. Rosinalda fulfills her agreement to the letter of the law but violates its spirit. In order to maintain fidelity to her absent husband, Rosinalda smears her breasts with chicken flesh and her genitals with mutton fat. Understandably, when King Cacavus visits her house to claim his prize, he is repulsed not by what he sees but by what he smells when he sinks his lips into her breasts and into her sex. He hastily abandons Rosinalda's bedroom and orders his troops to withdraw from the occupied territory. And thus, Rosinalda successfully balances an array of competing interests by keeping her word to King Cacavus without compromising her own self-interest.

This interpolated story reinforces some predominant themes in *Maluco*. Like Juanillo, Rosinalda displays an uncanny ability for acting and employing oral and body language to persuade her antagonist to cease his actions. Just as the official history about Magellan's voyage omits the human dimension of the expedition, so the formal agreement between Rosinalda and Cacavus fails to disclose why Cacavus found Rosinalda so sexually undesirable. Moreover, as I have suggested, this tale is one of disillusionment. Just as Juanillo and other members of Magellan's crew enlisted in the expedition with the expectation of improving their lot, so did King Cacavus agree to end the siege of the city with the expectation of enjoying Rosinalda's body. Neither plan is brought to fruition. Retelling this interpolated story allows the crew to escape the tedium of daily life aboard the ship and adds a dash of excitement to Charles V's otherwise bland existence at the monastery in Yuste.

At other moments, digressions function extratextually to establish subtle parallels between Juanillo's precarious situation in the late sixteenth century and that of many Uruguayans during the military dictatorship (1971–85). In the novel, Philip II has supposedly erased Juanillo's name from the roster of Magellan's crew and denied him a pension because Juanillo has been criticizing the truthfulness of the official history of the voyage. As punishment for his alleged crimes against the crown, Philip II removes Juanillo's name, just as military rulers "disappeared" alleged subversives who disagreed with the policies of the national government. Similarly, in part 2 of the novel, Juanillo recalls how the Inquisition coerced him into signing a statement declaring that he had not participated in the expedition.[50] When he approaches other survivors from the expedition, they pretend not to know him, maintain their distance, and refuse to vouch for his presence aboard the ship. During the military dictatorship in Uruguay and after running into trouble with the government, former friends of alleged subversives often refused to acknowledge the latter's existence.

The buffoon from Spanish Golden Age culture constitutes the principal strategy by which *Maluco* reinterprets Magellan's voyage around the world and challenges the historical truth produced by the conventions of the chronicles of the Indies. As a comedian, storyteller, and poet, Juanillo the buffoon parodies the conventions of the *relación* and brings to the forefront the performative nature of storytelling and its role in presenting the underside of the official historiography by reinterpreting the written record and speaking on behalf of previously silenced voices. In the sixteenth century, the buffoon reinforced the status quo and upheld the division of society along class lines. However, the insertion of the buffoon in *Maluco* releases the untapped subversive potential of this figure in that Juanillo defiantly and openly challenges his addressee, Charles V, to reject the official history as false and misleading. Although some critics have approached *Maluco* in the context of the picaresque literary tradition and praised the novel as a recent Spanish American example of postmodern historiographic metafiction, they have overlooked the fundamental role of the buffoon in the novel and discounted the role of storytelling in challenging the monolithic view of the past.[51] Against the backdrop of the heated polemics surrounding the quincentennial of Columbus's first voyage, *Maluco* provides a refreshingly humorous account of an episode from early New World historiography and invites the reader to evaluate historical records with a more critical eye.

While Juanillo in *Maluco* recasts Magellan's voyage as a narrative about storytelling and problematizes the reliability of the official accounts about the discovery and conquest, the sword-maker Ambrosio de Lara in *Esta maldita lujuria* focuses on rewriting the colonial historiography of the River Plate and the New World as a tale of the failed pursuit of material wealth and sexual fulfillment. While Baccino dedicates himself exclusively to writing fiction, Brailovsky (b. Buenos Aires, 1946) is a writer of wider-ranging vocational interests. As adjunct ombudsman for the city of Buenos Aires, a professor of Argentine natural resources at the University of Buenos Aires, and a regular contributor to weekly literary and cultural magazines, he has published numerous studies related to ecology, the environment, and the Argentine economy.[52] His literary writings to date include six novels— *Identidad* (1980, reissued as *Isaac Halevy, rey de los judíos* [1997]), *El asalto al cielo* (1985), *Tiempo de opresión* (1986), *Esta maldita lujuria* (1990), *Me gustan sus cuernos* (1995), and *No abrirás esta puerta* (1996)— and a collection of short stories, *Libro de desmesuras* (1984).

Using the historical moment of May 10, 1810, as a backdrop (a mere two weeks before the May Revolution of 1810), the novel narrates the founding and settlement of Carmen de Patagones in 1779 and recasts the colonial history of the New World as a tale of unrealized and frustrated dreams of conquering the elusive Ciudad de los Césares, the River Plate version of the El Dorado myth.[53] The novel assumes the form of a letter 182 pages long, divided into twenty-eight chapters and an afterword, from Ambrosio de Lara, a sword-maker in Carmen de Patagones, to the viceroy in Buenos Aires. In the letter Lara presents, in a rambling and disorienting fashion, key moments in his own life, such as the reasons for leaving his native Galicia and emigrating to the New World; his role in the establishment of the outpost of Carmen de Patagones; his participation in the failed expedition of 1782 to find the Ciudad de los Césares; and the suffering and hardship that he endured up to the writing of the letter in 1810. Interlaced throughout his testimonial account are digressive, scandalous vignettes about the conquistadors' failures to satiate their sexual desires. These anecdotes give credence to Lara's portrayal of the New World as a terrestrial inferno, a place where vice and human instincts reign supreme. In the process of retelling history, Lara exposes the underside of the topos of the New World as paradise and indicts the crown and the church for papering over the discrepancies between the utopia of the New World, depicted in the official historiography, and the harsh reality of life there in the late eighteenth century. Although Lara views himself as a common man who will render the "true history" of the River Plate and as a descendent of Bernal Díaz Castillo, who put forth the "true history" about the conquest of Mexico in the *His-*

toria verdadera de la conquista de la Nueva España,[54] he uses his marginal position to render a scabrous account of the conquest and to discredit the official historiography.

On one level, Lara's letter can be read within the tradition of reform-minded *arbitrista* writings of the eighteenth century. According to Sara Almarza, *arbitrista* writings in the New World responded to perceived problems in the colonies and were frequently addressed to a viceroy or another figure of authority. They usually included a presentation and analysis of a malady; offered remedies for solving the problem; expressed their ideas in a concise, accessible style; illustrated their points with philosophical quotations, historical events, passages from the Bible, and examples from European countries; and positioned the speaking subject as a loyal vassal of the king or another figure of authority to whom the writing was addressed.[55] *Esta maldita lujuria* follows the conventions of *arbitrista* writings in that Lara submits a letter to a government official (the viceroy of Buenos Aires), identifies the myth of the Ciudad de los Césares as responsible for fomenting the scramble for material wealth among explorers, and proposes a solution; namely, that the viceroy lead an expeditionary force to conquer and destroy, once and for all, the mythical city. Thus, the novel, at one level, is Lara's account of the state of moral degradation and disintegration of the River Plate region during the late eighteenth and early nineteenth centuries and his efforts to remedy the situation. His remoteness from the centers of power endows his writings with legitimacy not available to major figures in Spain.

On a second level, the novel implicitly protests the Argentine government's continuing censorship of sexually explicit references during the Proceso. Andrés Avellaneda, in his analysis of the discourse of censorship and cultural control in recent Argentine history (1960–83), argues that the state—primarily the military—elaborated between 1966 and 1983 a discourse of cultural censorship that culminated during the Proceso. Within this discourse, the so-called true cultural and artistic system possessed a noble mission, subordinated to a military-defined vision of "morality." By contrast, a "false" cultural system could be identified by its lack of adherence to the government's "moral" code and encompassed three primary areas. The first of these is obscenity: the idea of sex as an absence of decorum, homosexuality, prostitution, and antifamily activities (adultery, abortion, discord among siblings, and the degradation of marriage). The second is an insult or attack on religious institutions, the Catholic Church, or Christian morality. The third is aggression against national security interests (i.e., sovereignty and territorial integrity, the obligation to defend the country and the right of the state to require such defense, and the maintenance of order to avoid a disassociation of the continuum of those values).[56] Within this context, Ambrosio de Lara, as a loyal servant of the king and viceroy, assumes the role of the informant who reports life in the outpost of Carmen de Patagones as an example of a "false" cultural system, because the explorers and conquistadors as well as church officials violate the standards for obscenity and fail to uphold their self-professed Christian values. However, the carnivalesque tone with which Lara recounts such transgressions of Christian morality implies a critique of and attack on such standards as well as on the actual moral behavior of the authority figures promulgating such standards. For the twentieth-century Argentine reader, Lara's retelling of the New World historiography as a series of exempla against the dangers of *lujuria* levels a devastating and caustic critique of the reasons that the *junta* invoked to justify repressive measures in its crusade to eliminate alleged subversives from the body politic. Those chapters of the novel that rewrite foundational myths from the River Plate region, early New World historiography, and crucial events from the late eighteenth century are germane in inviting the reader to decipher the text against the backdrop of events from the colonial period of the New World as well as from Argentine history of the late twentieth century. *Esta maldita lujuria,* exposing the underside of the conquest, can be read as an "historia no-natural e immoral" [unnatural and immoral history], a compendium of the corruption and moral decline afflicting the River Plate region.

In his analysis of desire in four Argentine novels about the discovery—Antonio Di Benedetto's *Zama* (1955), Posse's *Daimón* (1978), Saer's *El entenado* (1983) and Brailovsky's *Esta maldita lujuria*—Fernando Reati argues that sexual desire in *Esta maldita lujuria* is the driving force behind the conquistadors' search for utopia in the New World.[57] He posits, moreover, that their search for an object of desire and their failure to find it are inscribed within the paradigm of the geographical and spiritual journey.[58] While I fundamentally agree with Reati that the novel deals with the failure to satisfy sexual desires, I would also argue, as I have noted, that the novel's extensive discussion of *lujuria,* as it relates to the New World historiography, mocks the official policy of the Argentine military governments that regarded unbridled sexuality as a threat to the stability and well-being of the Argentine nation.

To illustrate the role of sexual obsession as a motivating force in the discovery of the New World, Lara revisits the early exploration of the rivers and coastline of the River Plate area (1516–30). According to the official historiography, Juan Díaz de Solís, a Portuguese navigator in the employment of the crown of Castile, was the first European to explore the River Plate and seek the southwestern route to the Far East and India. In 1516 Solís and a handful of men landed on the east bank, where they were summarily butchered by a band of Querandí Indians.[59] In the novel, however, Lara deflects attention from the ending of Solis's life and refocuses it on his secret fear, and by extension that of other explorers: the fear of returning unexpectedly home to discover the infidelity of one's wife. Lara is not the originator of this tale, for he retells a story that Basilio Villarino, the second pilot of the Royal Armada in Carmen de Patagones, heard at a bar from Silvestre Antonio de Rojas, leader of the 1707 expedition to the Ciudad de los Césares. In *Esta maldita lujuria,* João Dias (the Portuguese name for Juan Díaz de Solís) pretends to leave one day prior to his scheduled departure and returns home to find his wife in bed with another man. In response to this startling situation, he pulls out his sword, and as Lara calmly recounts, in an understated tone, Solís murders her for her infidelity: "[L]e clavó su espada en el mismo lugar en que el mozo le clavara. [. . .]"[60] [He thrust his sword into the same spot where the youth had presumably plunged his own. . . .] As a result of his crime of passion, Solís misses the expedition leaving for the Orient, flees his native Portugal, and finds refuge in Spain, where the crown grants him asylum and names him captain of another fleet. Dias then changes his name to "Juan Díaz de Solís."[61] Once again, Ambrosio de Lara takes a famous explorer of the River Plate, attributes an obsession to this figure, and entertains the reader with a scandalous account.

While Solis's fear of his wife's infidelity dictates his actions, Ferdinand Magellan's fear of the powers of Patagonian women leads him to restrain his sexual impulses. As I have detailed in the discussion of Baccino's *Maluco,* Magellan, while circumnavigating the world, traversed the strait that bears his name, brushed the Patagonian coast, and met his death in 1521 at the hands of the native populations in the modern-day Philippines. In *Esta maldita lujuria,* tales about Magellan's voyage are intimately related to an exuberant eroticizing of the New World landscape. According to Lara, Magellan feared the mythological female Patagonian giants because their breasts were "más de un pie de longitud"[62] [over a foot long]. He didn't even attempt to make love with them out of fear that he would get lost in their breasts, referred to as "un océano de tetas que le fuera más difícil salir que del mismísmo Estrecho [de Magallanes]"[63] [an ocean of breasts from which it was more difficult to emerge than from the very Strait of Magellan]. The retelling of Magellan's landing at Patagonia is one of the few episodes in the novel in which an explorer is able to restrain his sexual impulses, not out of reasoned logic but out of fear of being devoured by the unknown. Lara's reinterpretation of the Solís and Magellan episodes from the early exploration of the River Plate area defamiliarizes the official history of such accounts by suggesting that the explorers' sexual insecurities influenced their public actions. Behind the retelling of such episodes, moreover, the reader perceives Lara's perverse enjoyment and reveling in narrating such episodes and at shocking the refined sensibilities of the viceroy. His status as a marginal figure gives him the liberty to perform such a scandalous critique.

Lara's revisionist historiography of early expeditions to the River Plate extends to the reinterpretation of foundational myths from the second wave of colonization that occurred between 1536 and 1556. One such myth concerns Pedro de Mendoza's founding of Puerto Nuestra Señora Santa María del Buen Aire (modern-day Buenos Aires) in 1536. According to the official historiography, Mendoza's expedition, large and highly organized in comparison with most early Spanish ventures to the New World, was a debacle. Within eighteen months of its arrival, starvation, diseases, and a war with the Querandí Indians (the same tribe that allegedly ate Solís) reduced the expedition to a third of its original size, and according to the German chronicler Ulrich Schimdel, the Spaniards slaughtered most of their cattle and horses, and ultimately were driven to cannibalism.[64] In the novel, Lara renders a similar account about the disastrous fate of the expedition but puts forth an alternative explanation as to Mendoza's motivation for establishing Buenos Aires in the first place. According to Lara, Mendoza sought to fulfill a promise to the Virgin of Buenos Aires in hopes that she would cure him from syphilis, which he had contracted from an "abadesa" (abbess) in Rome.[65] Lara concludes recounting this incident by noting that Mendoza died en route to Spain, baffled as to why the Virgin "no había querido curarlo del mal que lo trajera esta maldita lujuria"[66] [had not wanted to cure him of the malady brought on by that accursed lustfulness]. The founding of Buenos Aires as recorded in the official history loses its luster in Lara's version of that event, in which it is not as a story of praising God but a desperate effort to cure a disease that resulted from *lujuria*.

Unlike Mendoza, motivated by his hopes of curing syphilis, Pedro de Gamboa ventured to Tierra del Fuego in 1556 to search for the Ciudad de los Césares. In *Esta maldita lujuria* Lara proceeds to revisit this episode on the pretext that he wants to understand why Spain even bothered to establish the Carmen de Patagones outpost, referred to as the "último culo del mundo"[67] [the furthest asshole in the world]. He paints Gamboa as an explorer of delusional grandeur who believed his own lies about the area's wealth of natural resources and led an ill-equipped expedition that littered the lands with corpses, or in Lara's words, "sembrada de huesos españoles"[68] [spread Spanish bones across the land]. The prospect of finding and conquering the Ciudad de los Césares in Tierra del Fuego, however, sustains the Spaniards' unwarranted optimism. In this case, the lust for material wealth leads to the pursuit of an ill-conceived venture based on a distorted vision about the possibilities of the New World.

The Solís, Magellan, and Gamboa episodes from the period of exploration and conquest deal with noted historical figures that achieved prominence in the colonial history of the River Plate region and reiterate the message of the New World as the continent of unfulfilled promises. In addition to these stories, the novel retells canonical episodes dealing with the exploration and discovery of other regions, and such episodes reproduce a similar pattern of hope converted into disillusionment. Columbus, for example, becomes an object of ridicule in *Esta maldita lujuria,* as Lara espouses irreverent, behind-the-scenes explanations of some of Columbus's famous words from his *Diario de a bordo*. Chapter 4, "Bestiario," puts forth a series of examples to support Lara's contention that boundaries between the human and animal kingdoms are nonexistent in the New World. Columbus is presented as a lustful explorer whose sexual needs influenced his behavior aboard the ship and his dealings with Queen Isabel. According to Lara's account, Columbus smuggled on board a young woman disguised as a man and named every bay and peninsula in her honor.[69] In the novel, only after making love to her seven consecutive times did Columbus exclaim the famous phrase "¡Este es el Paraíso Terrenal!"[70] [This is the Earthly Paradise!], even though he was surrounded by an inhospitable environment of snakes and crocodiles. Later Lara asserts that Columbus was arrested and returned to Spain in chains because his crew overheard the screams of the woman, whose breasts were eaten by bats.[71] When Columbus finally returns to the royal court as an honored guest of King Ferdinand and Queen Isabel and is warmly received for his so-called accomplishments, parrots from the New World disclose the adulterous relationship between the queen and Columbus: "—¡Prr: dame otra vez Cristóbal, una vez más! ¡Prrrr!"[72] [Mmm, do it to me again, Christopher . . . Mmm, do it to me again!] The parrots' irreverent comments serve to degrade Columbus's heroic portrait and reduce him to a caricature of the legend. The foundational figure of Latin American continental identity is reduced to a mere skeleton of his former self.

The Portuguese explorer Vasco da Gama fares no better than Columbus in Lara's version of the past. En route to Africa, da Gama retrieves at Gibraltar a statue of the goddess Venus, who resembled a live woman: "[T]enía completas sus partes de mujer [. . .] y al calor de la costa africana esas partes estaban húmedas y tibias. [. . .] [T]enía brazos y piernas articulados para mejor devolver los abrazos."[73] [Her female parts were all there . . . and on the humid African coast they were warm and moist. . . . Her elbows and knees were articulated to better return embraces.] Since the statue of Venus is the only "woman" aboard the ship, the entire crew fantasizes about making love with her. Da Gama, however, resists their entreaties and refuses to "prostituir" [prostitute] his woman. When the expedition reaches the African coast, animal urges overcome him. On shore he seeks to satiate his sexual desires with an "hembra gorila"[74] [female gorilla]. Da Gama's act of bestiality provides just one more opportunity for the narrator to violate cultural taboos about sexuality and corroborate his thesis that the uncharted South American and African continents awaken lascivious impulses.

Lara's scabrous rewritings of Columbus and Da Gama's close encounters of another kind also encompass the escapades of Alvar Núñez Cabeza de Vaca in modern-day Paraguay. In the early 1540s, the historical Cabeza de Vaca traveled to the River Plate to assume the post of *adelantado* (governor in perpetuity) of the region and restore order at the Jesuit missions, which had achieved the reputation as colonies of unbridled *lujuria*. In the novel, however, the morally self-righteous Cabeza de Vaca of the official history resembles a grotesque figure from Ramón Valle Inclan's *Luces de bohemia* (1925). His body is disproportionately shaped ("todo su cuerpo era enorme"[75] [his entire body was enormous]), with the exception of his small and delicate penis, with which he could "penetrar a una mujer dormida sin que ella lo notara"[76] [penetrate a sleeping woman without disturbing her]. Here, since Cabeza de Vaca is ashamed about the size of his penis, he decides to visit a Guaraní folk doctor, who recommends that he rub it with a magical rock. Accordingly, Cabeza de Vaca rubs the rock against his penis all night long. By the next morning it has achieved "proporciones desmesuradas"[77] [huge proportions] and is described as "inverosímil"[78] [astonishing]. His friends, who earlier had teased him about his size, now marvel at this transformation. They no longer call him Alvar Núñez Cabeza de Vaca (Alvar Núñez Head of Cow) but "Alvar Núñez Verga de Toro"[79] [Alvar Núñez Shaft of Bull]. In the end his visit to the Guaraní doctor solves one problem (the small size of his penis) but creates another. He is now unable to find any woman with whom he can have intercourse. In desperation, Cabeza de Vaca kidnaps a Guaraní woman and rubs her genitalia with the magical rock until he transforms her into an anatomically suitable partner. Lara concludes his retelling of this episode by noting that the couple lived happily ever after, though Cabeza de Vaca occasionally "lamentábase de no poderle serle infiel, ya que nunca pudo encontrar otra mujer de su tamaño"[80] [lamented his inability to be unfaithful, since he could never find another woman of his size].

The Cabeza de Vaca tale in *Esta maldita lujuria* captures the frustration of all adventurers to unexplored lands. They traveled with dreams and expectations of satiating their every desire in an earthly paradise, but instead returned disillusioned and dejected, having discovered an earthly inferno. Once again "heroes" from the historiography are viewed through the lens of "esta maldita lujuria," that uncontrollable and excessive passion which leads them to realize a perverted and distorted version of their dreams and aspirations.

Within this revision of Spanish American colonial historiography, Lara also tells his own story about events in the River Plate region prior to Argentina's declaration of independence from Spain. As with other explorers, Lara's own life story is a tale of disillusionment with the promise and reality of the New World. To communicate his own failure, he retells Dante's unsuccessful pursuit of Beatrice in the *Divine Comedy* and suggests parallels between the textual reality and the experiences of explorers. According to Lara's version, Dante fell madly in love with Beatrice, a Florentine, though she was also the object of desire of a rival suitor, who showered her with gifts and eventually won her heart. Nonetheless, Dante persisted in pursuing Beatrice and visited her daily. Finally her husband fell deathly ill. One day, when it appeared that her husband's death was imminent and inevitable, Beatrice promises to marry Dante: "—Cuando ocurra lo inevitable —le dijo—seré tuya."[81] ["'When the inevitable happens,' she told him, 'I'll be yours.'"] At this moment the story takes an unexpected turn: the next day Beatrice died and her husband was miraculously cured. Dante was so horrified at the prospect of not fulfilling his desire for Beatrice that he "decidió revolver cielo e infierno en busca de ella"[82] [resolved to move heaven and hell to find her]. In the end, after incessant searching, Dante found Beatrice. But before they could even embrace each other, she vanished, because she had "la consistencia del aire"[83] [the consistency of air].

Ambrosio de Lara retells the Dante/Beatrice story to communicate similarities with his own experience in the River Plate. He always makes a point to establish analogies between the landscape in the *Divine Comedy* and that in Carmen de Patagones. Both the landscape and the river Dante crosses in hell resemble the "desiertos casi patagónicos"[84] [almost Patagonian deserts] and the "río Negro"[85] [Black River], respectively. Such retellings of works from European medieval literature constitute another strategy whereby Lara represents the nature of the New World experience and the irresistible power of lust over the actions of men. Like Dante, Lara arrives with the illusion of satiating his desires, yet becomes frustrated and disillusioned for not realizing his dreams. America, he states in a later chapter, is the place where "nunca se cumplían los sueños. [. . .] [L]as esperanzas eran una ilusión continuamente burlada [. . .]"[86] [dreams never came true. . . . [E]xpectations were no more than constantly frustrated illusions. . . .]

Interwoven into the textual fabric of Lara's autobiography is a stinging critique of the church and the imperial government of the late eighteenth century. Regarding the church, Lara points out the divergence between official policy and actual practice. Upon the arrival of Lara's ship in Lima in 1779, an official from the Inquisition detains the youngest African woman, with whom the entire crew had satisfied its sexual desires. The clergyman promises to protect her from further savagery and to instruct her in Christian doctrine.[87] Shortly thereafter Lara comments on the outcome of the official's successful religious indoctrination: "[S]e la salvó de tal modo que la muchacha estaba encinta en Río de Janeiro."[88] [The girl's soul was saved in such a fashion that she was pregnant and living in Río de Janeiro.] In addition to the church's hypocrisy, Lara shows its predisposition to vulgarity and profanity. In chapter 10, "Jodidos," a priest from the expedition explains in detail the etymology of the infinitive *joder* by reviewing the lecherous behavior of the Roman emperors Julius Caesar, Caligula, and Claudius, and by claiming that the church adopted the word in 1353. Given that the word *joder* has connotations of lechery and lust, Lara pokes fun at the church for adopting a word loaded with meanings contrary to its own ideology.

Spain's dispute with Great Britain in the late eighteenth century over the Falkland Islands, also known as the Islas Malvinas in modern-day Argentina, constitutes a focal point of Lara's indirect criticism of the Spanish government, on the one hand, and, on the other, of the military junta's decision to invade the Falklands Islands in 1982. According to historical accounts, a British expedition occupied and took possession of Port Egmont on West Falkland Island in 1764. As a British-controlled base, Port Egmont posed a singular threat to the Spanish empire in that armed ships could prey upon Spanish colonial ports and shipping in times of war and engage in contraband trading in times of peace.[89] In response to these developments, Spain created the governorship of the Malvinas in May 1766 and placed the island under the jurisdiction of the nearest constituted authority, the captain general of Buenos Aires, Don Francisco Bucareli. This administrative reorganization, however, failed to dislodge the British occupying force. Four years later, in May 1770, a heavily armed Spanish expedition consisting of a squadron of five frigates bearing 1600 troops sailed from Buenos Aires to Port Egmont with orders to end the English establishment.[90] Shortly thereafter, the on-site British commander surrendered and returned to England. For the time being, Spain had recaptured the Malvinas. However, the story does not end here. After protests from the British government over the humiliating expulsion of the colonists, Spain disavowed the decision of Captain General Bucareli in Buenos Aires and restored all of Britain's stores and effects previously seized at Port Egmont. The restitution did not preclude the claims to sovereignty by one or the other of the powers, though it recognized British possession and rights to occupy Port Egmont.[91] In 1774 the British inexplicably abandoned the island, and in 1780 the Spaniards destroyed the remnants of the British settlement, never establishing a colony there because they preferred the more accessible Puerto Soledad.[92]

Against this historical context about the dispute between Britain and Spain over the Falkland Islands in the eighteenth century, Lara's retelling of the dispute in *Esta maldita lujuria* achieves fuller meaning. For the late twentieth-century Argentine reader, retelling eighteenth-century disputes with Great Britain over the Falklands resonates with fresh memories about the Falkland Islands War in 1982. Lara's words ring prophetic for the modern-day reader when he remarks: "[U]n día u otro, una potencia extranjera se apoderá de lo que antes fue nuestro: quizás la que nos lo vendió una vez, o puede ser la que nos convenció de abandonar las Malvinas."[93] [One of these days, a foreign power will seize what was once ours; perhaps the power that once sold it to us is the one that convinced us to abandon the Malvinas.] Indeed, the British convinced the Argentine government to return the Falkland Islands to British control again in 1982. Such comments invite the modern reader to interpret this passage as a reminder of Argentina's recent humiliating defeat.

Esta maldita lujuria also presents an encoded critique of governmental and ecclesiastical institutions during both the colonial period and the Proceso de reorganización nacional. What connects both periods is Lara's and the military junta's disillusionment with the New World and Argentine society, respectively. At both historical moments, these authorities perceived an unraveling of the moral fabric of society and proposed desperate measures to reverse this trend. *Esta maldita lujuria* exposes the seamier side of the discovery and conquest. Lara mocks the church's feigned concern with the moral order of the universe, an attitude that coincides with the ideology of the military junta during the Proceso. Lara emplots the history of the River Plate region, the New World, and, by extension, modern-day Argentina as a tale of men driven by the force of uncontrollable sexual desires.

Esta maldita lujuria demands a competent reader, well-versed in allusions to River Plate culture of the colonial period and to Argentine culture during the Proceso. Elliptical allusions to the adventures of the explorers and discoverers as well as to prominent events such as the Falkland Islands war in 1982 demand careful readers, who must decode a series of clues to understand more fully the novel's purpose of demythifying the official historiography's vision of the New World as a utopian space. Lara retells the history of the colonial period as a challenge to the Spanish crown and church in the eighteenth century, which represent the New World as a land of abundance.

In a published interview with the literary critic Clark Zlotchew, Brailovsky recalls how as a journalist during the Proceso he learned how to write articles so that readers would read "entre las líneas"[94] [between the lines] and he could escape the wrath of government censors. Likewise, the reader of *Esta maldita lujuria* must be adept at reading between the lines and realize that revising the colonial history of the River Plate region functions as a pretext to critique not only the abuses of power in the remote past but also the sociopolitical situation of Argentina in the late twentieth century.

Baccino's *Maluco* and Brailovksy's *Esta maldita lujuria* employ invented, socially marginal figures who narrate and expose the seamier side of the New World historiography. *Maluco* reinscribes the story of Magellan's voyage within the Spanish medieval and Renaissance tradition of buffonesque literature and makes it an extension of Francesillo de Zúñiga's *Crónica burlesca*. It appropriates and mocks the conventions of the *relación de servicio* and buffonesque narrative in an effort to undermine the authoritativeness of the official New World historiography and to empower Latin America to restore its voice to the initial encounters between Europe and the Americas. *Esta maldita lujuria* presents the life story of the sword-maker Ambrosio de Lara and of the early conquistadors as a double-directed narrative that mocks and dismantles the authoritative discourses that the Spanish crown and church from the colonial period and the Argentine military junta and church during the Dirty War invoked to justify their crusades against alleged "enemies" and "subversives."

The Brazilian novelist and literary critic Silviano Santiago has argued that what characterizes much recent Brazilian fiction is the search for alternative angles from which to reconstruct Brazil's past and give forgotten or marginalized groups a voice.[95] Santiago's comments are equally applicable to River Plate narratives such as *Maluco* and *Esta maldita lujuria,* which employ a buffoon and a sword-maker to rewrite the discovery, conquest, and colonization of the New World, and in the process, to comment on recent historical events under dictatorship. The preponderance of these new angles suggests the importance of the marginal speaking position of the narrative voice and irreverent humor as fundamental strategies in dismantling the official historiography of the period and legitimating alternative visions about the past. In the next chapter, the focus will shift to marginal and vilified figures from the conquest of Mexico, who are invoked to rewrite the diffuse cultural myths of *mestizaje* and the black legend in the late twentieth century.

3
Rewriting Stories about Vilified Figures from the Conquest of Mexico

De su vida [Gonzalo Guerrero] quedan muchas incógnitas que resolver, trabajo mucho más extenso y que yo considero que les toca a los poetas y a los escritores, y no porque se suponga que ellos tienen más imaginación, sino que ya todo lo demás que se pueda decir de él, si no se descubren más datos, es parte del cuento o la novela, o de la leyenda o del poema. [. . .]
—José Armando Ceballos y Borjas, *Gonzalo Guerrero (Apuntes para su biografía)*

[Many unknowns about the life of Gonzalo Guerrero remain to be resolved. This is a much more extensive task, and one that I think should be undertaken by poets and writers. It's not that they necessarily have more imagination, but that if no new information is forthcoming, everything else that can be said about him may be best expressed in the short story or the novel, in the realm of legend or of poetry. . . .]

Este infausto 1994 se ha visto marcado [. . .] por el levantamiento armado en los altos de Chiapas, que ha venido a recordarnos que quinientos años después la iniquidad y la ambición mantienen sobre los indígenas la injusticia que han sido víctima desde la época del despojo.
　Así, saldando parte de la deuda que nuestro teatro tiene con la historia de estas tierras, la obra de Víctor Manuel Castillo Bautista toma la negra figura del conquistador Nuño de Guzmán para remembrar su tristemente célebre paso por los caminos y sobre los indios del occidente mexicano. [. . .]
—José Caballero, "Presentación," in *Nuño de Guzmán o la espada de Dios (Obra en un acto)*, by Víctor M. Castillo Bautista

[This unhappy year of 1994 was marked by the armed uprising in the Chiapas highlands. We are reminded that five hundred years after the dispossession of the indigenous population, iniquity and ambition continue to condemn them to the injustice they have suffered since that time.
　The work of Víctor Manuel Castillo Bautista seeks to square some of the debt that our theater owes to the history of this land. Castillo

> Bautista revives the lamentable figure of conquistador Nuño de Guzmán to recount his infamous travels in western Mexico and the outrages that he committed against the Indians along the way....]

IN CHAPTER 1, I DISCUSSED HOW *CÓMO CONQUISTÉ A LOS AZTECAS* AND *EL largo atardecer del caminante* recast the canonical *Cartas de relación* and *Los naufragios* as editor-mediated autobiographies that incorporate what has been silenced, denied, or repressed in New World historiography. These novels revisit the accounts of Cortés and Cabeza de Vaca to interrogate the truthfulness of the official historiography and to establish striking parallels between the abuses that the conquistadors perpetrated against the indigenous populations in the sixteenth century and those that the Argentine military regime committed against its citizens during the Dirty War.

Revising tales from early New World historiography, however, is not limited exclusively to un-writing *relaciones* of renowned historical figures. As I showed in chapter 2, peripheral marginal figures from the discovery and conquest of the River Plate have been invoked to render irreverent and contestatory accounts about episodes from that region and to critique obliquely the recent historical past in Uruguay and Argentina. The novels I examine in this chapter, however, provide the perspectives of a different type of figure: Spaniards vilified by conventional Eurocentric historiography, Gonzalo Guerrero and Nuño de Guzmán. In Eugenio Aguirre's *Gonzalo Guerrero* (1980) and Herminio Martínez's *Diario maldito de Nuño de Guzmán* (1990), these characters render testimonial accounts of their experiences in New Spain and implicitly rewrite the cultural myths of *mestizaje* and the black legend and engage their significance for contemporary Mexico.

Eugenio Aguirre (b. Mexico City, 1944) is a novelist and short-story writer who has served as president of the Asociación de escritores mexicanos and director of the literary division of the Sociedad general de escritores. Among his nineteen published novels, *Gonzalo Guerrero* has received the most critical and popular acclaim. He received the Gran Medalla de Plata awarded by the Academia Lutece in Paris, and in 1990, his novel was translated and published into French.[1] Herminio Martinez (b. Guanajuato, 1949), a member of the Institute for Humanistic Studies at the University of Guanajuato in Celaya, has published five novels (*Hombres de temporal* [1988], *Diario maldito de Nuño de Guzmán* [1990], *Las puertas del mundo: Una autobiografía hipócrita del Almirante* [1992], *Invasores del paraíso* [1998], and *El regreso* [1999]), two collections of short stories (*La jaula del tordo* [1986] and *La eternidad no tiene mirasoles* [1996]), and a collection of poetry (*Ruido de hombres* [1985]).

Gonzalo Guerrero re-creates, primarily in the form of a memoir, the story of Gonzalo Guerrero's transformation from a Spanish sailor into an acculturated Mayan of substantial social standing. According to fragmentary evidence from sixteenth-century Spanish chronicles, Guerrero, while en route from Darién (modern-day Panama) to Hispaniola, was shipwrecked off the coast of Jamaica in 1511, was washed ashore on the Yucatán Peninsula, and was captured and enslaved by indigenous groups. He subsequently climbed the social ladder and became a military leader, married an indigenous princess, fathered four children, and refused to return with Spaniards who tried to rescue him in 1519. He later led indigenous resistance against the military conquest of the Yucatán and finally died combating Spanish forces in Hibueras (modern-day Honduras) in 1536.[2]

The *Diario maldito,* on the other hand, narrates in the form of a travel diary the actions of Nuño de Guzmán from his arrival at Pánuco (the modern-day state of Tamaulipas) in 1526 through his return to Spain, where he wrote his final journal entry in 1544. Historical documents yield more information about Guzmán's life and career then they do about Gonzalo Guerrero. Nuño de Guzmán arrived in New Spain in 1526 to assume the post of resident governor of Pánuco, a post he held until 1528. As governor, he issued licenses for the branding and exportation of Amerindian slaves from Pánuco to Hispaniola—an act for which he would be denounced for generations to come. In 1528 Charles V named him president of the Primera audiencia of New Spain (1529–33), specifically to act as a counterweight to the growing power of Cortés. (Guzmán repeatedly clashed with Cortés and Juan de Zumárraga. The latter was a Franciscan, the first bishop and archbishop of New Spain [1527–48], and the leader of the Mexican Inquisition [1536–43].)[3] During his tenure as president of the Primera audiencia, Guzmán would often leave the city to conquer territory, and in 1530 he left on an expeditionary campaign to conquer lands extending to the Pacific Ocean, which included the modern-day states of Michoacán, Jalisco, Zacatecas, Nayarit, Sinaloa, Sonora, and Durango.[4] On his way through Michoacán, Guzmán—accompanied by a band of Spanish soldiers, local settlers, and allied Indians—tortured and publicly executed the Cazonci (hereditary ruler of the Purhépecha Indians), along the banks of the Lerma River on February 14, 1530.[5]

By the end of the sixteenth century, Guzmán had acquired an immutable reputation for greed and cruelty and come to symbolize Spanish atrocities against the Amerindians in the New World. His name had become synonymous with the black legend of Spanish colonialism.[6] In large measure this uniformly negative portrait originated from the publication of Bartolomé de las Casas's *Brevísima relación de la destrucción de las Indias*

(1552).⁷ Since the publication of the *Brevísima relación,* generations of historians and intellectuals have taken their cues from Guzmán's political rivals (mainly Cortés and Zumárraga) and reproduced the content of the documents left behind, all of which depict Guzmán as cruel, brutal, and lascivious.⁸

Gonzalo Guerrero rewrites the conquest of Mexico as a benevolent encounter and de-traumatizes the inception of *mestizaje,* contending explicitly with the vision of the union of Cortés and La Malinche as a rape. While the Gonzalo Guerrero episode is not even included as a footnote in history textbooks, this historical figure from Aguirre's novel, by contrast, is accorded the narrative space to tell his own story and to respond to criticisms that sixteenth-century Spanish chroniclers leveled against him, especially the accusation that he had betrayed Spanish culture by allying himself with the Maya. *Gonzalo Guerrero* endeavors to come to terms with the violent origins of the Mexican nation—Cortés's rape of La Malinche and the birth of Martín Cortés—by casting Guerrero as a modern-day Mexican hero, who officially married the indigenous Ix Chel Can out of love and fathered the first mestiza, Ix Mo, in 1515, years before the birth of Martín Cortés. In the novel the Guerrero/Ix Chel Can dyad displaces Cortés/La Malinche as the founding couple of Mexican cultural identity and inscribes this new beginning within the prevailing ideology of *mestizaje.*

Whereas Guerrero's experience in Mexico is largely ignored, Mexican historians have summarily denounced Guzmán as a megalomaniac and tyrant. The *Diario maldito,* however, goes beyond this simplistic, one-dimensional assessment of Guzmán's career in New Spain. By recasting Guzmán's experiences through a travel diary, the novel underscores the multifaceted nature of his character, presents a human being of uncontrollable passions, and brings to the forefront the ideological contexts in which historical writings have forged Guzmán's image as the incarnation of the black legend of Spanish colonialism.

Gonzalo Guerrero and the *Diario maldito* retell diffuse cultural myths, traceable to specific texts and interpretative traditions, about the conquest of Mexico. *Gonzalo Guerrero* proposes an alternative beginning for the cultural narrative of Mexican nation and inscribes it in the dominant ideology of *mestizaje,* without challenging the continued subordination of the indigenous populations in the tale. The *Diario maldito,* in contrast, gives the Spanish black legend a human face and revels in exaggerating stereotypical images of Nuño de Guzmán in order to lay bare the interests at stake in writing history. In the end, however, these novels are ideologically ambiguous and contradictory. On the one hand, they vindicate the indigenous side of Mexican identity by reformulating the foundation of *mestizaje* and by further denouncing the atrocities of the black legend. On the other hand, the novels maintain the focus on the realm of the Spaniards. As always, indigenous people are merely pretexts. After defining the concept of *mestizaje* as the cornerstone of Mexico's narrative of cultural identity and considering the pertinence of Octavio Paz's discussion of Cortés and Malinche in his essay "Hernán Cortés: Exorcismo y liberación" (1985), I will argue that *Gonzalo Guerrero* renovates the concept of *mestizaje* without challenging its underlying premises. I will then examine how the *Diario maldito* transforms the historical Guzmán's *relación* into a fictional travel diary that plays with conventions of the *relación* in order to rehumanize this maligned historical figure and to examine the ideological context in which history casts figures as villains. By revising these cultural myths, both novels grapple to explain how institutions of power employ myths for controlling the vision of the past and legitimating the present.

The notion of Cortés and Malinche as the founding couple in the narrative of *mestizaje* harks back to the 1920s. José Clemente Orozco's mural *Cortés and Malinche* (1926), found over the staircase in the National Preparatory School in Mexico City, portrays this couple as the Adam and Eve of the Mexican nation. According to Benjamin Keen, a naked and somber Cortés and Malinche clasp hands, and their union represents the union of Spanish and Indian elements in a new synthesis.[9] This union, however, is contingent upon Cortés's subjugation of the indigenous people, represented in the fresco by a prone and naked figure under the Spaniard's right foot.[10] Cortés's left arm prevents Malinche from interceding on behalf of the indigenous people and acts as a final separation from her former life. The image of Cortés and Malinche symbolizes synthesis, subjugation, and the ambivalence of her position in the story of the nation's colonial past,[11] ambivalence in the sense that she has been cast as the mother of the first *mestizos,* but these *mestizos* suffer from a complex of being *hijos de la chingada* (products of a mother who has yielded to violation).[12]

Octavio Paz, however, gives a different interpretation of the Cortés/Malinche encounter. In "Hernán Cortés: Exorcismo y liberación," Paz argues that this symbol of origin is not the symbol of tranquility but one of violence: sexuality is not innocent but criminal. The history of Mexico, Paz continues, does not begin with the peaceful union of a Spanish Adam and an indigenous Eve, as suggested by the Orozco mural, but rather with the murder and death of the indigenous populations.[13] This predominating myth about cultural origins, Paz argues, divides Mexicans and poisons their souls. Mexico's hatred of Cortés is not hatred of Spain: it is hatred of one's self.[14] In order to move beyond this situation, Paz advocates the demythification of Cortés and his relocation to the field of history.

Gonzalo Guerrero, however, offers an alternative solution for moving beyond Cortés. The novel proposes the tale of Guerrero as a new mythical point of origin and shifts attention away from Cortés and La Malinche during the foundational moment of the Mexican nation. In fact, Rolando Romero, in a discussion of the representation of Gonzalo Guerrero in the Spanish chronicles, views Guerrero as a counter-Malinche figure:

> Gonzalo Guerrero . . . serves . . . as a new model of cultural syncretism. This model is not based on the violation and destruction suggested by Paz's Malinche, but on the respect and willing acceptance of the culture of the Other. Guerrero as a counter model to the conquest shows that the territory that the Spaniards found on their way to the Orient changed both the Old and the New World. . . .[15]

For Romero, Guerrero embodies the dynamics of mutual exchange between Spaniards and indigenous peoples and offers a more auspicious beginning for the Mexican nation, a beginning based on resisting invasions and loving one's family. Although the Guerrero tale does not wreak the violence and destruction suggested by Paz's interpretation of the encounter, one remains dubious as to what extent Guerrero accepted the culture of the Other. After all, was not Guerrero's decision to go native motivated by his desire to improve his social standing? Had he returned to Spanish culture, would he have enjoyed the same level of prestige and status that he had attained in Mayan culture?

In order to construct a new idea of *mestizaje, Gonzalo Guerrero* focuses on the protagonist's conversion from a Spanish sailor into an acculturated Mayan leader. The novel consists of ten chapters and an academic bibliography. Chapter 1 begins with the words of an extradiegetic narrator, who regards Guerrero as an adventurer, and proceeds with Guerrero's reflections about the state of his life in Darién two weeks before his departure for Hispaniola. Chapter 2, narrated exclusively by Guerrero, covers the first nine days of the voyage and culminates with the shipwreck off the coast of Jamaica. In chapter 3 Guerrero recalls the ensuing seven days of physical and psychological hardship at sea that he and the crew endured until they washed ashore in the Yucatán. In chapter 4 he addresses the expedition members' efforts to regain their physical and psychological strengths and to formulate a rescue plan. Before they can act, however, indigenous tribes ambush them, kill their victims and eat their flesh, and take as captives Guerrero, Jerónimo de Aguilar, and other crew members. By the end of the chapter Guerrero, Aguilar, and others have managed to escape. In chapter 5 Guerrero remembers scenes from the crew's capture by another indigenous group and their enslavement as temple builders at the hands of the Mayan leader Taxmal. By the middle of the chapter Guerrero and Aguilar are reassigned as domestic workers and experience an improvement in their status.

In chapter 6 the extradiegetic narrator from chapter 1 interrupts Guerrero's narrative to recount Guerrero's experiences as a slave of Na Chan Can, and frequently re-creates events between 1512 and 1516 based on identified and unnamed sixteenth-century chronicles about the Yucatán. In chapter 7 Guerrero documents his continuing acculturation and acceptance into Na Chan Can's culture as evidenced by his marriage to the princess, Ix Chel Can. At the end of the chapter, Ix Chel Can announces that she is pregnant with Guerrero's child. In chapter 8, based on the often anthologized episode from chapters 25–29 of Bernal Díaz del Castillo's *Historia verdadera de la conquista de la Nueva España,* Guerrero re-creates his fortuitous reunion with Jerónimo de Aguilar, who had spent the previous five years as a slave with another indigenous group on the peninsula. In chapter 9, covering events between 1518 and 1523, Guerrero sacrifices his daughter Ix Mo at a *cenote* (deep-water-filled sinkhole) in Chichén Itzá to placate the gods, increases his involvement in resisting the Spanish invaders, and fathers another boy and girl. In chapter 10, corresponding to the period 1523–36, Guerrero recalls the numerous expeditions of Francisco Montejo and Alonso Dávila to the Yucatán Peninsula and his efforts to mount an effective campaign of resistance. He views his stance against the Spaniards as a defensive measure to protect his wife and children and meets his death at the hands of the Spaniards in 1536 at Champotón. The chapter concludes with the voice of the extradiegetic narrator from chapters 1 and 6, who lauds Guerrero's contributions to Mexico because of his actions in the Yucatán. Chapter 10 is followed by a bibliography of books and articles that Eugenio Aguirre consulted in his fictional re-creation of the Guerrero episode.

Gonzalo Guerrero is a hybrid of the nineteenth-century historical novel that recounts colonial history to construct national heroes and the Spanish American New Historical novel, as defined by Seymour Menton. It resembles the traditional historical novel in that the narrative progresses chronologically and tells a story; an extradiegetic narrator functions as an overarching authority that reinforces the main theme of Guerrero as a hero of the Mexican nation; the narrative adopts an attitude of admiration toward the indigenous cultures; and it concludes with a bibliography of historical documents that ostensibly inform the narrative—a technique reminiscent of Manuel de Jesús Galván's *Enriquillo* (1878). But, *Gonzalo Guerrero* shows narrative innovations typical of the New Historical novel. Guerrero retells his own story, as does the fictional Lope de Aguirre in Abel

Posse's *Daimón,* from an enunciative position of the late twentieth century. He also occasionally comments on and amends the official version of his life as immortalized in sixteenth-century Spanish chronicles, and the ideological stance is more critical in comparison to the unqualified admiration for the hero typical of the nineteenth century.

The publication of *Gonzalo Guerrero* represents the first widespread dissemination in novelistic form of the *mestizaje* tale from the Yucatán.[16] In comparison to many novels discussed in this study, *Gonzalo Guerrero* has been the subject of one book chapter and several journal articles. In his 1994 dissertation on the Mexican historical novel (1980–94), Manuel Medina argues that Aguirre's novel employs discursive strategies from the New World chronicles in order to undermine the conventional representation of Gonzalo Guerrero as a traitor and to question the criteria by which historians designate figures as "heroes" or "traitors."[17] What accounts for the novel's success, according to Medina, is its selection of a narrator, a focalizer, and the chronological presentation of events of Guerrero's life.[18] In a similar vein, Alice Reckley argues that *Gonzalo Guerrero* improvises on historical tradition by fabricating and amending information from the chronicles and subsequent historical investigations to alter the way history is remembered.[19] Deviations from the conventional structures of acceptable fictionalization create new memories of the Guerrero episode and take into account contemporary preoccupations in Mexico.[20] Monique Sarfati-Arnaud situates *Gonzalo Guerrero* within the context of Spanish American novels that question the official historiography about a historical figure and adopt the vantage point of "la visión de los vencidos" (the vision of the vanquished) as a fundamental strategy in challenging such historiography.[21] She further contends that the novel represents an uncritical defense of the ideology of *mestizaje* and ignores the violence against indigenous cultures that defined the conquest.[22]

On one level, my reading agrees substantially with those of Medina and Reckley. Indeed, the novel, like the works discussed in chapter 2, converts a marginal figure into a protagonist and uses techniques reminiscent of the New World chronicles to rewrite history and to generate new remembrances of this episode. Nonetheless, both scholars minimize the sociopolitical implications and cultural politics of proposing Gonzalo Guerrero and his wife Ix Chel Can as the founding couple of Mexican cultural identity. They discount the degree to which the novel marginalizes indigenous contributions to *mestizaje* in Mexico. In my estimation, Sarfati-Arnaud correctly approaches the novel as an uncritical defense of the ideology of *mestizaje.*

I would like to elaborate on her contention. Though *Gonzalo Guerrero* replaces Cortés/La Malinche with Gonzalo Guerrero/Ix Chel Can as the founding couple, it downplays the violence inflicted on the indigenous populations and their subordinate role in the ideology of *mestizaje*. Jorge Klor de Alva succinctly enumerates the critical elements of the official narrative of *mestizaje* in twentieth-century Latin America, which include that *mestizaje* is the felicitous product of the coming together of the various "races"; that it draws from all these races and becomes the essence of American reality; and that it is a unique expression of a synthesis that culminates with Christianity, the Spanish language, and the embrace of the West. In this narrative of *mestizaje,* adds Klor de Alva, the application of the concept becomes a euphemism for the overwhelming presence of Western influences and an excuse for eliding and dismissing that which is indigenous.[23] *Gonzalo Guerrero* manifests in the early 1980s strains on the ideology of *mestizaje,* which has undergirded the concept of Mexican identity since the Mexican Revolution in 1910.[24] The novel attempts to make such an ideology palatable as a vehicle for articulating a national and cultural identity.[25] But it simultaneously questions the canonized view of Gonzalo Guerrero as a traitor and remythifies him as a hero of the Mexican people, without fundamentally altering the asymmetrical power relations between the superior Spaniards and the "inferior" indigenous populations in the ideology of *mestizaje.*

As Medina perceptively notes, the novel endeavors to make Guerrero the father of Mexican *mestizaje.* In order to achieve this transformation, the account lays out, in a chronological fashion, his ostensible conversion into an acculturated Mayan who struggles to reconcile his Spanish roots with Mayan culture. In chapters 1–4, Guerrero's comments about the slaves (*los cafres*) aboard the ship signal an evolution in his thinking about their predicament and foreshadow his own self-transformation during captivity. The slaves, defined by their "mentes limitadas"[26] [limited intellects], initially receive his qualified pity from a position of absolute superiority: "Me conmovió, debo confesarlo, su mansedumbre; la aceptación que de su condición hacían y hube de retirarme con una ligera irritación."[27] [I pitied them, I must confess, for their servility, the acceptance of their condition that they showed. Slightly irritated, I was compelled to withdraw.] Shortly after Jerónimo de Aguilar informs him that the church is profiting from their enslavement, Guerrero becomes angry and experiences "rencor en mi pecho"[28] [a fervid resentment], which later explodes into an all-out rebellion against the values of his culture: "Sus palabras [. . .] habían incubado en mi razón la pozoña de la rebeldía, de la inconformidad ante el inhumano comercio que se venía haciendo con la carne de aquellos desdichados. [. . .] Me hallé repudiando a mi raza y a [. . .] mi religión. [. . .]"[29] [The church's words . . . had incubated within me the poison of rebellion, an utter inconformity with this inhuman trade in the flesh of those unfortunates. . . . I found myself repudiating my race and . . . my religion. . . .] His acknowledgment of the slaves' mistreatment at the hands of Spaniards leads him to question the infallibility of his own culture. When it becomes evident that the ship is about to sink, Guerrero, who now views the slaves as "desgraciados"[30] [unfortunates], makes an unheeded request that Captain Valdivia unchain them so that they might survive. This abrupt shift in attitude toward the slaves later enables Guerrero to see parallels between the Spaniards' treatment of the *cafres* aboard the ship and the treatment of the Spaniards as slaves by the Yucatán indigenous people: "¿No hacíamos, acaso, eso con los negros que nos traían al Darién o que eran llevados a la Fernandina? ¿Cuándo se habían visto *cafres* enjaulados?"[31] [Did we not subject to the same imprisonment the Negroes that they brought to us in Darien or that were brought to Fernandina? When had Kaffirs been seen to be encaged?] By the beginning of chapter 5, Guerrero understands more fully the suffering of the *cafres* aboard the ship. As a slave of the indigenous peoples, he realizes that "Ser esclavo es lo más doloroso"[32] [to be a slave is most painful]. The evolution in Guerrero's attitude toward the slaves, from utmost contempt to qualified empathy for their plight, is a key step in his purported acculturation, his transformation from traitor to hero.

A second catalyst in Gonzalo's accommodation to Mayan culture is the shipwreck itself. Stripped of the features that anchored his personal identity, he undergoes a cultural rebirth. The shipwreck converts him and the crew into "bestias del océano"[33] [ocean monsters], and without his favorite weapon, the harquebus, Guerrero feels powerless. This experience interrupts his habitual thinking about the world and his role in it: "Recuerdo que durante todo este espacio cronológico pude invertir mis pensamientos, encauzarlos en un torrente de acontecimientos cotidianos y vulgares, efectuar una selección purificadora y adoptar una revolución meditativa, con la cual nunca antes había soñado. [. . .]"[34] [I remember that throughout this entire chronological space I was able to invert my thoughts, to refine a selection of them from among a torrent of quotidian and vulgar events, and to channel them fruitfully, experiencing a meditative revolution that I had never dreamed possible.] Consequently, according to the extradiegetic narrative voice in chapter 6, Gonzalo is more amenable to blending in with his new surroundings:

> La naturaleza y el continuo contacto con las gentes de la ciudad le forzaron a ir adoptando las formas de vida y costumbres de la ciudad, que eran más congruentes con su situación que sus tradiciones cristianas. No tenía por qué buscar en

la cruz el consuelo que le podía proporcionar la ceiba sagrada de inmediato; ni por qué rezar a los santos apóstoles cuando el adoratorio de las Bacabes estaba en el centro de su pueblo. [. . .]³⁵

[His continual contact with the people of the city forced him to gradually adopt their lifestyle and customs, which were more compatible with his situation than were his Christian traditions. He had no need to seek the comfort of the cross when comfort was ever available at the foot of the sacred ceiba; why pray to the holy apostles when the temple of the Bacabs was right there in the town center? . . .]

In chapter 7 Guerrero himself echoes the sentiments of the extradiegetic narrator. He strategically attires himself in the trappings of the indigenous culture in order to ensure his continued social ascent: "He advertido que, si deseo verme integrado a la comunidad como si fuese un natural, debo acogerme a sus costumbres y respetarlas absolutamente."³⁶ [I have realized that if I want to be integrated into the community as though I were a native, I should attend to its customs and respect them absolutely.] Evidently, total respect for indigenous cultures is compatible with preserving his own view of the world. As a reformed Spaniard, he both practices "pagan" ritual sacrifices and holds regular conversations with a Christian God,³⁷ though he views himself as a "Judas,"³⁸ suggesting his less than total comfort with indigenous practices. By the end of the novel Guerrero embodies the values of the Catholic Church: virility, fraternity, stoicism, love for one's family and country, and sacrifice.³⁹

By detailing the phases in Guerrero's acculturation, the novel transforms him from the traitor of the sixteenth-century Spanish chroniclers into a twentieth-century hero of Mexican mestizos. A closer reading of the novel, however, in line with the underlying assumptions of *mestizaje,* demonstrates that the indigenous cultures assume a subordinate role in the life of Guerrero, since Spanish culture ranks "first among equals" in his ideology of *mestizaje.* The novel makes it abundantly clear that Guerrero is at the core a Catholic who adopts the rituals of indigenous religions in order to secure and improve his social standing. In chapter 7 the extradiegetic narrator claims that Guerrero enriched his Spanish with elements from indigenous culture serving as mere decorations:

A la fe de Gonzalo Guerrero le fue sucediendo, en sentido inverso, lo que aconteció a los indios con sus creencias después de la conquista; se fue preñado de paganías, más decorativas que sustanciales, y adornando con un mundo de símbolos alucinantes y contradictorios, pero de gran efectividad. Realmente, nunca se despejó de su religión como se ha pretendido, sino que se enriqueció con otra, y con ambas, obtuvo la seguridad personal e inmunidad militar que le proporcionaron tantos éxitos. [. . .][40]

[Gonzalo Guerrero's faith was undergoing a process inverse to that which shaped Indian beliefs after the conquest. In practice he accepted the trappings of a paganism more decorative than substantial, a world of outlandish and contradictory symbols that were nevertheless highly instrumental. Though he feigned otherwise, his new religion enriched rather than supplanted the old. Together, they provided the personal safety and the military immunity that brought him so many victories.]

Essentially, Guerrero "respects" (i.e., tolerates) Mayan practices so long as they strengthen the unquestionable hegemony of Spanish culture and promote his own self-interest.

The junior-partner status of Mayan culture resounds loud and clear in Guerrero's descriptions of the inferiority of their weapons and fighting tactics. As Sarfati-Arnaud similarly points out, Guerrero becomes critical and contemptuous of their combat tactics.[41] Guerrero says,

Acostumbraban, estos indios, a pelear a la desbandada en masa informe y desordenada, muy expuesta a los blancos del enemigo. [. . .] Era, pues, necesario enseñarles algo de las artes marciales, de las que yo fui tan avezado y tan bien afortunado. [. . .] Aconsejéles, también, que su gritería y alharaca no fuese onomatopéyica, que esto estaba bien para asustar a las bestias, pero no a los guerreros, sino que la convirtiesen en algo racional, en un código de entendimiento entre ellos que tuviese utilidad. [. . .][42]

[These Indians were accustomed to fighting in a confused and disorderly mass, fully exposed to the fire of the enemy. . . . Thus, it was necessary to teach them something of the military arts, of which I was fortunately a highly seasoned practitioner. . . . I also advised them to modify the onomatopoeic bellowing that they used in battle. Such shrieking frightens beasts but not other warriors. They had rather to devise a rational set of cries that among them would be meaningful and expedient. . . .]

The novel implies that if Guerrero had not instructed the indigenous populations in the use of Spanish weapons and military tactics, they would have been unable to repel the Spanish invasions. At no point in the novel does the focus fall on the valor of indigenous warriors.

Although *Gonzalo Guerrero* posits itself as an alternative foundational myth of Mexican miscegenation and displaces Cortés and Malinche as the founding couple of the nation, it upholds the fundamental underlying asymmetries in power between the Spaniards and the indigenous cultures. Guerrero's story masks the cultural violence of the Spaniards' entry into the New World and legitimizes, though in a bloodless fashion, the cultural superiority of the Spaniards and the subordination of the indigenous cultures. At no point in the novel are indigenous voices allowed to speak for themselves: Guerrero speaks for them. He expresses admiration for the sophistication of the indigenous frescoes and compares them to those in Pompeii, but such comments are commonplace in Bernal Díaz's *Historia verdadera* and Cortés's *Cartas de relación*. In short, the message in between the lines of the novel is unmistakable: Spanish technological superiority in weaponry, which Gonzalo Guerrero introduced to the Mayans, enabled them to resist Spanish dominance for many years. As Sarfati-Arnaud notes, the fictional Guerrero appropriates the discursive strategies of power from the chronicles of the conquest to keep the indigenous cultures in a subordinate position.

In her dissertation on the rewriting of the myth of *mestizaje* in three fictional narratives published in Mexico in the 1990s—Carmen Boullosa's *Llanto: Novelas imposibles* (1992), Carlos Fuentes's "Las dos orillas" in *El naranjo, o los círculos del tiempo* (1993), and Ignacio Solares's *Nen la inútil* (1993)—Carrie Chorba argues that the crisis of nationalist sentiment in the later 1980s and early 1990s, caused by levels of political and economic crisis, spurred writers and Mexican intellectuals to revisit sixteenth-century events and to rewrite themselves as a nation in order to bridge the failures of the present with possibilities of the future.[43] Mexicans needed to tell and be told, argues Chorba, of their national strengths, be they cultural, historical, or mythical, in order to approach the 1990s and ultimately the new millennium.[44] She further argues that the urgency with which the birth of Mexico (the conquest and early colony) are narratively revised and reworked in the novels constitutes an attempt to revive Mexico's sense of its nationhood and to speak in new ways to the heterogeneous and often disjunctive reality that is contemporary Mexico.[45]

Though Chorba's study does not analyze Eugenio Aguirre's *Gonzalo Guerrero*, her insights are pertinent to the points I have enumerated earlier. *Gonzalo Guerrero* revisits the cultural myths of *mestizaje* to reaffirm Spanish cultural values. In the novel the reconstituted tale of origins addresses the ambivalence that Mexicans feel toward the conquest and proposes a more auspicious beginning for the nation. However, the Guerrero version of *mestizaje* has its underside: once again, the indigenous populations are mere pretexts to solidify and confirm the continued hegemony of the Spanish elements in the partnership.

Whereas *Gonzalo Guerrero* recasts the Guerrero episode as a new tale about the origins of Mexican *mestizaje*, the *Diario maldito de Nuño de*

Guzmán revisits the career of Nuño de Guzmán to counter his depiction as the embodiment of the black legend. Unlike the fictional Guerrero, who has access to and responds to the official historiography about his life in the Yucatán Peninsula, Guzmán records his role in events as a travel diary and limits his critique of contemporary historical figures such as Columbus and Cortés to his knowledge of their actions in the early sixteenth century. The *Diario maldito* represents a move in the direction of revising diffuse cultural myths about the conquest and assessing their explanatory power in the historical present.

The novel consists of forty-two unnumbered entries (chapters) of five pages each. They can be divided into four sections. The first section (chapters 1–9), covering Guzmán's departure from Spain in 1525 through his arrival as governor of Pánuco in 1526, sets the stage for his arrival in New Spain. It focuses on Guzmán's obsession with the acquisition of gold and his secret plan to establish the utopian kingdom of Guzmania. The second section (chapters 10–14) deals with his stint as governor of Pánuco and discusses his controversial decision to exchange enslaved Indians for cattle from Hispaniola. The third section (chapters 15–39) covers his tenure as president of the *Primera audiencia* in Mexico City and his subsequent military campaigns to conquer the western and northwestern regions of Mexico. The fourth section (chapters 40–42) records Nuño's incarceration and subsequent return to Spain, where he enters his final journal entry in 1544, fourteen years prior to his death in 1558.

With the exception of one book review and one book chapter, the *Diario maldito* has yet to receive sustained critical attention. In his book review Seymour Menton characterizes the novel as "una extraordinaria creación lingüística" [an extraordinary linguistic creation] and cites to substantiate his assertion the invention of words, the incorporation of lyrical devices such as anaphora, apostrophe, and alliteration, and the inclusion of allusions from classical mythology and books of chivalry.[46] According to Menton, the *Diario maldito* exhibits many affinities with novels from the Spanish American Boom.

Because plays with language assume a prominent role in the novel, one could characterize the *Diario maldito* as a neo-Boom novel. The *Diario maldito,* however, differs from other Boom novels in that it foregrounds the rhetorical conventions and topoi from the New World chronicles in order to engage the canonical reading of the Spanish chronicles in general—which has approached the text as an unproblematic storehouse of "true" facts—and of those about Guzmán in particular. More importantly, the novel gives Guzmán a human face. It employs the travel diary to incorporate metacommentary about the writing of history, anaphora and alliteration, and the stylization of rhetorical conventions and topoi from the chronicles in order to alter Guzmán one-dimensional, negative image.

Kimberle S. López focuses on the fictional Guzmán's paranoid persecution of sodomites—which, according to López, is the least documented in reference to the historical Nuño de Guzmán yet the most salient element of the novel. She argues that the *Diario maldito* represents the conquistador ironically as a homophobic sadist who is subject to homoerotic desire, and it does so to highlight the contradictions inherent in the gendered rhetoric of conquest.[47] While López provides an exemplary reading of Nuño de Guzmán as a homophobic sadist subject to homoerotic desire, I will argue further that the *Diario maldito* presents a more rounded portrait of the historical figure that inflates the flat notion of the black legend. Though in the end the novel does not completely overturn the black legend elements of the historical Nuño de Guzmán, the novel begs for a reexamination of this figure.

The *Diario maldito* presents a human being of uncontrollable passions and brings to the forefront the ideological contexts in which historical writings have forged Guzmán's image as the incarnation of the black legend. The novel retells the cultural myth of the black legend by giving it a human face and reveling in stereotypical images of Guzmán in order to lay bare the ideological interests at stake in writing history. In the following section I will examine how the *Diario maldito* transforms the historical Guzmán's *relación* into a fictional travel diary that plays with conventions of the New World chronicles in order to rehumanize this maligned historical figure and to examine the ideological context in which history casts figures as villains. By revising the cultural myth of the black legend, the novel attempts to explain how institutions of power employ myths for controlling the vision of the past and legitimating the present.

Stylistically, the novel departs significantly from the original *relación de servicio* that the historical Guzmán submitted to Charles V.[48] In the *relación* Guzmán recapitulates in chronological fashion his accomplishments in New Spain. He claims that he is the victim of the hatred of Cortés and his supporters; he argues for the importance of his military conquests for the crown and enumerates the hardships he endured to achieve his exploits; and he sums up his legislative achievements in Pánuco and Mexico City, especially his decision to exchange Indians for cattle. As Blázquez notes, the *relación* is distinctive for its dry, direct, and, at times, irreverent style and tone.[49]

The travel diary in the *Diario maldito,* however, departs significantly from Guzmán's actual *relación.* For example, the fictional Guzmán addresses the account to himself instead of Charles V, he employs a lyrical mode to communicate his interior state of mind, and peppers his account with colloquial exclamations and *refranes* (sayings) when he reflects on the actions of other conquistadors. Moreover, he uses the travel diary to record and reflect upon events as they happen, whereas the historical Guzmán submitted a retrospective defense of his actions. Whereas the historical *relación* functions to project the public image of Guzmán, the *Diario maldito* presents the autobiographical "private" selves, as *Cómo conquisté a los aztecas* did for the fictional Cortés and *El largo atardecer del caminante* did for Cabeza de Vaca, and includes discussion of such topics as his desire for women and his loathing of archenemies.

The fictional Guzmán's meanderings about his achievements and misfortunes defy easy classification and constitute a private record of historical events that will serve as the basis for his public *relación*. Through his travel diary, the fictional Guzmán brings to the forefront the human dimension strikingly absent from most Spanish chronicles. For example, the *Diario maldito* registers Guzman's anxieties about the fate of his story. In chapter 11 he worries that his secret diary will not survive and that he will not be regarded as an artistic writer. Upon leaving Pánuco to assume presidency of the *Primera audiencia* in Mexico City, he remarks:

[T]al vez [estas anotaciones] van a hallar su fin en alguna fogata o en los dientes de los roedores. [. . .] [S]é bien que en estas grescas de redacción se ha de escribir con aseo y propiedad, lo que mayormente me falta a mí, y que la primera frase la da Dios, las que siguen el tiempo y la última el autor, de donde vengo a sacar que lo mío nunca cuajará como obra de arte, por lo natural, rudo y simple de su estilo. [. . .]⁵⁰

[Perhaps these annotations will end up in some bonfire or in the teeth of rodents. . . . I know very well that to be accepted in the literary world one must compose with decorum and propriety, qualities that for the most part escape me. I am aware that God is responsible for the first phrase, that time determines what follows, and that only then does the author have his say, which leaves me convinced that my crude and unpolished effort will never be accepted as a work of art. . . .]

As he writes his travel diary, Guzmán expresses concern about the erudition of his style, which for the contemporary reader comes across as anything but "rudo y simple," given the interpolation of *refranes, romances,* and citations from ancient and sixteenth-century sources. In chapter 18 Guzmán reiterates his concern about how future readers will interpret his diary, especially when they realize that the Spanish conquistadors destroyed the indigenous cultures in order to impose their own vision of the world:

¿ [C]ómo reaccionarían los cristianos, si una mañana, en Roma, de pronto aparecieran batallones de hombres más fuertes que ellos, y a sangre y fuego impusieran otra índole de fe, y echaran por tierra, en la Basílica de San Pedro, las estatuas de Jesucristo y de María? Bueno, esta patraña, en su inverosimilitud, me responde que salvajes, tiranos, crueles, malditos, invasores, herejes, blasfemos, bárbaros y bandidos es la manera de como los llamaríamos. Y no sé si realmente haya pasado aquí lo mismo, pero allí está ese silencio en la mirada triste de los indios. [. . .][51]

[How would Christians react if several battalions of men stronger than they suddenly appeared one morning in Rome, pulled down the statues of Jesus and the Virgin in St. Peter's, and imposed their own faith by blood and fire? In such an unlikely circumstance, one would describe such men as wretched, cruel, and blasphemous aggressors, as savage, heretical tyrants, and as barbarous despoilers. I don't know if that is really the same as what happened here, but there is that silence in the doleful eyes of the Indians.]

Clearly, Guzmán empathizes with the fate of the indigenous populations and intuits that the conquistadors will be remembered for their cruelty to them. In the diary, Guzmán departs significantly from the conventional vision of the chronicles of the period, which usually downplay the human dimension of history and narrate public acts of valor in a formulaic style. In chapter 28 he differentiates his own account from other chronicles by emphasizing the quotidian dimension of the conquest: "Ésta (la mía) no es ninguna crónica que busque el renombre, sino una simple memoria de efemérides, sucesos, incidentes y fenómenos celestiales como el que anoche vimos cuando se iluminó el universo con una estrella gigante y derramada. [. . .]"[52] [This chronicle of mine does not seek renown. It is a simple record of daily events, incidents, and celestial phenomena such as the giant star we saw last night that spilled out light sufficient to illuminate the universe. . . .] For Guzmán history is the recording of the everyday events: "[H]istoria es ésta que escribo al cruzar la laguna, rodeado de tal estruendo de triquitraques; chirimías, cascabeles y caracoles que nos dicen basta nunca o hasta pronto quién sabe. [. . .]"[53] [History is what I write while I cross the lake, immersed in the din of shawms, bells, and conch shells that announce its immortality . . . or its imminent death, who knows? . . .] Thus, the quotidian events of the conquistador, not just his heroic exploits, constitute Guzmán's conception of history.

The fictional Guzmán further personalizes his *relación* when he unveils plans to establish the kingdom of Guzmania.[54] Like so many other conquistadors, Guzmán inscribes his plan within the projects of his predecessors. He credits Columbus's voyage to the Indies for inspiring his own: "De

él fue la idea de Guzmania; de él que me la trajo de no sé dónde. De él que me la dio; de él al que le debo esta ilusión tan de la vida mía. [...]"⁵⁵ [He inspired the idea of Guzmania; he bought it to me from I know not where. He gave it to me; though this dream may be my own, I owe it to him. ...]
As the novel unfolds, his vision for Guzmania comes into sharper relief and surpasses the most ambitious plans of previous utopians. In the opening chapter of the novel, Guzmán predicts that Guzmania will be "superior a cualquiera de las capitales europeas, y más rica aún que la Catay que nunca vio el de Génova [...]"⁵⁶ [greater than any European capital and richer than the Cathay that the Genoan Columbus never saw ...] but distinct from that of Cortés because Guzmania "no olerá jamás a sobaquina de marqués, que para tales hedores está Coyoacán en Mexico ...]"⁵⁷ [will never reek with the body odor of a marquis; for such a stench there is Coyoacán in Mexico ...]. At this stage of the novel Guzmán has clearer ideas about what his utopia will not resemble than about what it will.⁵⁸ However, by chapter 12, he has articulated a more coherent and detailed vision:

> Guzmania ha de refugiar en calles de oro, las cuales servirán de sol a todo el género humano. Por supuesto que agora es solamente un decir que me anda a vuelta y me estalla en la boca. Un proyecto que a muy pocos les he confiado. Será una República cuyo poderío naval y terrestre superará al de cualquiera de las naciones europeas o asiáticas, [...] ya a la que la fama les ha dado el nombre de intocables. Pero vayamos por partes, Nuño. [...]⁵⁹

> [Guzmania will be found with streets of gold, which will be as the sun to all humankind. Of course, it is now but a vision that runs through my head and bursts from my tongue, a project of which I have confided in few. It will be a republic whose naval and land power will exceed that of any European or Asian nation ... even those whose reputation holds them to be invincible. But patience, Nuño. ...]

Guzmán's confidence in establishing Guzmania, nevertheless, wanes after his tumultuous tenure as president of the *Primera audiencia*. He rationalizes postponing his dream as follows:

> Y si César no fue capaz de fundar una Cesarea para su nombre ni Aníbal una Anibalia yo sí lo haré un día en Guzmania, de cuyo prestigio se hablará en todas las cortes europeas y hasta el mismo Romano Pontífice, que es el padre de la cristiandad querrá venir a conocerla para darle. [...]⁶⁰

> [And though Caesar was unable to found a Caesaria to honor his name, nor Hannibal a Hannibalia, I will do so one day in Guzmania, a Guzmania whose name

will be praised in all the courts of Europe. Even the pontiff of Rome, the Father of Christianity, will want to come see it. . . .]

After the king orders Guzmán's arrest and forced deportation to Spain in 1538, Nuño renounces his scheme for founding Guzmania and, in the spirit of the conventional *relación de servicio* reaffirms his undivided allegiance to the crown: "[M]is obras tuvieron un solo fin: servir a la estirpe hispana y enaltecer la gloria ibérica, pues Guzmania era nada más que un decir, y en su lugar, quedaron las villas de Guadalajara, Compostela, Tepic, Durango y Culicán, a más de otras hechas y tragedias por nosotros, allá donde el sol se pone tinto en sangre. [. . .]"[61] [My works had only one end: to serve the race of Hispania and extol the glory of Iberia. Guzmania was but an expression; in its stead we built the cities of Guadalajara, Compostela, Tepic, Durango, and Culicán, cities built by us but immersed in tragedy, places where the sun is reddened with blood. . . .] As with other conquistadors, finding utopia remains illusory and invariably leads to cruelty toward the native populations.

In his efforts to restore the human dimension behind public and private moments, Guzmán employs a lyrical mode to communicate the intensity of his emotions, which contradicts his lack of depth as the embodiment of the black legend. The public Guzmán in the opening chapter underscores his obsession and that of other conquistadors with finding gold through the repetition of the phrase "Todo era de oro" [everything was of gold]. In later chapters he likewise employs anaphoras to connect public events with personal memories of his family life. In chapter 4 Guzmán re-creates the atmosphere at the court, where Charles I officially appointed him governor of Pánuco and the color red permeated the setting: "Roja era la alfombra y rojos los terciopelos del gran salón [. . .] ; Rojo era el uniforme de los ujieres y las bragas de los pajes que nos ofrecían entremeses de queso y bandejas de platas. Rojos los gorros de seda de los chiquitines. [. . .]"[62] [Red was the carpet and red the velvets of the great hall . . . Red were the uniforms of the ushers and red were the pantaloons of the page boys who offered us bits of cheese on silver trays. Red were the silk caps of the little ones. . . .] In this passage the color red connects the exterior splendor of the occasion, as evidenced by the attire of the attendees, to a rhythm reminiscent of *modernista* poetry such as Rubén Darío's "Marcha triunfal." Such repetition adds a lyrical dimension to the chronicles and underscores the presentness of the historical moment. In the same chapter Guzmán later reiterates the presence of red to shift the focus from himself to the state of mind of the attendees:

> Rojos los licenciados [...] y los móncigos arribistas. Rojos no de ropa, más bien por los efectos de los muchos alcoholes ingeridos durante la fiesta [...] ;[63] Roja era la fraseología de los sobones, quienes, digo, hacían votos porque mi viaje nunca llegara a playas venturosas. ¡Casi los oigo pensar . . . ! Y rojo de emoción me sentía yo entre los funcionarios y esos gamoños. [. . .][64]

> [Red the most meritorious among them . . . and red were the most ambitious. Not that their clothing was crimson, but they were red from the alcohol of which they had partaken during their celebration. . . . Red were the clever phrases of these tricksters, who I can tell you were praying that my voyage would never lead me to auspicious lands. I could almost hear them think . . . ! And red with ire I felt among those functionaries and those disagreeable others. . . .]

Nuño de Guzmán captures the depth of the attendees' jealousy and hatred through the color red. Through anaphoras, red serves as the focal point around which Guzmán artistically organizes and re-creates the atmosphere surrounding his appointment as governor of Pánuco.

Anaphoras with color also build bridges between present public moment and memories of a distant, private past. Guzmán's observation of the blueness of the skies along the route from Vera Cruz to Mexico City triggers a chain of nostalgic memories from his bygone youth. He makes multiple, random associations with this color:

> Azules volutas ascienden hacia el cielo, que también es azul como los ojos de la taberna María Engracia o las capitas de aquellas estudiantes de Santa Ursula, en Barrio Bello de mi solar Guadalajara [Spain]. Azules volutas de mi cigarro de la vena azul de mi memoria que se hincha con los pechos sueltos de esa María Engracia y los alardosos cadereos de las colegiales. [. . .]
>
> Azules los años que evoco aquí y ahora, haciendo una pausa en el trayecto que seguimos rumbo a la ciudad de México. [. . .][65]

> [Blue spirals ascend to the sky, which is also blue, as blue as the eyes of the taverness María Engracia or the capes of the schoolgirls at Santa Ursula in Barrio Bello of my ancestral Guadalajara in Spain. The blue spirals of my remembered blue-veined cigar, swelling at the unfettered breasts of María Engracia and the flagrant hips of the schoolgirls. . . .
>
> Blue the years that I evoke here and now, pausing on our journey toward Mexico City.]

Just as the color red functions to reconstruct the splendor of a public event, in the scene where he is appointed governor of Pánuco, so the color blue communicates his reaction toward events from his private life.

The fictional Guzmán further inflects his *relación* by parodying the conventions of other New World chronicles. A self-proclaimed voracious reader of the chronicles, he emulates their conventions, with a twist of humor. One such example is the glossing and exegesis of passages from Columbus's writings and Cortés's *Cartas de relación*. In chapter 7, hundreds of young indigenous men on an island allegedly "moon" Guzmán and his crew aboard the ship: "[E]n señal de protesta por nuestra visita, se bajaron los tapacojones y, sin un ahí te va o ahí te viene, nos mostraron el rubio trasero, como dicen que lo hacen, en las plazas de Londres, unos individuos llamados «hooligans».[66] [To protest our visit, they dropped their loincloths and in a flash presented us with a view of their fair buttocks, as it is said that some individuals called "hooligans" do in the plazas of London.] The association of British "hooligans" with the indigenous populations in the sixteenth century jolts the reader's traditional conception of the indigenous populations as passive victims of Spanish atrocities. Guzmán immediately attributes this obscene gesture to their interracial composition (black slaves and Indians) and uses this anecdote as a pretext to illuminate the following phrase from an apocryphal letter by Columbus: "El Nuevo Mundo, que no las Indias, ¡tierra de Dios, do se acuesta uno y amanecen dos!"[67] [The New World, if not the Indies, is certainly God's country, for one lays down and two arise!] This irreverently humorous explication of a line from Columbus's writings alludes to the Spaniards' predisposition to rape indigenous women and pokes fun at the more serious glossing by later chroniclers such as el Inca Garcilaso de la Vega in the *Comentarios reales*. Later in chapter 10, the strong gusts of wind at sea prompt Guzmán to remember a friend's theory as to why Columbus detested the wind. Although the wind often blew Columbus off course, it led, more significantly, to an embarrassing moment before the Catholic monarchs: "la otra, por haberle arrancado la peluca delante de los Reyes Católicos, haciéndole quedar en ridículo, con su calva monda y lironda, cual pelota de billar a la intemperie. [. . .]"[68] [the other, for having blown off his wig before the Catholic monarchs, for having exposed him to ridicule, his scalp a peeled fruit, a billiard ball unprotected from the inclemency. . . .] This off-the-cuff remark about Columbus reflects Guzmán's irreverent attitude and latent contempt for his predecessor, who inspired his own project. By the end of the novel, Guzmán openly ridicules Columbus for his so-called discovery of the Indies. Guzmán writes:

> Una sarta de tonterías nos trajo él del descubrimiento. Runfla de patrañas, ya lo dije. Algunas más descabelladas que su cabeza redonda, pero muy bien tejidas para creerse y admirarse, como aquella de las criaturas que se paren en sí mismas, ¡hase de ver!, y el cuento de los obluggos que son seres del tamaño de una

uva, sólo que tan fieros en el guerrear que acaban con un ejército en cuestión de minutos. ¡Paparruchas! Paparruchas y nada más que paparruchas!⁶⁹

[The discoverer brought us a string of stupidities, a canard, nothing but tall tales, some of them balder than his cue-ball head, but so skillfully woven as to inspire belief and even admiration, like those convincing but false displays of import by certain small creatures, or those stories of beings that though miniscule are sufficiently fierce to annihilate an army in a matter of minutes. Hogwash! Hogwash and nothing but hogwash!]

Irreverence toward this heroic founding figure of Latin American culture lays the groundwork for demythifying other historical and cultural icons of Mexican national culture and for continuing to alter the image of Guzmán as the black legend.

Thus, in the *Diario maldito* Cortés fares no better than Columbus. Mention of the indigenous populations in New Spain, referred to as "paganos," serves as a stimulus for citing a passage from the *Segunda carta,* in which Cortés describes the populations of Tenochtitlán:

Sin quererlo, me viene a la mente un párrafo de la tal carta, precisamente aquel que revienta de este modo (lo incluyo en mi relación como testigo garante de lo muy lamiscón y fantoche que es el capitán de Sus Altezas): "Sus Majestades, las tiaras de los reyes paganos de esta ciudad de Tenochtitlán, tan magníficamente sustentada sobre las aguas de una laguna y ya descritas por mí en otras ocasiones, están verdaderamente cuajadas de gemas, que no de bizutería, como lo es de Santa Ana de Medellín, la tierra que idolatro por haber nacido en ella y que agora desearía besarla más que describirla. . . . ¡Bah!⁷⁰

[Without my wishing it, a paragraph of that letter comes to mind, precisely that part that bursts forth so (I include it in my *relación* just to demonstrate what an asswipe and a nobody is the Your Majesties' captain). "Your Majesties: the tiaras worn by the pagan kings of Tenochtitlán, this city so magnificently bolstered over the waters of a lake and described by me on other occasions, are truly brimming with gems, and not of glass as in Santa Ana de Medellín, the place I adore because I was born there, the ground I long to kiss more than words can say . . . Bah!]

Guzmán ridicules the incongruity between the excess with which Cortés manipulates language to profess his loyalty to the crown and his disobedience of Diego Velázquez's instructions from Cuba. An otherwise meticulous writer who consistently inserts the word "*sic*" after inserting indigenous words into his accounts, he forgets to include the second quotation mark, suggesting that even the thought of Cortés and his sycophancy disrupts his ability to express himself in a grammatically correct Spanish. Later, during a stroll through the streets of Mexico City, where he passes the houses that remind him of the Sad Night (August 13, 1521), Guzmán puts forth a comical explanation as to how the Spaniards emerged triumphant on that occasion. According to Guzmán, it was not the Spaniards' technological superiority but their ability to engage in artistry and stage the "miraculous" apparition of the patron saint Santiago that saved them from defeat in 1521:

> Todos vieron, dicen, cómo aquel caballero iba abriendo tajos fendientes y muy grande riza entre los escuadrones enemigos, mientras Cortés gritaba: «¡Santiago, cierra Santiago!», porque aquel torbellino era nada menos que el Apóstol enviado por Dios a socorrer a las huestes cristianas—dizque—, aunque después se supo que todo había sido una ardid del propio Hernán, al ordenarle a Francisco de Morla que se disfrazara de Santiago Apóstol y que montara su caballo rucio para entrar en liza y haber buen triunfo tras buen engaño, y yo sí creo que hubo tal añagaza, que ni Santiago ni otro célico mester pisaron aquellos aguazales ensangrentados. [. . .][71]

> [Everyone saw, they say, how that knight cut gaping holes of destruction through the enemy's ranks, while Cortés cried "Santiago, contain them!" because that whirlwind was the Apostle sent by God to come to the aid of the Christian host, they say, although it was later revealed that all was a ruse by Hernán himself, who had ordered Francisco de Morla to disguise himself as the Apostle Santiago, mount his gray horse, and enter the fray, where he won the victory through deception. I do believe that the victory was won by deceit, that neither Santiago nor any other heavenly apparition was present on that blood-soaked field.]

Guzmán's version of the miraculous escape of the Spaniards on the Sad Night deflates their heroism by showing they resorted to theatrical representation to escape death. While under house arrest as a prisoner of the court, Guzmán runs into Cortés, whose physical grandeur no longer corresponds to that ascribed to him by chroniclers when he conquered the Aztecs in 1521:

> Mucho me extrañó el encontrar a Cortés así de graso. Cuando yo tenía entendido que era más bien esbelto de muy buen mirar; por lo menos esto es lo que oí entre las putas de Santo Domingo, quienes me lo pintaron como un mancebo hermoso y asaz travieso en materia de amores; no sólo en ellas en sus mentes livianas lo dibujaron así, también algunas españolas vecinas de aquel lugar que hubieron algún que ver con el dicho garañón. ¡Bello, majo, mozo, ardiente! ¡Mmmm! Qué contraste con el que yo vi en la corte, cargado de lutos y que no cabía en su tamaño y con una cogullada de muy mala faz; repugnante y horrible; cínico y malfajado. [. . .][72]

[It was a surprise to see Cortés so pudgy. I had thought him a leaner and more attractive man, at least that is what the whores of Santo Domingo had told me. They described him as a handsome youth, exceedingly transgressive in questions of love. But it was not only those simpleminded women who described him so; they were seconded by local Spanish ladies who had encountered the stallion. A striking youth of manly beauty, handsome, passionate! Mmmm! What a contrast with what I saw at court: a mournful and cynical man with an overgrown waist and unsightly jowls. Repugnant, horrible. . . .]

The demythification of Columbus and Cortés as heroes from the age of discovery and conquest accompanies the transformation of Guzmán from a symbol of the black legend to a conquistador driven by psychological insecurities.

The *Diario maldito* systematically demythifies episodes and figures from the colonial period that function as touchstones in the cultural narrative on identity. In the novel Guzmán directs barbed criticisms at his archrival, Juan de Zumárraga, archbishop of Mexico City. Guzmán questions Zumárraga's interest in serving as the protector of the Indians and alleges that the latter staged the apparition of the Virgin of Guadalupe in 1531 to consolidate his power and the authority of the church in New Spain. In an imagined conversation with Zumárraga, Guzmán asserts:

> No me extrañaría, por ejemplo, que la mandaras pintar en colores indianos y hasta hacerle capilla con titularidad, para ser venerada por todas las naciones de tu dominio espiritual. Pero lo más administrativo estaría que, una vez pintada, soltaras el borrego de que se le apareció a un indio, pidiéndole óbolos y gabelas. [. . .][73]
>
> [It would not surprise me, for example, if you had her painted in Indian colors and had a chapel built in her name, so that she would be venerated by all the nations within your spiritual domain. But the cleverest of all would be if once she was so painted, you spread the rumor that she had appeared to an Indian asking for obols and other donations.]

Guzmán's words are prophetic, because he reports toward the end of the novel the "apariciones" of the Virgin of Guadalupe throughout New Spain.[74] For the modern Mexican reader, asserting the fraudulent apparition of the Virgin of Guadalupe, a symbol of Mexican identity, represents an assault on the most sacred of cultural icons.

The *Diario maldito* calls into question the conventional approach to reading the chronicles about the conquest of Mexico in general and Guzmán's *relación* in particular as documents that offer direct access to irrefutable facts about the nature of the conquest and Nuño de Guzmán. The stature of this maligned figure is enhanced in that he is no longer viewed as a one-dimensional demonic conquistador bent exclusively on destroying the indigenous populations. Through the travel diary, the novel profiles a conquistador not only obsessed with acquiring gold and establishing a personal utopia but also having a flair for writing well-crafted prose. In short, the novel relocates the historical Guzmán from the myths of the past to the realm of history, in which figures display their imperfections and humanity.

Though the novel in no way condones Guzmán's actions in the New World, it seeks to bring out his human side. While the history of New Spain is revived in the *Diario maldito,* the novel obliquely criticizes the tendency in Mexican colonial historiography of the nineteenth and twentieth centuries to view the conquistadors as one-dimensional symbols of evil. And this approach to Mexico's colonial history is consistent with a larger trend in cultural studies to rewrite the myths of national identity. As the anthropologist Alfredo Corona Ibarra argues in the preface to the historical Guzmán's *Memoria,* reissued by the Secretaria de Educación y Cultura Jalisco in 1990, rethinking the colonial history of Mexico cannot occur until historians see the conquistadors as "Ni ángeles, ni demonios; simplemente, hombres"[75] [neither as angels or devils, but simply as men]. In the realm of contemporary Mexican fictional narrative, the *Diario maldito* represents a move in that direction. And such a move resonates with recent historical reinterpretations of the career of Nuño de Guzmán, particularly his role in the conquest of Michoacán and the execution of the Cazonci.

In his monograph on the history of early colonial Michoacán (1521–65), James Krippner-Martínez argues that Guzmán's actions were extremely functional for the founding of Spanish colonialism in Michoacán and cannot be understood simply as the acts of a deviant individual. Guzmán did not act alone in executing the Cazonci, but rather fulfilled the aspirations of most of the Spanish settlers in the region. These settlers had experienced substantial resistance in their attempts to occupy Michoacán, proving that they and Cortés misunderstood the nature of their alliance with the Cazonci. The ultimate moral responsibility for the Cazonci's death, argues Krippner-Martínez, lay with those who killed him: namely, Spanish settlers, Guzmán, the army under his command, the colonial and royal authorities who placed all of the above in the New World, and, of course, the king.[76] While many of Nuño de Guzmán's actions in New Spain were cruel and brutal, they were not in the end exceptionally and uniquely so.

In *Gonzalo Guerrero* and the *Diario maldito* marginalized figures from the conquest of Mexico function to displace the tale of Cortés and the defeat of the Aztecs as the only tale from the early colonial period. *Gonzalo*

Guerrero shifts attention from events in Mexico City to events in the Yucatán Peninsula prior to Cortés's arrival in 1519, and proposes Gonzalo Guerrero instead of La Malinche as the symbol of Mexican *mestizaje*. Although the fictional Guerrero achieves standing in the Yucatán and outwardly acculturates into Mayan society, he never relinquishes his deep-seated belief in the innate superiority of Spanish culture and civilization. The Spaniards are "first among equals" in comparison to their indigenous counterparts. By shifting the origin of Mexican national and cultural identity from Cortés/La Malinche to Gonzalo Guerrero/Ix Chel Can, the novel fails to address the underlying asymmetry in power between the Spaniards and the indigenes. Consequently, the novel merely puts forth a more sanitized view of the encounter between Spaniards and the indigenes in the New World. It leaves intact the tale of *mestizaje* as the mythical origin of the Mexican nation. The *Diario maldito,* on the other hand, stylizes conventions from sixteenth-century Spanish chronicles and exaggerates them with the intent of presenting Nuño de Guzmán solely as a cruel and bloodthirsty conquistador. The novel rehumanizes him as a conquistador with grandiose dreams. Though the novel in no way condones Guzmán's actions in the New World, it seeks to bring out his human side. While the history of New Spain is revived in the *Diario maldito,* the novel obliquely criticizes the tendency in Mexican colonial historiography of the nineteenth and twentieth centuries to view the conquistadors as one-dimensional symbols of evil.

As both the Gonzalo Guerrero and Nuño de Guzmán tales originate primarily in the Yucatán Peninsula and the western and northwestern provinces of Mexico, retelling episodes from the early historiography of modern Mexico may be a significant indicator of the waning power of institutions in Mexico City to impose a definition of national culture that does not take into account the diversity of historical experiences of the outlying provinces. Carrie Chorba argues that the employment of marginal voices to relate a mainstream version of history is much in keeping with historical and society trends in Mexico in the 1980s and 1990s. The 1980s, Chorba notes, was a decade of historical revisionism, and as a result of events such as the 1968 massacre at Tlatelolco and the 1985 Mexico City earthquake, Mexico's population lost much faith in "great men" as society's leaders. With this breakdown of consensus and trust arises interest in microhistories, the telling of events from a wide variety of perspectives, not always the "official" ones.[77]

Gonzalo Guerrero and the *Diario maldito* revisit cultural myths of *mestizaje* and the black legend to reaffirm Spanish cultural values. In *Gonzalo Guerrero* the reconstituted tale of origins addresses the ambivalence that Mexicans feel toward the conquest and proposes a more auspicious beginning for the nation. However, the Guerrero version of *mestizaje* has its underside: once again, the indigenous populations are mere pretexts to solidify and confirm the continued hegemony of the Spanish elements in the partnership. The *Diario maldito,* likewise, endeavors to debunk the myth of the black legend and to lay bare the ideological context in which historians construct versions of history. By recasting Guzmán's tale in the mold of a travel diary, the novel delves into the multifaceted nature of his psyche and underscores the quotidian nature of the conquest, and thus rehumanizes this maligned and nearly forgotten historical figure.

In the 1950s prominent writers such as Octavio Paz in *El laberinto de la soledad* (1950) investigated the essence of the Mexican national character. In the 1980s and 1990s Eugenio Aguirre and Herminio Martínez likewise returned to these issues in novelistic form, focusing this time on the process of writing history and constructing identities. That these topics should reemerge in the 1980s and early 1990s suggests that Mexico has been seeking to reinvent its identity and to find something that can bind the nation together. In the final chapter, I will return to a major historical figure—Columbus—and examine the use of him in Augusto Roa Bastos's *Vigilia del Almirante* and Herminio Martínez's *Las puertas del mundo.*

4
Restaging Columbus

[E]n el esquema convencional de la historia de la literatura hispanoamericana, los textos de Colón constituyen el inicio de la tradición narrativa, el principio sin principio, la escritura de la fundación. Colón fue el primero en poner nombre a las cosas [. . .] [pero] no fue el único, sino sólo el primero; su figura representa a los cronistas del descubrimiento y conquista. [. . .]
—Roberto González-Echevarría, "Colón, Carpentier y los orígenes de la ficción latinoamericana"

[In the conventionally stated history of Latin American literature, Columbus's texts constitute the inauguration of the narrative tradition, the point of departure, the foundational texts. Columbus was not the only one who gave names to new things . . . but he was the first. Thus the figure of Columbus represents the chroniclers of discovery and conquest.]

¿En qué forma Cristóbal Colón anticipaba hacia 1492 al desprevenido jinete manchego esforzado en conseguir de la gente la aceptación vital de su máxima ilusión? Los cortesanos sostenían la cuadratura terrestre con el mismo empecinamiento con que Sancho hablaba de las aspas del molino cuando los seres dotados de una mágica aureola se esforzaban en navegar a las Indias, descubrir parajes desconocidos y combatir gigantes robustos en las llanuras de la Mancha. . . .
—Alvaro Miranda, "Apuntes a propósito de *Don Quixote*"

[How did Columbus anticipate in 1492 the improvident Quixote endeavoring to gain the forbearance that was vital to his ultimate fantasy? While those at court maintained their position on terrestrial quadrature with the insistence of Sancho Panza on the nature of the windmill, other beings with a kind of magical aura about them stubbornly sailed to the Indies, discovered unknown lands, and fought burly giants on the plains of La Mancha. . . .]

IN CHAPTERS 2 AND 3 I DISCUSSED HOW INVENTED AND HISTORICAL MARginal figures have been employed in River Plate and Mexican novels to contest the official historiography about the New World and to rewrite diffuse cultural myths. I will now like to return to a major historical figure—

Columbus—and his re-presentation in Augusto Roa Bastos's *Vigilia del Almirante* (Paraguay, 1992) and Herminio Martínez's *Las puertas del mundo: Una autobiografía hipócrita del Almirante* (Mexico, 1992). Augusto Roa Bastos (b. Asunción, 1917), Paraguay's most widely acclaimed fiction writer, has published six novels—*Hijo de hombre* (1960), *Yo el supremo* (1974), *Vigilia del Almirante* (1992), *El fiscal* (1993), *Contravida* (1994), and *Madama Sui* (1995). He has written seven collections of short stories—*El trueno entre las hojas* (1953), *El baldío* (1966), *Madera quemada* (1967), *Los pies sobre el agua* (1967), *Cuerpo presente, y otros textos* (1972), *Antología personal* (1980), and *Contar un cuento, y otros relatos* (1984). And he has written two collections of poetry—*El ruiseñor de la aurora y otros poemas* (1942) and *El naranjal ardiente, nocturno paraguayo: 1947–1949* (1960).[1] As I discussed in the previous chapter, Herminio Martínez is a novelist, short-story writer, and poet from Guanajuato.

In 1992 the legacy of Columbus and his first voyage to the New World remained a matter of heated contention. According to one interpretation, the 1492 discovery of the Americas was a benign event that enlarged the material and spiritual resources of humankind. The Spaniards' arrival and occupation of the New World was the greatest accomplishment of the Christian West. The opposing interpretation, that Columbus opened the door to tragedy, is more pessimistic. Disastrous yet foreseeable consequences unfolded that far surpassed any other tragedy in history up until then and perhaps ever since. More people died in plagues (according to some estimates, close to seven million people), wars, and religious persecution because of the confrontation between the European and native civilizations than in World Wars I and II, the Vietnam War, the Crusades, the U.S. Civil War, the French Revolution, and all other battles that have ever occurred. From this vantage point, the discovery and conquest constituted a monumental crime in world history.[2]

Proponents of the first view refer to Columbus's reaching the Americas as a "discovery"; in the second view, it was only an "encounter," since you can only discover that which you don't know but already exists. The "discovery" group argues that Columbus's landfall on October 12, 1492, was a glorious moment in history that should be celebrated with an annual holiday and centennials; the "encounter" group believes that it should be remembered only by a moment of mournful silence. From these viewpoints, then, two opposing portraits of Columbus emerge: hero or villain, saint or scoundrel.[3]

Columbus and his four voyages to the New World (1492–1503) have captured the interest and fascination of historians and literary writers alike. The North American historian Samuel Eliot Morison argues in *Admiral of the Ocean Sea* (1942), the most authoritative contemporary biography on Columbus, that Columbus was a genius and mariner of deep religious convictions who changed the course of history. Morison's biography focuses on Columbus the man and casts him in a favorable light. The journalist Kirkpatrick Sale in *The Conquest of Paradise* (1990) holds Columbus responsible for opening the door to a natural and human holocaust of unimaginable proportions. According to Sale, the pattern Columbus and the first voyage set in 1492 has governed Europe's relationship to the New World to this day. Such twentieth-century biographies have reinforced Columbus's image as either a brilliant mariner or as a man who marked the beginnings of European colonialism in Latin America.[4] Biographical and historical discourses about Columbus have shaped social reality, and undoubtedly similar preoccupations about the nature of Columbus have been staged in the Spanish American historical novel of the 1970s and 1980s. For instance, Alejo Carpentier's *El arpa y la sombra* (Cuba, 1979) and Abel Posse's *Los perros del paraíso* (Argentina, 1983) view Columbus as a symbol of holocaust and gloom. In their eyes, he is a destroyer, a treacherous liar, and an ignorant mariner. Because Latin America has suffered as a result of the so-called discovery of 1492 and its subsequent conquest, Columbus is regarded as the originator of all pains.[5]

In the year of the Columbian quincentennial, then, it is no surprise that other Spanish American novelists should once again have retold the voyages of Columbus and his enduring legacy for the New World. According to Sandra Ferdman, whenever Spanish American writers have explored the issue of their cultural and literary identity, they have returned to the writings of Columbus and rewritten his life story to find their foundations and figures.[6] Such is the case with Roa Bastos's *Vigilia del Almirante* and Herminio Martinez's *Las puertas del mundo*. Both novels return to Columbus's life and writings to reveal how the conventional images of Columbus have been constructed by historical, biographical, and other discourses. *Vigilia* freely intermingles documented and apocryphal episodes about Columbus's life with historiographical debates about the voyages. *Las puertas*, on the other hand, recasts Columbian writings as a delirious and dizzying journal account of the four voyages and their aftermath for his life.

Vigilia and *Las puertas* exemplify two distinct interventions in the debates surrounding the commemoration of the five-hundredth anniversary of Columbus's arrival in the New World. *Vigilia* rehumanizes the historical Columbus and explodes the myths that have portrayed him as saint or sinner. It invites the reader to relive episodes from Columbus's life in order to understand his legacy for the present and proposes another beginning for Latin American culture beyond the binary opposition of good and evil. By staging struggles among competing discourses in novelistic discursive space, *Vigilia* obliges the reader to contemplate how Columbus and his enterprise have come to be understood and to acknowledge that a historical figure's behavior performs and constructs an identity. Whereas *Vigilia* draws on the historiography about Columbus in order to engage the polemics in a serious fashion, *Las puertas* adds layers of discourse to present an iconoclastic yet negative assessment of Columbus and his voyages. By presenting a parody of Columbus's writings that contrasts his image in the official historiography to that in his private diary, *Las puertas* encourages the reader to adopt a negative stance toward Columbus and the quincentennial. As Columbian writings have constituted the basis from which polemicists have gathered their "facts" about Columbus and his voyages to the Indies, *Las puertas* parodies the conventions of the *relaciones* and mocks the strategies by which the historical Columbus endowed his writings with authority.[7]

Vigilia del Almirante consists of an introductory preface, four epigraphs (the first from Lope de Vega's drama *El mundo nuevo* [1614], the second from Cervantes's *Los trabajos de Persiles y Sigismunda* [1617], the third from a Guaraní shaman, and the fourth from the contemporary French poet Edmond Jabes's *El libro de las preguntas* [1972]), followed by fifty-three roman-numeraled and titled sections ("Partes") and an acknowledgments section ("Reconocimientos"). The fifty-three sections, which constitute the majority of the novel, alternate between the fictional Columbus's 1506 deathbed remembrances of his life and the philosophical meanderings of a narrator, who in 1992 revisits controversies surrounding the life of Columbus, the genesis of the first voyage of discovery, and the impact of the discovery on the course of Spanish American history. Within this framework, the novel interweaves fragments from Columbus's *Diario de a bordo,* the *Capitulaciones de Santa Fe* (the document that Columbus and the monarchs signed in April 1492 and that laid out the rights and responsibilities of all parties involved in the enterprise of the Indies), historiographical writings about the nature of the discovery, and purely invented scenes based on gossip and legends about Columbus's actions in the Caribbean. And thus, the novel creates the space in which readers are asked to review the historical, biographical, autobiographical, and legendary discourses and to question the conventional portraits of Columbus and interpretations about the significance of his first voyage. Through this confluence of discourses, readers acknowledge the oversimplification involved in reducing Columbus to an ideological symbol. In the final scenes of the novel, the fictional Columbus apologizes for the destruction of the Indies that his voyages inaugurated. *Vigilia* rewrites the ending of Columbus's life, and by extension, the beginnings of Latin American culture. It incorporates the myth of the

Piloto Desconocido (Anomymous Pilot) and extends the analogy between the historical Columbus and Don Quixote—as proposed by the German historian Jacob Wasserman in *Christopher Columbus: Don Quixote of the Oceans* (1929) and by later Columbus biographers—to challenge Carpentier's characterization of Columbus in *El arpa y la sombra* as a liar and scoundrel and to reveal the complexities of assessing the significance of Columbus's life and voyages. *Vigilia* serves as a unique discursive space to stage this issue.

The body of commentary on *Vigilia* focuses on the postmodern concept of history as a discursive construction, as a contentious product of competing discourses. In his 1994 dissertation, "La nueva novela histórica latinoamericana: El descubrimiento revisitado en Roa Bastos, Carpentier y Posse," José Urbina analyzes *Vigilia* in relation to Carpentier's *El arpa y la sombra* and Posse's *Los perros del paraíso*. Urbina examines these novels' points of convergence and divergence in the representation of Columbus and situates his findings within trends in postmodernism. Rosalía Cornejo-Parriego argues in her article that the intertextual dialogue that *Vigilia* establishes between historical and fictional discourses destroys the initial goal of affirming the power of historiography and displaces the written authority of historical texts,[8] while Robin Lefere analyzes the biographical-historical, symbolic, and autobiographical dimensions of the novel as part of an overarching strategy to demythify the dominant narrative about the "Discovery."[9] Two other article-length studies analyze *Vigilia* within the trajectory of Roa Bastos's previous novelistic production. José Ortega argues that the novel interrogates historical discourses about the discovery and Columbus the man. Moreover, he posits that *Vigilia* is dialectically related to poetic and historical truths about Spanish American reality, which has been subjected to mythification and manipulations by institutional political powers.[10] Similarly, Milagros Ezquerro views *Vigilia* as a significant milestone in Roa Bastos's career and inventories the novel's dominant narrative strategies for reinventing Columbus, which include the incorporation of literary and historical anachronisms, the quixotification of Columbus's final days in 1506, and the preponderance of the Piloto Desconocido legend.[11] As Ezquerro herself concedes, her comments about the novel are "schematic" and "intuitive" and require further analysis.[12] In a book-review article, Seymour Menton gives *Vigilia* as an example of a Latin American New Historical novel that mechanically incorporates the ingredients of a postmodern recipe and displays less originality in its conceptualization than *El arpa* and *Los perros,* to which it is indebted.[13]

Indeed, *Vigilia* is indebted to other historical, biographical, and literary discourses. However, by attending to the specific strategies by which Roa

Bastos confronts these discourses to reveal their competition, I will contend that *Vigilia* presents a direct response to Carpentier's portrayal of Columbus as an inveterate liar and irresolvable enigma. The novel rewrites Columbus's deathbed memories in part 2 ("La mano") from *El arpa* and interweaves metahistorical commentary about the writing of history in order to move beyond the polemics of characterizing Columbus as saint or sinner. It blurs the boundaries between historical and literary representations of the past and encourages the reader to adopt a critical and skeptical attitude toward truths manufactured by both discourses. I will discuss the similarities and differences in narrative structure between *El arpa* and *Vigilia* and show how Cervantes's *Don Quixote* and the legend of the Piloto Desconocido are incorporated to dislocate Columbus from the realm of myth and relocate him in the realm of historical and literary discourse.

A contemporary literary antecedent of *Vigilia, El arpa* consists of three parts. In part 1 Giovanni Mastei, the future Pope Pius IX, travels to the New World in 1823, where he first considers the idea to canonize Columbus. The proposal for canonization is shown to be motivated exclusively by a political strategy to impose a new colonialism on the independent Latin American nations. In part 2, the fictional Columbus rewrites his accounts of the first voyage of discovery as recorded in the *Diario de a bordo* and confesses to exaggerations, errors in judgment, deception, and outright lies regarding the New World. In his final discourse in the novel, Columbus laments that in four centuries since the discovery, historiography has been unable to portray him adequately, because, as he states, "salido del misterio, volví al misterio [. . .]"[14] [I came from mystery, I returned to mystery . . .].[15] Part 3 takes place in the last decade of the nineteenth century and relates a tribunal's proceedings concerning Columbus's beatification. *El arpa* attempts to resolve the mystery of Columbus by portraying him in a uniformly negative fashion.

With regard to its narrative structure, *Vigilia* shares many key features with *El arpa*. For example, the narrative in *Vigilia* is constructed around two enunciative moments: one in the early sixteenth century and another in the late twentieth century. In the sixteenth century, a moribund Columbus reviews his personal and professional life and acknowledges his shortcomings in those areas. In this respect, the chapters from *Vigilia* resemble part 2 of *El arpa,* for the fictional Columbus in both novels reviews incidents from his life prior to dying and acknowledges his shortcomings. Furthermore, an unidentified twentieth-century narrator reconsiders the controversies surrounding Columbus in a fashion similar to the way that nineteenth-century theologians in *El arpa* reviewed the historiography in deciding whether to canonize Columbus. The structural resemblances between *Vigilia* and *El arpa* end here, however. In *Vigilia* the moribund Columbus not only laments the destruction of the indigenous populations that his voyages inaugurated but also renounces his role in the enterprise. His final moments of life are retold through the last chapters of *Don Quixote,* whereas the fictional Columbus in *El arpa* is not elevated by such lofty comparisons.

As I noted earlier, Rosalía Cornejo-Parriego examines the intertextual dialogue that *Vigilia* establishes between historical and fictional discourses. She looks particularly at the intertexual connections among literary texts (principally *Vigilia* and *Don Quixote*) and literary and historical texts (*Vigilia* and Juan Fancisco Manzano Manzano's *Colón y su secreto: El predescubrimiento* [1982]). The latter is the latest monograph that advances the hypothesis that the Piloto Desconocido was a precursor of the discovery and gave Columbus maps and information that enabled the Admiral to "discover" the New World. She argues that *Vigilia* parodies the literary character Don Quixote as well as the narrative armature of Don Quixote in order to reflect upon the purposes of historiography and literature and the fragility of the borders between reality and fantasy.[16] I agree with Cornejo-Parriego's contentions and would add that such a strategy serves to redefine the conventional characterization of Columbus as either saint or villain.

Part 25, "El Caballero de la Triste Figura," from *Vigilia* inverts historical chronology and portrays Columbus as the direct antecedent of Don Quixote. The fictional historian states:

> Cien años después vendría el *Quijote.* Pero el futuro Almirante ya lo había presentido con esa especie de premonición absorta que los héroes soñados inspiran a sus lectores ingenuos y alucinados y los impulsan a imitarlos. Héroes que únicamente las grandes novelas acogen y hacen revivir en sus páginas. [. . .][17]

> [*Quixote* would arrive one hundred years later, but the Admiral had already experienced that kind of stunning premonition that is inspired by imagined heroes, heroes found only in the pages of great novels and brought back to life there. Those are the heroes that actually transport their most receptive readers and inspire them to imitation. . . .]

The fictional historian in this *historia fingida* (novel) merely echoes the sentiments of actual biographers of *historias documentadas* (histories), who have depicted Columbus as a quixotic figure. For example, the Colombian historian Germán Arciniegas, alluding to Spanish American biographies about Columbus that establish parallels between Columbus and Don Quixote, regards the historical Columbus as Don Quixote's antecedent in that the former's readings of fabulous medieval texts inspired and sustained his vision of the Indies, just as the books of chivalry molded Don Quioxte's understanding of his world. This comparison suggests that truth is stronger than fiction and that the historical Columbus became a motivating impulse for later creative writing. Arciniegas asserts that the historical Columbus

> Tenía la cabeza llena de fábulas y fue de oscuro nacimiento. Acabó codeándose con reyes y llamándose Almirante del Mar Océano y Visorrey y gobernador general de las Indias. Se llamaba Cristóbal Colón. De la misma manera como ocurrió al de la Mancha [...] Colón decidió llamarse *don Cristóbal*. Tan exacto es lo del quijotismo de Colón que casi no hay biografía suya que no lo registre. Para muestra, estas líneas en la [biografía sobre Colón] de Madariaga: «El espíritu quijótico de Colón inspira a todas estas páginas históricas. El descubridor andante se describe a sí mismo desde el principio como *don* Cristóbal Colón, antes de que nadie le haya autorizado a llamarse así». [...][18]

> [was of uncertain birth and had a head filled with fables. He ended up mingling with kings and calling himself admiral of the ocean sea, viceroy, and governor general of the Indies. His name was Cristóbal Colón, but like the man of the Mancha ... he decided that he should be called *don Cristóbal*. Columbus's quixotism is so clear-cut that nearly every biography mentions it. As an example, I give you these lines from a biography of Columbus by Madariaga: "Columbus's quixotic spirit imbues every page of this history. Like the knight-errant, the itinerant discoverer describes himself from the beginning as *don* Cristóbal Colón, before anyone has authorized him to do so...."]

The analogy highlights how historical discourse affects the reader's view of literary discourse. Roa Bastos in *Vigilia* takes this commonplace in Spanish American biographies about Columbus and fuses episodes from the life of Columbus with key chapters from *Don Quixote* in order to redefine the conventional characterization of Columbus as either saint or villain.

Roa Bastos's strategy for displaying discursive struggles in novelistic discourse is not new for him in *Vigilia*. In her analysis of Roa Bastos's *Yo el supremo,* Helene Carol Weldt-Basson applies Gerard Genette's concept of hypertexuality—any relationship between a text (hypertext) and a prior text (hypotext) upon which it is based in a manner other than commentary— to discuss the relationship between chapters from *Yo el supremo* and those from *Don Quixote*.[19] Specifically, she examines how the association between El Supremo and Don Quixote ultimately contributes to the construction of the dictator's portrait. Similarly, the narrative strategy of juxtaposing multiple discourses about Columbus extends to encompass the juxtaposition of Columbus and Don Quixote in *Vigilia* in order to prompt the reader to interrogate received images about the past, to question attempts to glorify Columbus as a saint and man of science or to condemn him as a sinner.

According to the conventional account derived from Ferdinand Columbus's *Vida del Almirante* (1571) and Las Casas's *Historia de las Indias* (1554), Columbus spent the last three years of his life imploring the crown to restore his privileges. In the final moments of his life on May 20, 1506, depicted by Ferdinand Columbus and Las Casas in their respective accounts, the historical Columbus summoned his son Ferdinand Columbus, his brother-in-law Francisco, and one of his loyal servants to his bedside. Fifty years later, Las Casas described Columbus's final moments in the *Historia de las Indias* as follows:

> Y así pasó desta vida en estado de harta angustia y amargura y pobreza e sin tener, como él dijo, una teja debajo de que meterse para no se mojar o reposar en el mundo. El que había descubierto por su industria otro nuevo y mejor que antes sabíamos, felicísimo mundo. Murió desposeído y despojado.[20]
>
> [And so he passed from this life in a state of heightened anguish, bitterness, and poverty, and without, as he said, as much as a roof tile under which to repose or merely to shelter himself from the rain. He had discovered a new and happier world, an improvement upon that we had theretofore known, and had done so thanks to his own industry, but he died an indigent, stripped of his wealth.]

Columbus's agony and suffering that surrounds this final episode of his life in Las Casas's account is replaced in Roa Bastos's novel with the serenity and peacefulness of the Don Quixote from Cervantes's novel. In chapter 52 and 53 in *Vigilia,* the depicted scene resembles the final chapters of the *Quixote* in that the priest, who administers the last rites, declares el "loco caballero navegante" [the mad knight-errant of the sea] sane; the fictional Columbus declares himself sane (Yo fui loco y muero cuerdo [. . .] [I was mad, but I die sound of mind . . .]); and Columbus dies in the presence of many, including the *ama* (housekeeper) and the *sobrina* (niece) from the *Quixote*.[21] The restoration of Columbus's and Don Quixote's sanity at the end of their lives reassures the reader of the possibility of returning to a point of equilibrium and stability, of reversing the process of deviating from conventional norms and reestablishing a sense of normalcy.

Establishing parallels between the historical Columbus and Don Quixote sets up expectations for the reader that the narrative will bring closure about the significance of the historical Columbus's life. However, these expectations are dashed. These chapters diverge from those in the *Quixote,* as the fictional Columbus predicts historians' fascination with his life for the next five hundred years:

> —Esta buena gente [los historiadores] se ha quemado los ojos, despepitado el ánima, dejado la vida en la penosa y larga tarea de cinco cientos años para averiguar quién era yo. [. . .] Cada individuo es infinito y misterioso como el universo mismo, y ante cada uno la imaginación tiembla sin saber por dónde comenzar para entenderlo y menos aún en qué punto terminar. Por lo cual ninguna historia tiene principio ni fin y todas tienen tantos significados como lectores aya. [. . .][22]

> [—For five hundred long years, these good people, the historians, have worked late into the night and dedicated much effort to the soul-crushing labor of trying to define me. . . . But every individual is as infinite and mysterious as the universe itself. Where does one begin in the effort to understand a man? The imagination trembles at the very thought, and trembles even more when deliberating where to stop. Indeed, while no history has either beginning or end, it has as many meanings as readers. . . .]

Whereas the historical Columbus, as constructed by Renaissance chroniclers, attempted to impose univocal meaning on the significance of his life by seeing it as the tale of an instrument of God fulfilling a prophecy from ancient texts, the fictional Columbus in this passage imputes numerous meanings to his life and implicitly replies to the interpretation of his life as proposed in Carpentier's *El arpa.* Once again the novel becomes the space in which literary and historical discourses compete to construct the social reality about Columbus. By establishing analogies between the biographies of Columbus and Don Quixote as well as between significant events in the official historiography and chapters from *Don Quixote,* Roa Bastos's *Vigilia* seeks to reverse the spectral negative presence of Columbus as the inaugurator of the extermination of the indigenous populations and to propose a more sober acceptance of the past.

In addition to dealing with struggles over history, biography, and literature, the novel also encompasses legends, thereby expanding the discursive struggle to include the less formal kind of popular knowledge about Columbus. In particular, the novel revisits the controversy surrounding the role of the Piloto Desconocido to show the complexities surrounding the genesis of Columbus's first voyage. The legend of the Piloto Desconocido, which has its origins in the early sixteenth century, has undergone numerous reelaborations from then to the present.[23] As early as 1494, both popular and learned circles held that Columbus first obtained knowledge of the newfound land by way of a shipwreck survivor's testimony. The basic legend posited the existence of a Spanish sea merchant whose sailing vessel, caught in a heavy storm, was pushed from either the Canary Islands or the Madeira Islands far westward into the unknown reaches of the Ocean Sea. When the pilot and his crew landed on the island that Columbus later named Hispaniola, the pilot recorded what he saw and subsequently found his way back, though without full knowledge of his bearings and with much hardship. The survivors, who eventually returned with him to Spain, were cared for by Columbus. In this way, Columbus inherited knowledge of the existence of the lands he later "found" because of the testimony of the pilot, who was the last survivor to die.[24]

According to Edmundo O'Gorman in *La invención de América* (1958), the legend of the shipwrecked pilot emerged in the context of the ideological controversies among the European intelligentsia surrounding the newfound lands and reveals itself as a point of departure for a discourse that questioned the established European conception of the cosmic order.[25] According to Hortensia Calvo-Stevenson, this myth of origin authorizes the finder of the text by making him the possessor and, subsequently, the actualizer, the performer of secret knowledge.[26] Similarly, in 1992, *Vigilia* resuscitates the Piloto Desconocido myth, not only to bring into dialogue numerous discourses about the nature of Columbus but also to question the established conception of Columbus as an erudite genius who single-handedly formulated his plan to discover the Indies.

Parts 8 and 9 from *Vigilia,* chapters corresponding to a historian's reflections in 1992, directly address the controversy surrounding the Piloto Desconocido and his significance in the genesis of Columbus's plan to reach to the Indies. As is the case with many issues from the Columbus controversy, the acceptance or rejection of the legend of the pilot is inextricably linked to the ideological framework in which historians have approached the Admiral. According to the fictional historian in the novel, most skeptics of the legend are "los defensores más acérrimos del Almirante como el sólo y único descubridor del Orbe Nuevo. [. . .]"[27] [the staunchest defenders of the Admiral as the lone and unique discoverer of the Nova Orbis . . .]. By contrast, less ideologically committed ones remain unconvinced about the ultimate significance of the Piloto in Columbus's developing his voyage to the Indies, because they require written documentation, which often is nonexistent: "¿[P]uede esperarse que existen tales documentos sobre un fantasma o sobre un mito que ya se ha instalado en la tradición oral, en la memoria colectiva y hasta en los anales de la ciencia histórica?"[28] [Would one expect to find such documents concerning a ghost or a myth that has become part of the oral tradition or the collective memory, or even been incorporated into the history of science?] According to the fictional historian, the absence of written documentation in oral histories does not automatically discredit the veracity of an account, though their truth claims should be cross-checked with more conventional documented histories, because oral and written histories are inherently complementary:

> ¿Cómo optar entre hechos imaginados y hechos documentados? ¿No se complementan acaso en sus oposiciones y contradicciones, en sus respectivas y opuestas naturalezas? ¿Se excluyen y anulan el rigor científico y la imaginación simbólica y alegórica? No, sino que son dos caminos diferentes, dos maneras distintas de concebir el mundo y de expresarlo. Ambas polinizan y fecundan a su modo [. . .] la mente y la sensibilidad del lector, verdadero autor de una obra que él la reescribe leyendo, en el supuesto de que lectura y escritura, ciencia e intuición, realidad e imaginación se valen inversamente de los mismos signos. [. . .][29]

> [How does one choose between imaginary and attested particulars? Don't they complement each other in their oppositions and contradictions, in their opposed natures? Do scientific rigor and symbolic-allegorical imagination exclude or negate each other? No, they are simply divergent paths, different ways to conceptualize the world and to express it. Each enriches and stimulates . . . the mind and the senses in its own way, and the reader is the real author of the work, rewriting it as he reads, for reading and writing, science and intuition, reality and imagination are inverse applications of the same symbolic system. . . .]

Readers of *Vigilia* are empowered to select the "truth of the facts" from oral and written accounts—such as the legends from Caribbean natives or from Las Casas's *Historia de las Indias*—to arrive at their own understanding about the significance and relevance of the Piloto Desconocido for the first voyage to the Indies.

As he did between Don Quixote and Columbus, the fictional historian within the novel subsequently establishes analogies between the notable achievements of the Piloto and the historical Columbus. If the Piloto is regarded as the precursor of the discovery because he landed in the New World before Columbus, then Columbus is the precursor of the so-called *encubrimiento* [concealment] because he mistakenly took the islands of the Caribbean for the Indies in Asia[30] and projected his knowledge, based on his readings of ancient and medieval sources, onto the New World:

> El nuevo mundo continente ya estaba descubierto en los libros. El orbe ignoto y enorme salió de la escritura falsa y falsificadora. Pero los hombres y los hechos que salieron de ella no hicieron más que falsear y convertir el descubrimiento en encubrimiento. [. . .] El piloto desconocido es otra invención del resucitado Almirante. [. . .][31]

[A new continent had already been encountered in books, but the vast and undiscovered new world differed from its depictions in these false and dissembling documents. And the men who returned from the continent falsified what they had seen; their stories concealed more than they revealed. . . . The anonymous pilot is one more invention of the resurrected Admiral. . . .]

The dissatisfied fictional historian then proceeds to reread the accounts of such chroniclers as Gonzalo Fernández de Oviedo, López de Gómara, Peter Martyr, Las Casas, and the Inca Garcilaso de la Vega[32] and underscores the subjection of all those accounts to ideological manipulation. *Vigilia* once again brings into relief that the novel provides the discursive space in which competing discourses enter into dialogue and question the notion of a monological truth about Columbus.

This meditation about the Piloto myth, in turn, leads to other comments about the similarities and differences between a *historia documentada* (history) and a *historia fingida* (novel), that is, between history and literature:

> Las dos son géneros de ficción mixta; sólo difieren en los principios y en los métodos. Las primeras buscan instaurar el orden, anular la anarquía, abolir el azar en el pasado, armar rompecabezas perfectos, sin hiatos, sin fisuras, lograr conjuntos tranquilizadores sobre la base de la probanza documental. [. . .] Las historias fingidas, en cambio, abren la imaginación al espectro incalculable del azar tanto en el pasado como en el futuro: abren la realidad al tejido de oscuras leyes. En esa tela de araña invisible tejen su propia realidad, su propia necesidad, su espacio, su tiempo, en una tercera y aun en una cuarta dimensión, que no es la del sueño solamente. Sus inventores no son ni buenos ni malos ni astutos ni cínicos ni embaucadores ni impostores. [. . .] Su lenguaje es pues simbólico, no descriptivo. A partir de hechos míticos, fabrican alegorías.[33]

[They are two genres of commingled fiction, differing only in their methods and principles. The former seeks to impose order, to banish anarchy, to discount the role of chance in the past, to construct solvable jigsaw puzzles without chinks or gaps, to erect reassuring edifices on documentary foundations. . . . *Historias fingidas,* on the other hand, open the imagination to the full spectrum of chance in both the past and the future. Reality is exposed to a web of questionable elements. In this invisible spider's web they weave their own reality, their own necessity, their space, their time, in a third or even fourth dimension, which is more than just the world of dreams. Their inventors are neither good, nor bad, nor deceivers, nor impostors. . . . Their language is symbolic, not descriptive. From mythic events they weave allegories.]

And so, *Vigilia,* a *historia fingida* according to the definition of the work's fictional historian, interweaves documented and apocryphal accounts of Columbus and his voyages in order to recast our memory of this often praised and maligned historical figure. Likewise, in the preface of the novel, Roa Bastos claims that *Vigilia* blurs the boundaries between history and the novel and proposes an alternative hybrid mode of writing to recuperate the humanity of the historical Columbus: "[La novela] es por tanto una obra heterodoxa, ahistórica, acaso anti-histórica, anti-maniquea, lejos de la parodia y del pastiche, del anatema y de la hagiografía. [. . .]"[34] [The novel is thus a heterodox form, ahistorical or antihistorical, anti-Manichaean, far from parody and pastiche, from anathema and from hagiography.] Recuperation of Columbus's humanity is achieved by creating a novel in which competing discourses enter into dialogue and conflict about his nature and by avoiding sterile binary oppositions. By reimagining Columbus in this manner, the novel opens other possibilities for retelling the tale of Spanish American culture. It would no longer be told solely as a story of violence and destruction inflicted on the indigenous populations in the New World; it could also serve as the foundation for a more hopeful future for Spanish America. This challenges the ending of *El arpa,* in which Columbus is denounced as an inveterate liar motivated exclusively by greed and condemned to remain forever misunderstood.

While the examination of the controversy surrounding the Piloto Desconocido and his role in the genesis of Columbus's first voyage of discovery serves to redefine the conventional ideological debate about Columbus as an erudite genius, the invocation of chapters from *Don Quixote* and its protagonist, Alonso Quijano/Don Quixote, functions to buttress Columbus's image as a misunderstood, noble-minded individual and to move the reader to reinterpret Columbus's voyage as the point of departure for a more hopeful future. In the novel the fictional Columbus writes Juana la Loca an apocryphal letter to express his grief over the death of Queen Isabella. He renounces his title of Caballero Navegante and returns to his prevoyage identity as Columbus:

> Yo he vivido loco y muero cuerdo, por manera que conozco este tránsito en que el alma transida se abre por fin luminosa al sosiego de la cordura sin abjurar ni abominar los delirios de la noche del alma. [. . .][35]

> [Having once been mad and dying now whole, I recognize the transition of the tormented soul, newly illumined, to the tranquility of reason, neither renouncing nor despising the delirium of its dark night.]

These paraphrased words of Alonso Quijano ennoble the character of the historical Columbus and prepare the reader to reassess received images of Columbus.

In Part 52 actual chapters from the *Quixote* are superimposed over final scenes of Columbus's life as recorded in the official historiography. Present at his bedside are his son Hernando, his brother Bartolomé, the two Diegos (son and brother), Las Casas, the *ama* and *sobrina* from the *Quixote* (who I mentioned earlier), and the seven squires referred to as the "Sancho Panzas," who followed King Ferdinand's retinue from town to town.[36] In his farewell address to friends and family, the fictional Columbus highlights his reconversion to his earlier self:

> Yo fui loco y muero cuerdo. Fui Almirante, Visorrey y Gobernador perpetuo de todas las Indias. ¡Ah locura de los que ponen su quimera en los honores y riquezas de este mundo! No vuelvo a ser agora más que el grumete ligur, el peregrino de la tierra y del mar, el judío errante convicto y converso, que siempre fui con honra y sin provecho. Pueda yo, con la ayuda de vuesas mercedes, con mi arrepentimiento y mi verdad última, la única genuina y valedera, volver a ganar la estimación que de mí se tenía.... —¿Qué es lo que vuesa merced está diciendo, señor? —preguntó el Ama con lágrimas en los ojos? — Nada, almas mías... —dijo el Almirante — sino que me voy muriendo a toda prisa. Y antes de que la lengua se me aquiete para siempre en el ataúd de mi boca, sólo quiero rogaros que perdonéis la locura desta historia, los grandes disparates que en ella se describen como ciertos, y que únicamente lo son para mí. [...][37]

> [I have been mad and die now whole. I was admiral, viceroy, and governor for life of the Indies. What madness, those who value the honors and riches of this life! Once again I am but a Ligurian cabin boy wandering land and sea, a wandering Jew, a convict and a converso, what I have always been, with honor if to no advantage. If I could, with the help of Your Excellencies, with my repentance and my final truth, the only genuine and worthy truth, regain the esteem that I once enjoyed.... "What are you saying, Your Excellency?" asked the *ama*, tearfully. Nothing, my souls, ... said the Admiral, just that I am dying forthwith. And before I am eternally silenced and my tongue entombed in my mouth, I want to beg your forgiveness for the folly of this narrative, the absurdities that are described therein as fact, though they be so for me and no other....]

From this point forward, however, the ending of the novel diverges from the final scenes of *Don Quixote*. The fictional Columbus replies to the ending of *El arpa*, in which Columbus proclaims himself an indecipherable mystery, and acknowledges multiple approaches to interpreting Columbus:

> [C]ada individuo es infinito y misterioso como el universo mismo, y ante cada uno la imaginación tiembla sin saber por dónde comenzar para entenderlo y menos aún en qué punto terminar. Por lo cual ninguna historia tiene principio ni fin y todas tienen tantos significados como lectores aya. [...][38]

[Every individual is as infinite and mysterious as the universe itself. Where does one begin in the effort to understand a man? The imagination trembles at the very thought, and trembles even more when deliberating where to stop. Indeed, while no history has either beginning or end, it has as many meanings as readers. . . .]

Whereas Alejo Carpentier in *El arpa* seeks to impose a univocal reading of Columbus as an inveterate liar motivated solely by the search for gold, Roa Bastos in *Vigilia* approaches the historical Columbus and his life as a complex conglomeration of legends, histories, and myths that can be recombined to tell many stories, because the novel provides the space for the historical, biographical, literary, and legendary discourses to enter into dialogue and to underscore the social constructedness of truths about Columbus's life and voyages.

Vigilia employs a complex narrative structure that interweaves historical and apocryhal voices and documents to transform the reader's remembrance of Columbus as either a hero or a villain. It re-creates Columbus's life and interrogates the past to promote a more productive discussion about both the past and the future of Latin America. The reexamination of the Piloto Desconocido legend leads into a discussion about the boundaries between histories (*historias documentadas*) and novels (*historias fingidas*) and to the recognition that both modes manufacture knowledge that serves diverse ideological interests. Furthermore, the filtering of episodes in Columbus's life through chapters of *Don Quixote* serves to portray Columbus as a complex individual and responds to such Spanish American novels as *El arpa,* which attempt to reduce the historical Columbus to an ideological symbol and stifle the debate about the legacy of Columbus for Spanish American culture.

While *Vigilia* provides a space in which multiple discourses enter into dialogue about the nature of Columbus and his legacy for modern Spanish America, Herminio Martinez's *Las puertas del mundo* centers on Columbus the man as recorded in his private diary, which spans the four voyages and records remembrances from his private life. The novel, comprised of an epigraph from Seneca's tragedy *Medea* and twenty-six chapters, can be divided into five major parts. Part 1 (chapters 1–6) deals with episodes that occurred during the first voyage and Columbus's recuperation at the Franciscan monastery at La Rábida in 1493. Part 2 (chapters 7–13) records the second voyage and his visit with King Ferdinand and Queen Isabella. Part 3 (chapters 14–18) re-creates the third voyage to South America, Columbus's subsequent incarceration and forced deportation to Spain at the hands of Bobadilla, and his visit with the monarchs, who eventually restore his freedom. Part 4 (chapters 19–22) touches on the fourth voyage of discovery, and part 5 (chapters 23–26) discusses the death of Queen Isabella in 1504 and Columbus's ensuing fall from royal favor. In all major parts of the novel, the fictional Columbus engages in dialogue with himself, reimagines conversations with the royal monarchs, assesses the sinister motives of his archenemies, and remembers his sexual relationships with women, especially Raquel—the sister of Luis de Santángel, who accompanies the fictional Columbus on the first voyage as an "hembra de placer" [woman of pleasure].

The second part of the novel's title, "Una autobiografía hipócrita del Almirante" [A hypocritical autobiography of the Admiral] alludes to those chapters from the fictional Columbus's private journal in which he critiques his official reports to the Catholic monarchs and contradicts the official historiography, which omits the seamier underside of the Columbian enterprise. The novel deals in anti-Semitic stereotypes and portrays Columbus as a greedy, Jewish hypocrite who betrays his community and expresses no qualms about the crown's financing his voyages with unlawfully confiscated properties from Jewish communities. The fictional Columbus skillfully manipulates the rhetoric of Christianity in order to conceal and advance his own economic self-interest. Moreover, he is presented as an impulsive, degraded figure who suffers from delusions of grandeur and moments of delirium in which he uses language to create a deceptive image of the New World. In the spirit of popular debates in 1992 that sought to denigrate the heroic image of Columbus, *Las puertas* performs an irreverent revision of Columbus and his writings. Whereas *Vigilia* stages a conflict among various discourses to construct a single interpretive position for readers that sees Columbus more ambivalently, *Las puertas* builds and adds layers of discourse to construct an iconoclastic yet negative exploration of Columbus. Though *Vigilia* appears more dialogical and *Las puertas* more monological, both arrive at specific ideological interpretations about Columbus. Unlike *Vigilia,* which juxtaposes multiple discourses about Columbus to underscore the socially constructed nature of truths, *Las puertas* endeavors to impose a uniformly negative and humorous assessment of Columbus and employs learned citations of medieval authoritative sources in a novelistic context to explode such an image.

In stylistic terms, *Las puertas* diverges radically from the original Columbian writings. The novel employs modern-day syntactical structures and vocabularies, with passages cast in a lyrical mode, and accumulates surrealistic images about the New World geography that overwhelm the comprehension of an impatient reader. It dramatizes for the reader the linguistic dilemma that Columbus confronted in making the New World reality fit into his medieval notion of the world. The interlacing of the narrative with popular *refranes,* citations from ancient, medieval, and modern authorities, and Mexican interjections challenges the reader to interpret the text by contrasting their meaning in the original context to that in novelistic discourse of the late twentieth century.

The epigraph in *Las puertas* previews the recasting of the original Columbian writings from official reports to the crown into a frivolous and impassioned account of the voyages. This epigraph, an adaptation of a passage from book 7 of Seneca's *Medea* and included in Columbus's *Libro de las profecías* (1501–03)—a working manuscript composed of sources and ideas for a long apocalyptic poem—underscores Columbus's role as a reader of ancient texts in order to find authorities to legitimate his first voyage. In the *Libro de las profecías* Columbus extracted this passage from *Medea* as evidence from classical literature that the discovery of the Indies had been prophesied centuries ago and that it was now his task to serve as the instrument to fulfill that prophecy. The *Medea* passage reads as follows in the *Libro* and the novel, respectively:

> Vernán los tardos años del mundo ciertos tiempos en los quales el mar Oçéano alfoxerá los atamentos de las cosas, y se abrirá una grande tierra, y um nuebo marinero como aquél que fue guya de Jasón que obe nombre Tiphi, descobrirá nuebo mundo y entonces non será la ysla Tille la postrera de las tierras.[39]

> [In the latter years of the world will come certain times in which the Ocean Sea will relax the bonds of things, and a great land will open up, and a new mariner like the one who was the guide of Jason, whose name was Typhis, will discover a new world, and then will the island of Thule no longer be the farthest land.][40]

> En edades tardías venir han unos siglos en que el Océano relajará las cadenas del mundo se abrirá una tierra inmensa. Tetis revelará un nuevo mundo y Tule ya no será la postrera de las tierras.[41]

> [In late days to come in some centuries the Ocean will loosen the chains of the world (and) an immense land will be opend. Tetis will reveal a new world and Tule will no longer be the farthest of lands.]

As Gabriella Moretti has noted in her article about the significance of the *Medea* passage in the *Libro de las profecías,* the historical Columbus goes beyond a literal transcription of the Latin passage and performs an interpretative translation. He replaces Tehthys (goddess and wife of Father Okeanos in *Medea*) with Typhis (a famous mariner who, according to Greek mythology, served as guide in leading Jason to the Golden Fleece) in

Las puertas. Like Typhis, Columbus was the new mariner who would discover a new world.[42] Just as the historical Columbus read, collected, compiled, and interpreted ancient and medieval texts to create antecedents for his own enterprise and viewed himself as the instrument to fulfill that prophecy, the fictional Columbus in *Las puertas* likewise reads and glosses sources to legitimize his thoughts aboard the ship. In the epigraph from *Las puertas,* however, the fictional Columbus retains the figure of Tehthys from the *Medea* passage, and thus unwrites the passage transcribed from the *Libro*.

A cursory comparison of the translation found in the *Libro* and that in *Las puertas* illustrates that the novel does not reproduce the medieval syntax and orthography of the original quotation but rather transforms the context of the original locution. The epigraph functions to underscore the fundamental strategy of citation and intertextuality to rewrite Columbus's voyages and to alter our collective memory of the enterprise. The fictional Columbus does indeed discover another world; nonetheless, the cataloguing of the physical attributes of the new lands is subordinated to the overarching task of revealing the interior landscape of Columbus's own soul.

In the historical Columbus's writings, the authority of experience from the first voyage, as exemplified in the *Diario de a bordo,* is displaced in later *relaciones* from the third and fourth voyages by an appeal to written sources and traditions. The later *relaciones* combine Columbus's actual trials with purely intellectual experiences—his readings of ancient and medieval textual authorities—and rely upon the reader's literary competence to decipher their full sense.[43] In contrast to the compiler of the diary-like account of the first voyage, the narrative voice in the *relaciones* from the third and fourth voyages acquires an authorial, prophetic cast. The practical, descriptive, and often formulaic tenor of the *Diario* is replaced with an overarching, theoretical schemata in which experiences are situated and then interpreted. The cardinal referents in the texts are no longer actual lived occurrences but cultural fables that, according to E. Michael Gerli, deprive "lived" experiences of their actuality by removing chance, contingency, and accident from their representation and by inscribing them in the sphere of the legendary.[44]

As is the case in Columbus's writings, the rewritten accounts of the voyages in *Las puertas* feature variations on the authority of direct experience and of appeals to written sources, though with the underlying purpose of parodying those conventions. In chapter 5, the fictional Columbus undermines the authority of the medieval forensic rhetorical tradition in that what Columbus inventories in his eyewitness testimony is a chaotic series of surrealistic images about the New World. For instance, the fictional Columbus, who is recovering at La Rábida after his first voyage, recalls what he witnessed during the first voyage:

> En Némesis vi el río del odio del que habló Heberto el Grande en su *Crónica de lugares fantásticos,* y supe ahí de la existencia de los hombres [. . .] que tienen ojos bizcos que lloran lágrimas musicales y un lomo escamado como de pez. [. . .]
> Vi los zorros de Lebbal, armados con una garfa interminable para defenderse del ataque inminente de las garduñas lloronas de Aretta que, ocultas en la floresta, comían raíces venenosas antes de lanzarse sobre sus enemigos quienes, según aquella especie de mamíferos hórridos, en sus plateados cuerpos criaban el piojo de la eterna hermosura. [. . .][45]

> [In Nemesis I saw the river of hate of which Heberto el Grande spoke in his *Chronicle of Fantastic Places,* and there I learned of . . . cross-eyed men who cried musical tears and had fishlike scales on their back. . . .
> I saw the foxes of Lebbal, armed with immensely long claws to defend themselves from imminent attack by howling Aretta martens that, eating poisonous roots, waited, hidden among the foliage before hurling themselves upon their enemies, which, in the manner of that horrific mammal species, raised the lice of eternal beauty on their silvery bodies. . . .]

Such passages, which bring to the forefront Columbus as testimonial witness, add a lyrical dimension to an otherwise prosaic account and display his linguistic dexterity in creating a world.

The *Diario de a bordo,* the extant version of Columbus's account of the first voyage, is Bartolomé de las Casas's transcription and glossing of an original in his possession in the mid-sixteenth century. Our contemporary understanding of Columbus's account of his first voyage to the Indies, as Margarita Zamora has pointed out, is mediated by Las Casas's reading of the *Diario.* From this adapted version of the *Diario,* several salient stylistic features of the writing emerge. From the departure of the caravels on August 3, 1492, to their return at the port of Palos on March 15, 1493, Las Casas includes a date for each entry in the journal, summarizes the actions of Columbus, and, at times, even quotes the written word of the Admiral with expressions such as "Dize el almirante [. . .]" [The Admiral says . . .] or "Todas las palabras del Almirante son formales" [The Admiral writes formally]. Columbus meticulously records his observations about the geography and landscape and manifests an obsession with finding gold and other material wealth. As Zamora has noted, the *Diario* from the first voyage stands out as a typical exploratory nautical writing in that for the first forty-two days of the voyages, the text records technical navigational information regarding direction, speed, winds, currents, and other maritime phenomena relevant to the successful completion of the voyage. However, with the landfall entry of October 11, 1492, the *Diario* increasingly focuses on the events of the voyage as a coherent experience.[46]

In *Las puertas,* by contrast, the chapters that retell Columbus's first voyage record and probe the internal landscape of his mind. The comments and reactions to what he observes in the Caribbean are directed to himself, not to the Catholic monarchs, as is the case in the *Diario.* Moreover, each chapter, which corresponds to a journal entry, is undated and deals with current and past concerns from his personal life, such as his relationship with other crew members and past lovers. Whereas the Columbus in the official *Diario* constructs his discourse within the tradition of diary writing, the Columbus in the unofficial, confessional diary engages in digressive storytelling about himself and the enterprise of the Indies. The tone of this confessional diary is markedly gossipy and humorous, and thereby transcends the conventional images of Columbus as either saint or villain, which have come to dominate popular debates about the quincentenary.

In chapter 1, corresponding to the October 12, 1492, landfall at Guanahaní, the fictional Columbus unwittingly contradicts his image from the official historiography as a man of religious conviction and fervor. He invokes the rhetoric of Christianity in order to distract the reader from the self-interest of the enterprise. Whereas in the *Diario* the historical Columbus names the first island San Salvador for purportedly religious reasons, the fictional Columbus in *Las puertas* invokes religion to camouflage his genuine motivation to enrich himself financially: "[D]ecidí bautizar con el nombre de San Salvador, y no tanto porque yo sea un ferviente súbdito del Mesías de los católicos, sino antes bien por seguir la corriente de las apariencias hasta la total realización de mis proyectos."[47] [I decided to christen it with the name San Salvador not so much because I am a fervent devotee of the Catholic messiah, but rather to keep up appearances until my projects are fully realized.] What drives and sustains his vision of discovering the Indies is not the intensity and depth of his Christian faith but his sexual relationship with Raquel de Santángel aboard the ship. The fictional Columbus remarks of her importance on the voyage: "Qué bueno que [Raquel] va aquí a mi lado, porque en situaciones como la presente un par de tetas es más efectivo que toda la *Suma Teológica.*"[48] [How well it is that Raquel is at my side, because in situations such as this, a pair of tits is of more use than the entire *Summa Theologica.*] Sex—not his faith in God—drives and sustains his endeavors.

While descriptions about the gentleness of the inhabitants and the beauty of the landscape abound in the October 12 entry from the *Diario,* the interiority of the fictional Columbus's landscape and the crew members' encounters with the natives come to the forefront in the novel. Such interactions, of course, immediately assume carnal dimensions. The fictional Columbus records in a humorous and disturbingly lighthearted fashion the conquistadors' rape of indigenous women:

> Allá los [los conquistadores] descubro, ¡ea!, despojándose de las calzas, con una y hasta tres nativas de la mano, a las que conducen a los follajes para hacer lo que yo sé. Hay que dejarlos que hagan para que su espíritu descanse, al fin que, como dicen que escribió el hijo del maestre de Santiago [Jorge Manrique in the *Coplas para la muerte de su padre*], nuestras vidas son los ríos que van a dar a la mar; y en ellos tales ríos no son de muerte sino de deseo entre estas féminas desguarnecidas de todo atavío. [. . .]⁴⁹

> [There! I encounter the conquistadors, and in what a way! Divesting themselves of their breeches with one, two, or three natives at hand, leading them to the bushes for a purpose I know of. This they must be allowed, that they may be at ease, for as was written by the son of the master of Santiago, our lives are as rivers that run to the sea. But here among these wholly unclothed women, the rivers of my men's lives lead not to death; they flow with desire. . . .]

In Manrique's *Coplas* the verse "nuestras vidas son los ríos que van a dar a la mar" [our lives are as rivers that run to the sea] affirms the inextricable connection between life and death, though in the novel these words allude to the intimate connection between life and sexual desire. Just as the fictional Columbus rewrites the conventional historiography about the first voyage, he relocates a serious, oft-quoted line from the *Coplas* into a new and frivolous context. The *Coplas,* which present the elegy for a dying man, are emptied of their solemnity of tone and purpose and are invoked to talk about the rape of indigenous women and to critique the veneer of refined culture that portrayed the conquest as a benign event.

As the fictional Columbus cites passages from Spanish medieval literature and reinscribes them in a modern context, he also appeals to the popular wisdom of *refranes* to justify his mistreatment of the indigenous populations. Columbus's obsession with gold leads him to commit atrocities against the indigenous populations when they fail to comply with his requests. In the novel, Raquel de Santángel attempts to dissuade Columbus from quartering the local caciques when they fail to comply with his demands for gold. In order to justify the violence of his actions, Columbus resorts to a common *refrán:* "[P]ensé a lo hecho pecho, ¡y que siga saliendo el sol por Antequera! [. . .]"⁵⁰ [I thought, what's done is done and what will be will be! . . . .] The incongruence between the seriousness of his actions as they adversely affect the indigenous populations and the frivolity with which he applies a *refrán,* normally invoked to react to minor incidents in daily life, recasts the historical Columbus's atrocities and contempt for the indigenous populations in a disturbing form of mordant satire, as evidenced in the subsequent expression "Indio muerto, indio bueno"[51] [A dead Indian is a good Indian]. In the novel, the historical Columbus is recast first and foremost as a linguistic performer who uses language play to invent and alter the perceptions and memories of the New World and to conceal the violence unleashed by the conquest.

In his capacity as ethnographer, the fictional Columbus observes and reports on indigenous customs and implicitly critiques the Eurocentric lens through which the chroniclers interpreted indigenous cultures. Such rites and cultural practices, filtered through the colorful language of Columbus, run counter to European sensibilities about human nature. In chapter 2, Columbus describes a ritual by which adolescent candidates are admitted into a religious community in the province of Tiátome. Aspirants are subjected to a test:

> [L]as Vírgenes Divinas [. . .] encargadas de la ejecución de semejante examen, el cual consiste en que al candidato lo desnudan sobre una cama de flores acariciándole y besándole la entrepierna, de modo que si su miembro de varón no produce cambio, sino que se mantiene dormido, entonces él es un hombre digno de tal sacerdocio. Más si al contacto de manos femininas, besos, arrumacos y demás escarceos, la masculinidad del aspirante se contorsiona, tiembla, y se agita y yergue enhiesta como espada de un Mío Cid Campeador, en este caso el individuo es comido inmediatamente por toda la comunidad religiosa, entre lamentaciones y cánticos de liturgia.[52]

> [The Sacred Virgins . . . are charged with performing this test, in which they relieve the candidate of his clothing upon a bed of flowers, caressing and kissing him between the legs. If the young man is worthy of this priesthood, his male organ remains dormant, betraying no reaction. If, however, his masculinity awakens to the caresses and amorous ministrations of womanly hands and lips, if it becomes unquiet and ultimately stands to attention like the sword of Mío Cid Campeador, in such case the individual is promptly eaten by the entire religious community, accompanied by lamentations and liturgical song.]

The proliferation of euphemisms to refer to the penis ("la masculinidad" and "la espada de un Mío Cid Campeador") superimposes a humorous tone on a report renowned for its lack of style. This initiation rite into a religious order, which illustrates the perceived separation of spirituality from sexuality, is designed to ensure that those who repress their sexual instincts are promoted, while those who physically display their arousal are condemned to immediate death.

By recasting Columbus's *Diario,* a ship's log that outlines in minimal form his adventures and travels from island to island, as an introspective and meditative chronicle of emotions and reactions to the voyage, *Las puertas* goes against the conventional representation of Columbus as saint or sinner by bringing to the fore the sexual undertones of the New World enterprise. The Columbus in the novel explores the interiority of his soul and acknowledges sexual exploitation as a driving force behind the enterprise of the Indies. His hypocrisy resides in that he dons the robes of religious piety in order to conceal his economic motivations for discovering the Indies.

As Columbus's journal from the second voyage has been lost, its content is derived from numerous sources, which include Columbus's prefatory letter (April 1493) to Ferdinand and Isabella, letters 2 to 5 of the *Libro copiador,* and Columbus's own official report (dated January 30, 1494) about the colonization of Hispaniola, known as the Torres Memorandum.[53] In these writings, the historical Columbus discusses his thoughts and experiences concerning the establishment of the colony on Hispaniola, the exploitation of the Indies and the islands' natural wealth, the continuing search for the empire of the Grand Khan, relations between the Christians and between them and the Indians (including the capture of the cacique Cahonaboa and the skirmishes between his people and the Spaniards), the disastrous fate of *La navidad,* and the obsessive search for gold.[54] In *Las puertas,* by contrast, the fictional Columbus's account of the second voyage focuses largely on Columbus's remembering his experience at the royal court prior to his first voyage. There he expounds a detailed theory as to the role of spelling lessons in bringing about the insanity (*la locura*) of the young Juana La Loca[55] and gossips about an alleged relationship between Juana and the indigenous Tábari.[56] Rather than providing a physical description of the topography, the fictional Columbus describes an imaginary landscape of fantastic and surrealistic images. This section of the novel maintains the frivolous tone of the first section, features Columbus's linguistic dexterity, and documents his growing frustrations at not finding more gold in the Indies.

In an imagined visit to the palace of the Grand Khan, Columbus selects five women with whom he engages in sexual intercourse. The language of his comments reflects the underlying commercial and sexual dimensions of the encounter: "[Q]uisiera elegir yo cinco de las más bellas criaturas con que el Khan administra su anatomía y es feliz, muy feliz, pagándoles a peso de oro y diamantes cada braguetazo."[57] [I would like to select five of the prettiest creatures with whom the Khan satisfies his physical needs and is pleased, most pleased, paying them in coins and diamonds for each such engagement.] The Grand Khan, in short, views his genitalia as property to manage and administer to his entourage of women. Although gold is in short supply in the New World, sex is excessively abundant. In light of the absence of gold, Columbus classifies and inventories the sizes and shapes of female breasts:

> Hemos visto [. . .] pechos hasta casi enloquecer. Pechos de ricas y variadas proporciones: los ya hinchados y los que apenas se insinúan en ruborcillo de durazno o manzana. Los erguidos con erguío de mandona hidalga y los ya flojos o a punto de secarse, que aun así siguen siendo sujetos de incentivo o donaire, pues en nada se le comparan a los de ciertas europeas que en semejantes condiciones suelen parecer más calcetines con canica que jardines colgantes. [. . .][58]

> [We have seen . . . nearly enough breasts to drive us mad, breasts of many and varied proportions, some in their fullness and others merely suggesting themselves with a peach- or applelike blush. Upstanding breasts such as those of the imperious noblewoman, and less-proud breasts, or those whose days of plenitude are numbered, but that even so continue to attract with their grace, for by no means can they be compared to the breasts of certain European women, which in such circumstances resemble chalk-filled socks rather than hanging gardens. . . .]

As the historical Columbus employed analogies to make the New World comprehensible to a home audience that had never traveled to the Indies, the fictional Columbus compares New World female breasts to European ones in order to poke fun at the strategies by which the historical Columbus made his report comprehensible to Isabella and Ferdinand and to critique the whole New World enterprise.

In the third voyage, recorded primarily in the *Relación del tercer viaje* and in a portion (May 30–August 31, 1498) of a since-lost *diario* of the same voyage excerpted by Las Casas in his *Historia de Indias,* Columbus's task is less to relate the voyage than to interpret its significance.[59] Columbus quickly moves on from relating the navigation to an impassioned defense of his achievements and a treatiselike interpretation of the ultimate significance of his enterprise.[60] According to Zamora, the letters pertaining to the third voyage could be viewed both as personal epistles recounting Columbus's experiences and as manifestos that attempt to construct a framework within which Columbus's particular achievements are placed and then interpreted.⁶¹

During the sixteenth and seventeenth centuries, the New World was often gendered as an exploitable naked female. In *The Writing of History* (1988) Michel de Certeau vividly re-creates in words the scene from a drawing entitled *America* (c. 1575) by Jan van der Straet:

> Amerigo Vespucci, the voyager, arrives from the sea. A crusader standing erect, his body in armor, he bears the European weapons of meaning. Behind him are the vessels that will bring back to the European West the Spoils of paradise. Before him is the Indian "America," a nude woman reclining in her hammock, an unnamed presence of difference, a body which awakens within a space of exotic fauna and flora. . . . An inaugural scene: after a moment of stupor, on this threshold dotted with colonnades of trees, the conqueror will write the body of the other and trace there his own history. From her he will make a historied body—a blazon—of his labors and phantasms. She will be "Latin" America.⁶²

According to Margarita Zamora, this scene has become an emblem of the discovery: the reclining woman, nude in a luxuriant New World landscape, greeting the European man who stands on the shoreline before her, armored and bearing a staff with a crucifix in his right hand and an astrolabe in the other. Discreetly hidden under his tunic is a sword. Furthermore, she argues that Certeau's critical assessment of this "inaugural scene" is just one in a series of graphic and verbal representations of the discovery as an erotic encounter between a fully clothed European male and a naked Amerindian female.⁶³

The iconography of the New World as an exploitable naked female is evident in the *relación* from the third voyage, where Columbus believes to have located the terrestrial paradise in modern-day Venezuela. Here the historical Columbus challenges Ptolomy's conceptualization of the shape of the world as uniformly spherical and proposes it as something more pear-shaped:

> Yo no tomo qu'el Paraíso Terrenal sea en forma de montaña áspera, como el escrivir d'ello nos amuestra, salvo qu' él sea en el colmo, allí donde dixe la figura del peçón de la pera, y que poco a poco andando hazia allí desde muy lejos se va subiendo a él.⁶⁴

> [I do not think that the Terrestrial Paradise is the shape of a rugged mountain, like the writings about it show us, but rather that it is at the very top, which I described in the figure of the nipple of the pear, and that bit by bit traveling toward it from a great distance one ascends to it.⁶⁵

Likewise, the fictional Columbus in *Las puertas* comments on the discovery of the earthly paradise and its resemblance to the breast of a woman:

> Son las repúblicas del Edén, carajo. Se siente y se sabe en todo lo que vemos y en todo cuanto oímos [. . .] en esta elevación terrenal donde se siente suavidad del viento [. . .] tengo la certeza de que nuestros ojos son testigos de que los cielos giran y de que el mundo no es tan redondo como lo anunciara Tolomeo y demás sabios de su ciencia, sino más bien en forma de pera, o como quien tiene una pelota muy redonda y en un lugar de ella fuese como una teta de mujer, y que la parte del pezón fuera la más alta y más vecina del cielo. [. . .]⁶⁶

> [These are the republics of Eden, *carajo*. This we feel and know from all we heard and saw . . . at this terrestrial elevation where we feel the softness of the breeze . . . I'm sure that our eyes witnessed the spinning of the heavens and that the world is not as round as Ptolemy and other learned scientists claimed, it has instead the form of a pear, or rather of a very round ball, the breast of a woman, the nipple being the highest part and the closest to heaven. . . .]

The Mexicanization of this passage with the insertion of the interjection "carajo" pokes fun at Columbus's discovery of the supposed earthly paradise and deflates the elevated tone in which the historical Columbus recorded his original observations.

Las puertas del mundo assumes a satirical stance toward the legacy of Columbus and his four voyages of discovery to the Indies. Unlike the conventional histories that view Columbus as saint or sinner, the fictional recreation of the voyages depicts him as a degraded, hypocritical liar who manipulates the religious discourses to advance his own self-interest. The novel intermingles Columbian writings with inventions of pure fantasy and imagination. By recasting these early accounts of the discovery as a series of disconnected meditations and ramblings from a personal diary, the novel underscores the immediacy of the historical present and its resistance to totalizing schemes of historiography that eliminate the discontinuity of the historical process. By filling in the silences of the historical record, the novel presents the enterprise of the Indies as a tale of sexual exploitation and of an obsession for acquiring material wealth.

Vigilia del Almirante and *Las puertas del mundo* return to Columbus and his writings to problematize interpretations about Columbus the man and the significance of his voyages. While *Vigilia* rehumanizes Columbus in order to demythologize his conventional image as saint or sinner and points toward a future that breaks with the cycles of violence and destruction unleashed on October 12, 1492, *Las puertas* puts on display his psychological interiority to discredit his heroic image. Columbus's life and writings serve as a point of departure for Martínez to parody the rhetorical conventions of the chronicles and to undermine their authority as an explanation for the state of Latin American culture. In these novels, Columbus is no longer the foundational figure of Latin American culture but rather a figure worthy of ruminations and mockery.

Afterword

IN HIS SHORT STORY "PIERRE MENARD, AUTOR DEL QUIJOTE," JORGE LUIS Borges explains that there are basically three ways of rewriting in the present a few pages of Cervantes's novel that would be identical to the original: simply copying it, immersing oneself in the culture of the early seventeenth century to the point where a perfect re-creation of the Spanish masterpiece is possible, and re-creating the text from a twentieth-century perspective ("to go on being Pierre Menard and reach the *Quixote* through the experiences of Pierre Menard").[1] The latter represents an endeavor not only of archaeological reconstruction, but also of radical recontextualization, in which expressions already existing three centuries earlier now acquire an entirely different meaning. The result, according to Borges's narrator, is that "Cervantes' text and Menard's are verbally identical, but the second is almost infinitely richer."[2] In other words, Menard's rewriting is an invitation to adopt a new technique of reading, by which older texts are enriched by a recontextualization in a later time period.[3]

Although the contemporary Mexican and River Plate writers whose novels I have analyzed do not propose to rewrite the chronicles of the Indies in the same way that Pierre Menard endeavored to rewrite the *Quixote,* they do recontextualize the Spanish chronicles and enrich their meaning for the modern-day reading public. Moreover, they bring to the forefront the issue of the location from which the speaking subject reconfigures the past. In this book, I have discussed a selection of novels that were written in the 1980s and 1990s and that rewrite episodes from the Discovery and conquest from the vantage point of major historical and invented marginal figures. In many respects, these novels represent continuity in trends in Spanish American novelistic production of the 1970s and 1980s, when writers such as Augusto Roa Bastos in *Yo el supremo* (1974), Carlos Fuentes in *Terra Nostra* (1975), Alejo Carpentier in *El arpa y la sombra* (1979), Fernando del Paso in *Noticias del Imperio* (1987), and Gabriel García Márquez in *El general en su laberinto* (1989) reread, rewrote, demythified history, and challenged hegemonic interpretations of the past. As this book has shown, however, the selected novels dramatize the impossibility of knowing the past, address an array of contemporary preoccupations about these nations' interpretation and understanding of the colonial period, and bring to bear how the location of the speaking subject affects historical rewritings. Major historical and invented figures from the discovery and conquest converge to revise episodes from early New World historiography and problematize in the late twentieth century the conventional ways of approaching the past.

The writers of the Mexican novels studied in this book seek to come to terms with the consequences of Cortés's defeat of the Aztecs and the violent origins of the Mexican nation and to challenge inherited images and cultural myths about the conquistadors. Posse and Brailovsky, the authors of the River Plate novels, retell the colonial past to render an oblique critique of the recent historical past in Argentina. Posse establishes parallels between the situation of Cabeza de Vaca in the sixteenth century and that of Argentine citizens during the Dirty War, while Brailovsky proposes similarities between the sword-maker Ambrosio de Lara's situation in Patagonia in 1810 and that of Argentine citizens who faced the military junta's repression of sexual expression. Literary and cultural anachronisms function as a principal strategy for establishing such parallels between the remote and immediate past. Baccino's *Maluco* and Roa Bastos's *Vigilia* bring to the forefront the problematic reliability of written historical records and creatively reconfigure the voyages of Magellan and Columbus to underscore the ways that historical, literary, mythical, and legendary discourses construct and impose a social truth about the past.

The novels, moreover, re-create tales of the discovery and conquest from a twentieth-century perspective in an endeavor of radical recontextualization, by which the original tale acquires a different meaning in the 1980s and 1990s. The novels with postmodern features problematize past cultural and discursive practices and recontextualize them within the present; they foreground conventions from the chronicles by exaggerating, subverting, and thematizing aspects of production and reception such as the act of reading and writing. Readers are asked to reexamine and question their own values and views about their constructed realities.

The novels about the discovery and conquest represent one more chapter of the late twentieth century in which writers reconceptualized the notion of cultural and national identity. Writers no longer viewed identity as a static "essence," as was the case when the Spanish chronicles were first included in the colonial canon in the mid-nineteenth century, but saw it as a dynamic interaction between discursive practices from the past and present. They did not regard identity as timeless and immutable but as historically contingent, changeable, and constantly renewable. This trend in the body of works echoes broader trends in contemporary literary and cultural studies that emphasize identity as a social construction, that delegitimize master discourses, and reconceptualize Latin America as plural, hybrid, and heterogeneous, which contrasts with the monologic discourse of *Hispanidad*.[4] Moreover, in all the novels examined in this book, eyewitness testimonies and retrospective autobiographical accounts are the preferred modes for recontextualizing the chronicles of the Indies and challenging hegemonic interpretations of the past. Retelling the lives of the Spanish explorers and conquistadors is no longer the tale of a homogenous category, but rather that of individuals who explore and divulge the interior landscape of their souls. Although novels such as *Cómo conquisté a los aztecas* and *Las puertas del mundo* demythify the heroic standing of Cortés and Columbus, respectively, they also seek a deeper understanding of these historical figures as well as of the contexts and purposes in which their life stories have circulated and been transmitted.

The rewriting of stories from the discovery and conquest in the Spanish American novel of the 1980s and 1990s took place within a broader cultural trend when the Columbian quincentenary provoked a wide-scale conversation about the historical significance and legacy of the discovery and conquest.[5] The Columbus debate was played out in the realms of official and popular culture. For the official celebrations of the quincentennial of 1992, millions of dollars were spent on international events, culminating in a grand regatta, an international fleet of tall ships that sailed from Spain and arrived in New York Harbor for the Fourth of July. At the same time, widespread activism subverted the official celebration. A group of Native Americans "landed" in Amsterdam, declared the land theirs, and set off for a European El Dorado rumored to be located somewhere near the Rhine. The Latino performance artists Coco Fusco and Guillermo Gómez Peña toured Europe and the United States, where they lived in a golden cage for three days, presented themselves as undiscovered Amerindians from an island in the Gulf of Mexico that had somehow been overlooked by Europeans for five centuries, and created a satirical commentary on Western concepts of the exotic, primitive other.[6] In the United States countless demonstrations, conferences, pedagogical projects, and media events created a counternarrative. Many didactic films and videos, such as *Surviving Columbus* (1990), *Columbus on Trial* (1992), and *Columbus Didn't Discover Us* (1992), revealed an anticolonial thrust and underscored the negative impact of Columbus's landing for indigenous populations.[7]

As part of this broader cultural trend, a similar phenomenon of rewriting life stories of figures from the discovery and conquest took place in Spanish American theater and Latin American film. Numerous plays staged this encounter with a focus on such Spanish figures as Columbus, Cortés, and Gonzalo Guerrero as well as Amerindian figures such as La Malinche,

Cuauhtémoc, and Moctezuma.⁸ The dominant tendency in these plays, argues Juan Villegas, was not to reread history from the vantage point of the vanquished, but rather to underscore the injustices of the dominant regime and its interpretations of history.⁹ Recent Mexican plays like Sabina Berman's *Aguila o sol* (1984), Vicente Leñero's *La noche de Hernán Cortés* (1992), and Hugo Rascón Banda's *La Malinche* (2000) follow the dominant tendency outlined by Villegas and employ a variety of dramatic techniques associated with postmodernism (parody, openness, discontinuity, marginality, and anachronism) to deform, decenter, and demythify received "historical" truths about the conquest of Mexico, which have underscored the Eurocentric vision of this event.¹⁰

As Richard Gordon has noted in his dissertation "Reviewing the Colony/Revising the Nation: Mexican and Brazilian Cinematic Dialogues with Colonial Texts" (2002), the last decade of the twentieth century also witnessed an explosion of cinematic renditions of texts and figures from colonial Latin America, prompted by the quincentenaries, in 1992 and 2000, of the arrival of the Spanish and the Portuguese, respectively, to the New World. Recent Latin American films that exemplify this tendency include Nicolás Echevarría's *Cabeza de Vaca* (Mexico-Spain, 1990); Juan Mora Catlett's *Retorno a Aztlán* (Mexico, 1989), which is on Náhuatl culture before the arrival of the Spaniards; and Eduardo Rosoff's *Ave María* (Mexico, 1998), in which the director revives Sor Juana Inés de la Cruz as a mestiza. In his analysis of five films—Humberto Mauro's *Descobrimento do Brasil* (Brazil, 1937), based on Pero Vaz de Caminha's letter of discovery; Emilio Gómez Muriel's *La monja alférez* (Mexico, 1937), based on the autobiography of Catalina de Erauso; Echevarría's *Cabeza de Vaca;* Pereira dos Santos's *Como era gostoso o meu frances* (Brazil, 1971), based on the tale of a sixteenth-century German, Hans Staden, and the final months of the luckless Frenchman Jean (who is captured by a tribe of cannibals called the Tupinambá); and Rossoff's *Ave María* (1998)—Gordon contends that Mexican and Brazilian directors converse with the colonial past in order to comment on the present. He explores the political and ideological implications of such dialogues in redefining Mexico and Brazil, especially in terms of the importance of indigenous populations in conceptions of national identity.¹¹

As a line for future inquiry, it would be productive to examine how theater/film and the novel approach a historical figure (for example: Cortés, in Ayala Anguiano's *Cómo conquisté a los aztecas* and Leñero's *La noche de Hernán Cortés* and Cabeza de Vaca in Posse's *El largo atardecer del caminante* and Echevarría's *Cabeza de Vaca*) and engage theoretical issues such as the possibility of writing history, the performative dimensions of constructing cultural and self-identities, and the ways that both genres position themselves in relation to the official historiography and attempt to give history a human face.

With Spanish American literary texts, no single conceptual tool, such as the postmodern concept of historiographic metafiction, is adequate to approach and explain the diverse and varied novelistic production dealing with the discovery and conquest of the New World. Although these novels do draw on postmodern strategies, they also address long-standing preoccupations in Spanish American literature about issues of national and cultural identity to reenvision our understanding of the discovery and conquest, the period traditionally viewed as the birth of Latin America. The chronicles of the Indies can no longer be read simply as an unquestioned storehouse of uncontestable "facts" but may now be seen as a constructed tale that has denied the multicultural origins of Latin American societies. In the 1980s and 1990s Mexican and River Plate writers delved into the New World historiography for revelations concerning the genesis and development of their contemporary reality. Since the chroniclers of the Indies made the earliest attempts to interpret America, it is fitting that contemporary Spanish American writers continue those efforts to comprehend the New World, and eventually, to probe even further the multicultural origins of Latin America.

Notes

Introduction

1. Aníbal González Pérez, "Imágenes de la conquista y la colonia en la novelística hispanoamericana contemporánea: Notas para una interpretación," *Revista de Estudios Hispánicos* (San Juan, Puerto Rico) 19 (1992): 431.

2. For an analysis of Spanish American historiography and the different historical genres of the chronicles of the Indies, see Walter Mignolo, "Cartas, crónicas y relaciones del descubrimiento y la conquista," in *Historia de la literatura hispanoamericana: Epoca colonial,* ed. Luis Iñigo Madrigal (Madrid: Cátedra, 1982), 56–125; and Mignolo, "El metatexto historiográfico y la historiografía indiana," *MLN* 96 (1981): 358–402. For further information about the transformation of colonial Latin American studies from an emphasis on literary studies to semiotic interactions, see "Second Thoughts on Canon and Corpus," *Latin American Literary Review* 20, no. 40 (1992): 66–69; and Idelber Avelar, "De Macondo al Huarochirí: El canon literario latinoamericano ante prácticas discursivas emergentes," *Dispositio* 18, no. 44 (1993): 193–214. For an overview of scholarship on the chronicles in colonial Latin American literary studies, see Rolena Adorno, "Colonial Spanish American Literary Studies: 1982–1992," *Revista Interamericana de Bibliografía/Inter-American Review of Bibliography* 38, no. 2 (1988): 167–76; Walter Mignolo, "La lengua, el territorio (o la crisis de los estudios literarios coloniales)," *Dispositio* 11, nos. 28–29 (1986): 137–60; and James C. Murray, *Spanish Chronicles of the Indies: Sixteenth Century* (New York: Twayne, 1994), especially chapter 1.

3. Mignolo, "Cartas, crónicas" 57–59.

4. José Miguel Oviedo, *Historia de la literatura hispanoamericana,* vol. 1: *De los orígenes a la Emancipación* (Madrid: Alianza, 1995), 76–78.

5. Roberto González Echevarría, "Humanismo, retórica y las crónicas de la Conquista," in *Historia y ficción en la narrativa hispanoamericana: Coloquio de Yale,* ed. Roberto González Echevarría (Caracas: Monte Avila, 1984), 160–64.

6. Ibid., 59.

7. González Pérez, "Imágenes" 432–33. In nineteenth-century Spanish American narrative, representative novels include *Xicoténcatl* (Mexico, 1826) by an anonymous writer, *Gonzalo Pizarro* by Manuel Asencio Segura (Mexico, 1839), *Guatimozín* by Gertrudis Gómez de Avellaneda (Cuba, 1846), *La novia del hereje* (Argentina, 1846) by Vicente Fidel López, *El inquisidor mayor: Historia de unos amores* by Manuel Bilbao (Chile, 1852), and *Enriquillo* (Dominican Republic, 1879–82) by Manuel de Jesús Galván. González Pérez, "Imágenes" 431–32.

8. Margarita Zamora, "Historicity and Literariness: Problems in the Literary Criticism of Spanish American Colonial Texts," *MLN* 102 (1987): 334–46.

9. Ibid., 338.

10. Doris Sommer has argued in *Foundational Fictions: The National Romances of Latin America* that nineteenth-century narrators could project an ideal future through novels

because the nonscientific method of history left epistemological gaps, and the writers filled in a history to help establish the legitimacy of the emerging nation and direct that history toward a future ideal. Doris Sommer, *Foundational Fictions: The National Romances of Latin America* (Berkeley and Los Angeles: University of California Press, 1991), 7. In his essay "The Historical Method" (1848), Andrés Bello polemicized against what others understood as modern historiography, and in the absence of basic historical data, he advocated self-consciously personal narratives over the pretense of objectivity; the personal narratives together seemed to deliver more autonomous and more accurate pictures than those offered by an informed "science" of history." Cited in Sommer, *Foundational Fictions,* 8. With regard to the discovery and conquest, Bello recommended that inquisitive readers delve into the eyewitness accounts of the chroniclers instead of the retrospective accounts by self-proclaimed historians: "Do you want to know, for example, what the discovery of America was like? Reading Columbus's diary, Pedro de Valdivia's letters and those of Bernal Díaz will tell you much more than Solís or Robertson." Cited in Sommer, *Foundational Fictions,* 8.

11. González Pérez notes that in the second period (1898 to 1968) of his scheme, major discussions in literary circles about the colonial period shifted from narrative to the essay. For example, Alfonso Reyes's *Visión de Anáhuac* (Mexico, 1917), José Carlos Mariátegui's *Siete ensayos de interpretación de la realidad peruana* (Peru, 1928), Mariano Picón Salas's *De la Conquista a la Independencia* (Venezuela, 1944), Pedro Henríquez Ureña's *Historia de la cultura en la América Hispánica* (Dominican Republic, 1947), and José Lezama Lima's *La expresión americana* (Cuba, 1957) reevaluated and transformed the vision of the colonial period as a medieval period in that, although they still viewed it as the origin of Spanish American culture, they also emphasized the cultural production of elites in urban centers and viewed the colonial period as inaugurating a process of fusing forms. González Pérez "Imágenes," (see n. 1), 435. Kimberle S. López has also noted the publication of the following novels between 1927 and 1969: Roberto J. Payró's *El mar dulce: Crónica novelesca del descubrimiento del Río de la Plata* (Argentina, 1927) on the expedition of Juan Díaz de Solís; Arturo Uslar Pietri's *El camino de El Dorado* (Venezuela, 1947) on the quest for El Dorado; Antonio Di Benedetto's *Zama* (Argentina, 1956) on the bureaucracy of the late colony; and Miguel Angel Asturias's *Maládrón* (Guatemala, 1969) on the contact between Europeans and Amerindians peoples in the conquest. Kimberle S. López, *Latin American Novels of the Conquest: Reinventing the New World* (Columbia: University of Missouri Press, 2002).

12. Alfonso Reyes, *Letras de la Nueva España* (Mexico City: Fondo de Cultura Económica, 1948), 46.

13. Enrique Anderson Imbert, *Historia de la literatura hispanoamericana,* vol. 1: *La colonia: Cien años de la República,* sixth ed. (Mexico City: Fondo de Cultura Económica, 1967), 20.

14. René Jara, "Crítica de una crisis: Los estudios literarios hispanoamericanos," *Ideologies & Literature* 4, no. 16 (1983): 337.

15. Gabriel García Márquez, "Fantasía y creación artística en América Latina y el Caribe," *Texto Crítico* 14 (1979): 4–5.

16. In her article on the growth of colonial Spanish American literary studies from 1982 to 1988, Rolena Adorno attributes the increased scholarship on the chronicles to the publication of Tzvetan Todorov's *The Conquest of America* (1982), the quincentenary of Columbus's first voyage, and, on a broader scale, to the attention Latin American novelists of the Boom cast on the origins of Latin American history and culture. Adorno, "Colonial Spanish American" 168. For instance, Carlos Fuentes in *La nueva novela hispanoamericana* (see n. 2), (Mexico City: Cuadernos de Joaquín Martiz, 1969) saw the mission of the writer as

one of inventing a language to fill in the lacunae from the official historiography of the continent and thereby giving a voice to the voiceless:

> [L]a novela latinoamericana se ofrece como un nuevo impulso de fundación, como un regreso al acto de la génesis para redimir las culpas de la violación original, de la bastardía fundadora: la conquista de América fue un gigantesco atropello, un fusilico descomunal que pobló el continente de fusiloquitos, de siete leches, de hijos de la chingada. (46)
>
> [The Latin American novel offers up a new foundational impulse, like a return to our genesis to expiate the guilt of the original violation, of the foundational bastardy, for the conquest of America was a monstrous crime committed in an extended fit of madness that populated the continent with its rabid progeny, with a mongrel race, with the totally fucked offspring of a historic rape.]

In his article "Colonialism Now and Then: Colonial Latin American Studies in the Light of the Predicament of Latin Americanism" Gustavo Verdesio takes issue with Adorno's and Mignolo's claim that that the area of colonial studies has undergone a paradigm shift. Verdesio argues that while the majority of the important theoretical contributions have privileged the study of texts and perspectives previously repressed by the rigid criteria of colonial canon formation, the majority of the works published in the field do not follow the theoretical paths opened by those theoretical contributions. Gustavo Verdesio, "Colonialism Now and Then: Colonial Latin American Studies in the Light of the Predicament of Latin Americanism," in *Colonialism Past and Present: Reading and Writing about Colonial Latin America Today,* ed. Alvaro Félix Bolaños and Gustavo Verdesio (Albany: State University of New York Press, 2002), 3. In short, little consensus exists with regard to intellectual production, and rather than discussing a paradigm shift, Verdesio proposes talking about the new scholarship as an emergent mode of production, but not as the statistically dominant one in the discipline (5).

For further discussion of the state of Hispano-American colonial studies, see Walter Mignolo, "The Darker Side of the Renaissance: Colonization and the Discontinuity of the Classical Tradition," *Renaissance Quarterly* 14, no. 4 (1992): 808–28; and Petra Schumm, "La 'cultura' en la crítica sobre los siglos coloniales en Hispanoamérica y el Brasil," *Dispositio* 18, no. 44 (1993): 79–98. See also two anthologies of critical studies: Santa Arias and Mariselle Meléndez, eds., *Mapping Colonial Spanish America: Places and Commonplaces of Identity, Culture, and Experience* (Lewisburg, PA: Bucknell University Press, 2002); and Bolaños and Verdesio, eds., *Colonialism Past and Present* (see n. 16).

17. Years before the paradigm shift manifested itself in colonial Spanish American literary studies, José Rabasa notes that the Mexican philosopher and historian Edmundo O'Gorman expressed in the introduction to Joseph de Acosta's *Historia natural y moral de las Indias* (1972) the need to rectify the emphasis that positivist historiography had placed on the exclusive appraisal of the chronicles as a source of information, as depositories of data from which a factual truth may be construed. O'Gorman, writes Rabasa, underscored the need to read and study the epistemological and ontological as well as rhetorical suppositions informing the historiography of the New World. José Rabasa, *Inventing A-M-E-R-I-C-A: Spanish Historiography and the Formation of Eurocentrism* (Norman: University of Oklahoma Press, 1993), 4–5.

18. Walter Mignolo, "La lengua, el territorio (o la crisis de los estudios literarios coloniales)," *Dispositio* 11, nos. 28–29 (1986): 139.

19. Birgit Scharlau, "Nuevas tendencias en los estudios de crónicas y documentos del período colonial latinoamericano," *Revista de Crítica Literaria Latinoamericana* 16, nos. 32–33 (1990): 366. Another factor might have been the arrival of New Historicism, which

encouraged critics to think historically and to compare literary texts with other contemporary nonliterary texts. In other words, the larger field of literary studies was feeling the impact of and, at the same time, influencing other fields, especially history and anthropology. I would like to thank Laura Podalsky for sharing those insights.

20. Ibid., 367.

21. Mignolo, "La lengua, el territorio" (see n. 18), 141.

22. Ana Pizarro, *America Latina: palavra, literatura, cultura,* vol. 1: *A Situação Colonial* (Campinas, São Paulo: Editora da Unicamp, 1993). For a more traditional approach to colonial literary history, organized by authors, genres, and periods, see Oviedo, *Historia de la literatura hispanoamericana,* vol. 1: De los orígenes a la Emancipación, (see n. 4); and Roberto González Echevarría and Enrique Pupo-Walker, eds., *The Cambridge History of Latin American Literature,* vol. 1: *Discovery to Modernism* (Cambridge: Cambridge University Press, 1996). For a comparative history of Latin American literature, see Mario J. Valdés and Djelal Kadir, eds., *Literary Cultures of Latin America: A Comparative History,* 3 vols. (Cambridge: Oxford University Press, 2004).

23. Abel Posse, "La novela como nueva crónica de América: Historia y mito," in *De conquistados y conquistadores: Realidad, justificación, representación,* ed. Karl Kohut (Frankfurt: Vervuert, 1992), 249–55.

24. Novels on the rewriting of the discovery and conquest in the recent Spanish American novel (1978–2000) include the following. From Argentina, comes Abel Posse's *Daimón* (1978), *Los perros del paraíso* (1983), and *El largo atardecer del caminante* (1992); Juan José Saer's *El entenado* (1983); and Antonio Elio Brailovsky's *Esta maldita lujuria* (1991). From Colombia, comes Flor Romero's *Malintizín: La princesa regalada* (1999). From Cuba, comes Alejo Carpentier's *El arpa y la sombra* (1979) and Antonio Benítez Rojo's *El mar de las lentejas* (1979). From Mexico, comes Eugenio Aguirre's *Gonzalo Guerrero* (1980); Homero Aridjis's *1492, Vida y tiempos de Juan Cabezón de Castilla* (1985) and *Memorias del Nuevo Mundo* (1987); Armando Ayala Anguiano's *Cómo conquisté a los aztecas* (1990); Carmen Boullosa's *Llanto: Novelas imposibles* (1992), *Duerme* (1994), and *Cielos de la tierra* (1997); Luis Humberto Crosthwaite's *La luna siempre será un amor difícil* (1994); Olivier Debroise's *Crónica de las destrucciones* (1998); Carlos Fuentes's *Cristóbal Nonato* (1987); Mario Huacuja's *El viaje más largo* (1993); Marisol Martín del Campo's *Amor y conquista: La novela de Malinalli mal llamada la Malinche* (1999); Herminio Martinez's *Diario maldito de Nuño de Guzmán* (1990), *Las puertas del mundo: Una autobiografía hipócrita del Almirante* (1992), *Invasores del paraíso* (1998), and *El regreso* (1999); Otilia Meza's *Gonzalo Guerrero: Símbolo del mestizaje mexicano; Novela histórica* (1994); Eugenio Partida's *La ballesta de Dios* (1991); Ignacio Solares's *Nen, la inútil* (1994); and Carlos Villa Roiz's *Gonzalo Guerrero: Memoria olvidada; Trauma de México* (1995); from Nicaragua comes Rosario Aguilar's *La niña blanca y los pájaros sin pies* (1992). From Paraguay comes Augusto Roa Bastos's *Vigilia del Almirante*. From Uruguay, Alejandro Paternain's *Crónica del descubrimiento* (1982) and Napoleón Baccino Ponce de León's *Maluco: La novela de los descubridores* (1990). From Peru, Félix Álvarez Saenz's *Crónica de blasfemos* (1986); from Puerto Rico, Olga Nolla's *El castillo de la memoria* (1996) and Edgardo Rodríguez Juliá's *La noche oscura del niño Avilés* (1984). And from Venezuela, Miguel Otero Silva's *Lope de Aguirre, príncipe de la libertad* (1979). I agree with Kimberle S. López's assertion that the majority of New Historical novels that rewrite the conquest and colony still tend to privilege the perspective of the "great (European) men" of history, erasing and silencing the voices of women and Amerindians, despite the corpus's marked emphasis on marginality. López, *Latin American Novels* (see n. 11), 11–12.

25. For further discussion of the proliferation of the historical novel in Latin America, see Seymour Menton, *Latin America's New Historical Novel* (Austin: University of Texas

Press, 1993); Fernando Aínsa, "La reescritura de la historia en la nueva narrativa latinoamericana," *Cuadernos Americanos* (nueva época), 28 (1991): 13–31; María Cristina Pons, *La novela histórica de fines del siglo XX* (Mexico City: Siglo XXI, 1996), especially 83–109 and 254–69); and Juan José Barrientos, *Ficción-Historia: La nueva novela histórica hispanoamericana* (Mexico City: UNAM, 2001). Both Menton and Aínsa attempt to distinguish the New Historical novel from the traditional historical novel (à la Walter Scott). Menton enumerates the characteristics of such narratives, which include (1) the subordination, in varying degrees, of the mimetic re-creation of a given historical period to the illustration of three philosophical ideas, popularized by Borges and applicable to all periods of the past, present, and future—namely, the impossibility of ascertaining the true nature of reality or history, the cyclical nature of history, and the unpredictability of history; (2) the conscious distortion of history through omissions, exaggerations, and anachronisms; (3) the utilization of famous historical characters as protagonists, including Columbus, Magellan, Felipe II, Goya, Francisco de Miranda, Maximilian and Carlota, and Santos Dumont; (4) metafiction; (5) intertextuality; and (6) the Bakhtinian concepts of the dialogic, the carnivalesque, parody, and heteroglossia. Menton, *Latin America's New Historical Novel*, 23–24. Both Aínsa and Menton cite as paradigmatic examples of this trend Alejo Carpentier's *El arpa y la sombra* (1979), Antonio Benítez Rojo's *El mar de las lentejas* (1979), Mario Vargas Llosa's *La guerra del fin del mundo* (1981), Germán Espinosa's *La tejedora de coronas* (1982), Posse's *Los perros del paraíso,* and Fernando del Paso's *Noticias del imperio* (1987). Menton attributes the publication of so many historical novels between 1979 and 1992 to the awareness since the late 1970s of the approaching quincentennial of the discovery of America. Menton, *Latin America's New Historical Novel*, 27.

26. González Pérez, "Imágenes" (see n. 1), 446–47.

27. Ibid. Following González Pérez's lead, Margarita Graetzer examines the intertextual relations between the chronicles of the Indies and selected contemporary works of Spanish American literature. Specifically, Graetzer studies the issue of identity as it relates to el Inca Garcilaso de la Vega's *Comentarios reales* (1609/1617) and Benjamín Carrión's prose narrative *Atahualpa* (Ecuador, 1933); the topos of the voyage as journey of discovery as it appears in Cabeza de Vaca's *Los naufragios* (1542/1556) and Carpentier's *Los pasos perdidos* (Cuba, 1953); and different versions of the same historical event in Columbus's *Diario de a bordo* (1492) and Posse's *Los perros del paraíso* (Argentina, 1983). Margarita Graetzer, "'Crónicas de Indias' y narrativa hispanoamericana: Espacio de encuentros" (PhD diss., University of Texas, 1994).

28. She focuses on Juan José Saer's *El entenado,* Homero Aridjis's *1492* and *Memorias del Nuevo Mundo,* Herminio Martínez's *Diario maldito de Nuño de Guzmán,* and Abel Posse's *El largo atardecer del caminante* to illustrate how this subcorpus constitutes a new way for the empire to write back.

29. López, *Latin American Novels* (see n. 11), 26–27. The other published monograph pertaining to the discovery and conquest is Bart L. Lewis's *The Miraculous Lie: Lope de Aguirre and the Search for El Dorado in the Latin American Historical Novel* (2003). Lewis analyzes the representation of the figure of Lope de Aguirre in five novels published during the mid-to-late twentieth century: Arturo Uslar Pietri's *El camino de El Dorado* (Venezuela, 1947), Posse's *Daimón,* Miguel Otero Silva's *Lope de Aguirre, Príncipe de la libertad* (Venezuela, 1979), Jorge Ernesto Funes's *Una lanza por Lope de Aguirre* (Venezuela, 1984), and Félix Álvarez Sáenz's *Cróncia de blasfemos* (Peru, 1986). Lewis shows how these novels appropriate and give Lope de Aguirre a revisionist voice. Other studies that analyze the figure of Lope de Aguirre in Latin American literature include the dissertations by Amir Hamed and Consuelo Ramos Nadal.

Dissertations by Viviana Plotnik, Graciela Michelotti-Cristóbal, José Leandro Urbina,

Carrie Chorba, Victoria Eugenia Campos, María Esther Quintana, Ahna Bishop-Jara, Francisco Eduardo Porrata, and Sara Ann Smith examine various Latin American historical novels set in the period of the discovery and conquest. Articles by Juan José Barrientos, Raymond Souza, Fernando Reati, Seymour Menton, Roberto González Echevarría ("Colón, Carpentier"), Elzbieta Sklodowska, Donald Shaw, and many others do also. Several critical anthologies include articles on these novels, such as the volumes edited by Anna Housková and Martin Prochazka and by Julio Ortega and José Amor y Vásquez; and two collections edited by Karl Kohut. There is one book-length monograph by Antonio Usable González. A critical anthology of articles edited by Santiago Juan-Navarro and Theodore Robert Young examines the representation of the conquest of the Americas in Iberian and Ibero-American literature and film.

30. The criticism on the respective novels will be discussed in the individual chapters of this book.

31. The criticism on *El arpa y la sombra* and *Los perros del paraíso* will be discussed in chapter 4 of this book. On *El entenado* see María Victoria Albornoz, "Caníbales a la carta: Mecanismos de incorporación y digestión del 'otro' en *El entenado* de Juan José Saer," *Chasqui: Revista de Literatura Latinoamericana* 32, no. 1 (2003): 56–73; María Luisa Bastos, "Eficacias del verosímil no realista: Dos novelas recientes de Juan José Saer," *La Torre: Revista de la Universidad de Puerto Rico* 4, no. 13 (1990): 1–20; Susana Beatriz Cella, "Una heterología por plenitud: Acerca de *El entenado* de Juan José Saer y *1492: Vida y tiempos de Juan Cabezón de Castilla* de Homero Aridjis," *Literatura Mexicana* 2 (1991): 455–61; Amaryll Chanady, "Saer's Fictional Representation of the Amerindian in the Context of Modern Historiography," in *Amerindian Images and the Legacy of Columbus,* ed. René Jara and Nicholas Spadaccini (Minneapolis: University of Minnesota Press, 1992): 678–708; Rita De Grandis, "*El entenado* de Juan José Saer y la idea de historia," *Revista Canadiense de Estudios Hispánicos* 18, no. 3 (1994): 417–26; idem., "*The Witness* by Juan José Saer: Paratextuality and Post-Modernism," *Latin American Literary Review* 41 (1993): 30–40; Arcadio Díaz-Quiñones, "*El entenado:* Las palabras de la tribu," *Hispamérica* 21, no. 63 (1992): 3–14; Amy Fass Emery, *The Anthropological Imagination in Latin American Literature* (Columbia: University of Missouri Press, 1996); Florencia Garramuño, *Genealogías culturales: Argentina, Brasil y Uruguay en la novela contemporánea (1981–1991)* (Rosario: Viterbo, 1997); Rita Gnutzmann, "*El entenado* o la respuesta de Saer a las crónicas," *Iris* (1992): 23–36; Brian Gollnick, "'El color justo de la patria': Agencia discursiva en *El entenado* de Juan José Saer," *Revista de Crítica Literaria Latinoamercana* 39, no. 57 (2003): 107–24; López, *Latin American Novels;* Jorge Monteleone "Eclipse del sentido: De *Nadie nada nunca* a *El entenado* de Juan José Saer," in *La novela argentina de los años 80,* ed. Roland Spiller, 2nd ed. (Frankfurt: Vervuert, 1993), 153–76; Viviana P. Plotnik, "La reescritura del descubrimiento de América en cuatro novelas hispanoamericanas contemporáneas: Intertextualidad, carnaval y espectáculo" (PhD diss., New York University, 1993); María Cristina Pons, *La novela histórica de fines del siglo XX* (Mexico City: Siglo XXI, 1996); Julio Premat, "El eslabón perdido: *El entenado* en la obra de Juan José Saer," *Cahiers du Monde Hispanique et Luso Bresilien/Caravelle* 66 (1996): 75–93; Gabriel Riera, "La ficción de Saer: ¿Una 'antropología especulativa'? (Una lectura de *El entenado*)," *MLN* 111 (1996): 368–90; Evelia Romano Thuesen, "*El entenado:* Relación contemporánea de las memorias de Francisco del Puerto," *Latin American Literary Review* 23, no. 4 (January–June 1995): 43–63 and "La ocasión para narrar: Historia, realidad y alegoría en un texto de Juan José Saer," *Nueva Revista de Filología Hispánica* 47, no. 1 (1999): 99–119; Sara Ann Smith, "Lost-Body Writing in Latin America's Contemporary Historical Novel" (PhD diss., Michigan State University, 2001); and Gustavo Verdesio, "The Literary Appropriation of the

American Landscape: The Historical Novels of Abel Posse and Juan José Saer and Their Critics," in Bolaños and Verdesio, *Colonialism Past and Present* (see n. 16), 239–60.

CHAPTER 1. REWRITING THE *RELACIÓN* as Autobiography

1. For further biographical information on Ayala Anguiano and Posse, see Mark Frisch, "Armando Ayala Anguiano," in *Dictionary of Mexican Literature,* ed. Eladio Cortés (Westport, CT: Greenwood Press, 1992), 57–58; and Silvia Pites, "Entrevista con Abel Posse," *Chasqui* 22, no. 2 (1993): 120–28.

2. Manuel Medina, "El pasado en el presente: La historia en la novela mexicana (1980–1993)" (PhD diss., University of Kansas, 1994), 221.

3. Kimberle S. López, *Latin American Novels of the Conquest: Reinventing the New World,* (Columbia: University of Missouri Press, 2002), 114–15.

4. Richard A. Young, "Cabeza de Vaca en la literatura y el cine: Lectura y representación de un relato histórico," *Anclajes* 4, no. 4 (2000): 194.

5. Kerstin Bowsher, "Shipwrecks of Modernity: Abel Posse's *El largo atardecer del caminante,*" *Forum for Modern Language Studies* 38, no. 1 (2002): 88.

6. David Bost, "Reassessing the Past: Abel Posse and the New Historical Novel," in *La Chispa'95: Selected Proceedings,* ed. Gilbert Paolini (New Orleans: Tulane University Press, 1995), 41, 46; Lola Colomina-Garrigós, "La reescritura de la Historia y el peso de la conciencia histórica en *El largo atardecer del caminante,*" *Tropos* 27 (2001): 7–9.

7. Seymour Menton,"La historia verdadera de Álvar Núñez Cabeza de Vaca en la última novela de Abel Posse, *El largo atardecer del caminante,*" *Revista Iberoamericana* 52, no. 175 (1996): 422–23.

8. Angel García Ronda, "La melancolía del caminante," review of *El largo atardecer del caminante,* by Abel Posse, *Quimera* 86–87 (1993): 54–55.

9. Sylvia Molloy, *At Face Value: Autobiography in Spanish America* (Cambridge: Cambridge University Press, 1991), 1.

10. Ibid., 2.

11. Ibid., 3.

12. For an authoritative overview of scholarship on colonial Spanish American convent literature, see Kathleen Ann Myers, "Bibliographical Essay: Autobiographical Writing in Spanish-American Convents, 1650–1800," in *Word from New Spain: The Spiritual Autobiography of Madre María de San José (1656–1719)* (Liverpool: Liverpool University Press, 1993), 209–15; and Stacey Schlau, "Wanted, Dead (to the World): Autobiographical Narratives by Colonial Nun Authors Gerónima Nava y Saavedra and Ursula Suárez," in *Spanish American Women's Use of the Word: Colonial through Contemporary Narratives* (Tucson: University of Arizona Press, 2001), 3–26. Other studies on this topic include Kristine Ibsen, *Women's Spiritual Autobiography in Colonial Spanish America* (Gainesville: University of Florida Press, 1999); Kathryn Joy McKnight, *The Mystic of Tunja: The Writings of Madre Castillo, 1671–1742* (Amherst: University of Massachusetts Press, 1997); and Kathleen Myers, *Neither Saints nor Sinners: Writing the Lives of Women in Spanish America* (New York: Oxford University Press, 2003).

13. Molloy, *At Face Value* (see n. 9), 3.

14. Roberto González Echevarría, "Humanismo, retórica y las crónicas de la Conquista," in *Historia y ficción en la narrativa hispanoamericana: Coloquio de Yale,* ed. Roberto González Echevarría (Caracas: Monte Avila, 1984), 160.

15. Ibid.

16. The following draws on the summary of the contents of the five *cartas* in Angel Delgado Gómez, ed., *Cartas de relación,* by Hernán Cortés (Madrid: Clásicos Castalia, 1993), 37–51.

17. Ibid., 37.

18. Beatriz Pastor Bodmer, *The Armature of Conquest: Spanish Accounts of the Discovery of America, 1492–1589,* trans. Lydia Longstreth Hunt (Stanford, CA: Stanford University Press, 1992), 95.

19. Ibid.

20. Delgado Gómez, *Cartas de relación* (see n. 16), 57.

21. Ibid., 73.

22. For an annotated bibliography on editions of the *Cartas* from the sixteenth century to the twentieth, see ibid., 71–89.

23. Ibid., 41.

24. Armando Ayala Anguiano, *Cómo conquisté a los aztecas* (Mexico City: Diana, 1990), 5.

25. Ibid., 6. The portrait that appears in the novel is a cropped image of the painting that used to hang in the Ayuntamiento in Medellín, Badajoz, Extremadura (Spain) until it was destroyed during the Spanish Civil War (1936–39). In 1957, the Ayuntamiento commissioned Juan Aparicio Quintana to paint a replica of the original. ("Los retratos de Hernán Cortés," http://www.medellin.es/pretratos_cortes.htm#Weiditz). October 28, 2005. Courtesy of the Ayuntamiento de la Villa de Medellín.

26. Ibid., 11.

27. Ibid., 41.

28. Defenders of Cortés (pro-hispanistas) such as Lucas Alemán in the nineteenth century have glorified the conquest and viewed Cortés as a hero and messenger of Christianity, while detractors (pro-indigenistas) have denounced him as the destroyer of indigenous culture and cited poems and accounts from the vantage point of the conquered, "la visión de los vencidos." For further discussion of this issue, see José Luis Martínez, *Hernán Cortés* (Mexico City: Fondo de Cultura Económica, 1990), 832–36.

29. Ayala Anguiano, *Cómo conquisté* (see n. 24), 169.

30. Ibid., 159.

31. Ibid., 163. Courtesy of Princeton University Library, Rare Books Division, Department of Rare Books and Special Collections.

32. Ibid., 3.

33. Ibid., 7.

34. Ibid., 9.

35. Ibid., 146.

36. Ibid., 92.

37. Ibid., 18.

38. Ibid., 19. Courtesy of Armando Ayala Anguiano.

39. This summary of *Los naufraugios* draws heavily from Enrique Pupo-Walker's "Notas para la caracterización de un texto seminal: *Los naufragios* de Alvar Núñez Cabeza de Vaca," *Nueva Revista de Filología Hispánica* 28, no. 1 (1990): 166–71.

40. Enrique Pupo-Walker, ed., *Los naufragios,* by Alvar Núñez Cabeza de Vaca (Madrid: Castalia, 1993), 105–11.

41. Ibid., 90–91.

42. Ibid., 93–95.

43. For an extensive bibliography on Cabeza de Vaca and his writings, see ibid., 155–74; and Rolena Adorno and Patrick Charles Pautz, eds., *Alvar Núñez Cabeza de Vaca: His Ac-*

count, *His Life, and the Expedition of Pánfilo de Narváez,* vol. 3 (Lincoln: University of Nebraska Press, 1999), 383–417.

44. Pupo-Walker, *Los naufragios* (see n. 40), 103.

45. Non-Hispanic literary re-creations of the Cabeza de Vaca episode in the New World include: Walter Brooks Drayton Henderson, *The New Argonautica: An Heroic Poem in Eight Cantos of the Voyage among the Stars of the Immortal Spirits of Sir Walter Raleigh, Sir Frances Drake, Ponce de León, and Núñez da Vaca;* John Upton Terrell, *Journey into Darkness;* Helen Rand Parish, *Estebanico;* and Daniel Panger, *Black Ulysses.* Pupo-Walker, *Los naufragios* (see n. 40), 157–63; and Rolena Adorno, "The Negotiation of Fear in Cabeza de Vaca's *Naufragios,*" *Representations* 33 (1991): 193 n. 3.

46. Abel Posse, *El largo atardecer del caminante* (Buenos Aires: Emecé Editores, 1992), 38.

47. John Beverly, *Against Literature* (Minneapolis: University of Minnesota Press, 1993), 70–71.

48. Posse, *El largo atardecer* (see n. 46), 11.

49. Ibid., 12.

50. Ibid., 12.

51. Ibid., 53.

52. Ibid., 54.

53. Ibid., 65.

54. Ibid., 60.

55. Ibid., 69.

56. Ibid., 46.

57. Ibid., 30.

58. Ibid., 33. David Bost makes a similar point that that Oviedo's critique of the fictional Cabeza de Vaca's testimonial implies that the pen will vanquish the sword, and that in his capacity as the chronicler of the Indies (*cronista mayor de Indias*), Oviedo will create an image of the New World that will be accepted as truthful fact. Bost, "Reassessing the Past" (see n. 6), 42–43.

59. Posse, *El largo atardecer* (see n. 46), 34.

60. Ibid., 11.

61. Ibid., 45.

62. Ibid., 214.

63. Ibid., 152.

64. José Rabasa, "Allegory and Ethnography in Cabeza de Vaca's *Naufragios* and *Comentarios,*" in *Violence, Resistance and Survival in the Americas: The Legacy of Conquest,* ed. William B. Taylor and Franklin Pease (Washington, DC: Smithsonian Institute Press, 1993), 60.

65. Posse, *El largo atardecer* (see n. 46), 216.

CHAPTER 2. FICTIONAL MARGINAL FIGURES AND THE REWRITING OF THE NEW WORLD HISTORIOGRAPHY

1. For a discussion of sixteenth-, seventeenth-, and eighteenth-century texts that analyze the lands and peoples of the geographic zone north of the River Plate, see Gustavo Verdesio, *Forgotten Conquests: Rereading New World History from the Margins* (Philadelphia: Temple University Press), 2001.

2. Daniel B. Baker, *Explorers and Discoverers of the World* (Detroit: Gale Research, 1994), 370.

3. Cited in Martin Torodash, "Magellan's Historiography," *Hispanic American Historical Review* 51 (1971): 313.

4. Ibid., 313.

5. Antonello Gerbi, *Nature in the New World: From Christopher Columbus to Gonzalo Fernández de Oviedo,* trans. Jeremy Moyle (Pittsburgh: University of Pittsburgh Press, 1985), 101–2. For a further discussion of Peter Martyr and his *Decades,* see ibid., 50–75; and Edmundo O'Gorman, *Cuatro historiadores de Indias, siglo XVI: Pedro Mártir de Anglería, Gonzalo Fernández de Oviedo y Valdés, Fray Bartolomé de las Casas, Joseph de Acosta* (Mexico City: Alianza Editorial Mexicana, 1989), 13–40. On Antonio Pigafetta, see Gerbi, *Nature in the New World,* 100–116; Humberto E. Robles, "The First Voyage Around the World: From Pigafetta to García Márquez," *History of European Ideas* 6, no. 4 (1985): 385–404; and Leoncio Cabrero, *Primer viaje alrededor del mundo,* by Antonio de Pigafetta (Madrid: Historia 16, 1985), 7–47.

6. Gabriel García Márquez, "La soledad de América Latina," *Anthropos* 187 (1999) [1981]: 46–47.

7. Gabriel García Márquez, "The Solitude of Latin America (Nobel Lecture, 1982)," trans. Marina Castañeda, in *Gabriel García Márquez and the Powers of Fiction,* ed. Julio Ortega (Austin: University of Texas Press, 1988), 87.

8. Juana María Cordones-Cook, "Contexto y proceso creador de *Maluco: La novela de los conquistadores,*" *Chasqui* 22, no. 2 (1993): 104.

9. Cited in ibid., 103–4; and Rubén Acevedo, "'Maluco': Crónica de las desesperanzas y locuras de un bufón," review of *Maluco: La novela de los descubridores,* by Napoleón Baccino Ponce de León, *Revista Iberoamericana* 160–61 (1992): 1187.

10. Viviana P. Plotnik, "La reescritura del descubrimiento de América en cuatro novelas hispanoamericanas contemporáneas: Intertextualidad, carnaval y espectáculo" (PhD diss., New York University, 1993), 157–58.

11. Malva E. Filer, "*Maluco:* Re-escritura de los relatos de la expedición de Magallanes," in *Actas Irvine-92: Encuentros y desencuentros de culturas, Siglos XIX y XX,* ed. Juan Villegas (Irvine, CA: Regents of the University of California, 1994), 4:293.

12. Ibid., 294. Fernando Moreno Turner also focuses on how *Maluco* employs intertexuality to parody such discourses as the picaresque, thereby underscoring the subversive nature of the buffoon's rendition of Magellan's voyage. Fernando Moreno Turner, "Parodia, metahistoria y metaliteratura (En torno a *Maluco* de Napoleón Baccino Ponce de León)," *Hispamérica* 28, no. 82 (1999): 3. Ahna Bishop-Jara focuses on the novel's mythopoetic appropriation and deconstruction of the primary sources of the writing of the discovery and conquest. Ahna Bishop-Jara, "Metahistories: Constructions of Memory in Contemporary Latin American Fiction" (PhD diss., University of Minnesota, 2001), 45.

13. Filer, "*Maluco,*" 294. Florencia Garramuño regards the prologue of *Maluco* as a hyperbolic rewriting of the prologue of *Lazarillo de Tormes* in that Juanillo addresses his letter to Charles V just as Lazarillo addressed his letter to Your Highness ("su Alteza"). Florencia Garramuño, *Genealogías culturales: Argentina, Brasil y Uruguay en la novela contemporánea (1981–1991)* (Rosario: Viterbo, 1997), 59 n. 46.

14. Magdalena Perkowska-Alvarez also takes issue with Filer's argument that *Maluco* parodies the picaresque genre. Magdalena Perkowska-Alvarez, "Historias híbridas: El posmodernismo y la novela histórica latinoamericana, 1985–1995" (PhD diss., Rutgers University, 1997), 185. Furthermore, she argues that irony and humor are the principal strategies through which the novel puts into question the system of inclusion and exclusion that gov-

erns history and challenges the silences, omissions, and falsifications of the official history (187). While the studies of Cordones-Cook, Moreno Turner ("Parodia, metahistoria" [see n. 12]), Perkowska-Alvarez, Plotnik, and Hugo Verani ("Napoleón Baccino Ponce de León: La imaginación del Nuevo Mundo: La ficcionalización de la historia," in *De la vanguardia a la posmodernidad: Narrativa uruguaya (1925–1995)* [Montevideo: Ediciones Trilce, 1996], 207–22) take note of the figure of the professional buffoon as a key element in rewriting the expedition of Magellan, my study specifically locates this figure in the Spanish Golden Age tradition of buffonesque literature.

15. In Mateo de Alemán's *Guzmán de Alfarache* (part 2, chapter 1), the *pícaro* assumes the role of buffoon to the French ambassador in Rome. He cites as key elements for success the ability to act and to perform, the study of letters, and an excellent memory about people. Cited in Fernando Bouza, *Locos, enanos y hombres de placer en la corte de los austrias: oficio de burlas* (Madrid: Ediciones Temas de Hoy, 1991), 35.

16. Francisco Márquez Villanueva, "Literatura bufonesca o del loco," *Nueva Revista de Filología Hispánica* 24 (1985–86): 506–8.

17. Napoleón Baccino Ponce de León, *Maluco: La novela de los descubridores* (Barcelona: Seix Barral, 1990), 9.

18. For critical editions of this *Crónica,* see Diane Pamp de Valle Arce, ed., *Crónica burlesca del emperador Carlos V,* by Francesillo de Zúñiga (Barcelona: Edición Crítica, 1981); and José Sánchez Paso, ed., *Crónica burlesca del emperador Carlos V,* by Francesillo de Zúñiga (Salamanca, Spain: Europa Artes Gráficas, 1989).

19. Jean Franco, "The Nation as Imagined Community," in *The New Historicism,* ed. Aram Veeser (New York: Routledge, 1989), 211.

20. José Antonio Sánchez Paso, "La sociología literaria de don Francés de Zúñiga," *Nueva Revista de Filología Hispánica* 24 (1985–86): 850.

21. Jorge Mariscal, "A Clown at Court: Francesillo de Zúñiga's *Crónica burlesca,*" in *Autobiography in Early Modern Spain,* ed. Nicholas Spadaccini and Jenaro Taléns (Minneapolis: Prisma Institute, 1988), 61.

22. Ibid., 63.
23. Ibid.
24. Ibid., 67.
25. Ibid.
26. Ibid., 70.
27. Baccino, *Maluco* (see n. 17), 8.
28. Ibid., 7.
29. Nick Caistor, trans., *Five Black Ships: A Novel of the Discoverers,* by Napoleón Baccino Ponce de León (New York: Harcourt Brace and Company, 1994), 3.
30. Baccino, *Maluco* (see n. 17), 8.
31. Caistor, *Five Black Ships* (see n. 29), 4.
32. Baccino, *Maluco* (see n. 17), 8–9.
33. Caistor, *Five Black Ships* (see n. 29), 5.
34. Baccino, *Maluco* (see n. 17), 205–6.
35. Caistor, *Five Black Ships* (see n. 29), 221–22.
36. Baccino, *Maluco* (see n. 17), 25.
37. Caistor, *Five Black Ships* (see n. 29), 22.
38. Baccino, *Maluco* (see n. 17), 65–66.
39. Caistor, *Five Black Ships* (see n. 29), 64.
40. Baccino, *Maluco* (see n. 17), 75.
41. Caistor, *Five Black Ships* (see n. 29), 75.

42. Baccino, *Maluco* (see n. 17), 77.
43. Ibid.
44. Caistor, *Five Black Ships* (see n. 29), 77.
45. For further commentary on other aspects of the novel's historical and literary intertextual dimensions, see Moreno Turner ("Parodia, metahistoria" [see n. 12]), Esther Quintana ("Los pícaros, bufones y cronistas de *Maluco, la novela de los descubridores*" [PhD diss., University of California, Berkeley, 1998] and "El bufón como narrador: *Maluco: La novela de los descubridores*," in *Pensamiento y crítica : Los discursos de la cultura hoy*, ed. Manuel F. Medina [East Lansing: Michigan State University, 2000], 123–38); and Cynthia Vich ("El diálogo intertextual en *Maluco*," *Revista Iberoamericana* 63, no. 180 [1997]: 405–18).
46. Baccino, *Maluco* (see n. 17), 99–103.
47. Ibid., 196.
48. Caistor, *Five Black Ships* (see n. 29), 210.
49. Vich cites the story about the Duchess Rosinalda as one example of the "marvelous real" dimensions of the novel as in Gabriel García Márquez's *Cien años de soledad*. Vich, 'El diálogo intertextual" (see n. 45), 411.
50. Esther Quintana also argues that *Maluco* re-creates metaphorically the situation of repression and censorship under the Uruguayan dictatorship of the 1970s and 1980s. Just as Juanillo suffers from the censorship of the Spanish Inquisition, intellectuals in Uruguay had to avoid political topics in order not be imprisoned or expelled from the country. Quintana, "Los pícaros, bufones y cronistas" (see n. 45), 2.
51. For a reading of the novel as an extended metaphor about the process of human self-discovery, see María Luisa Luján Campos, "*Maluco* y la pendularidad de sus opuestos," in *Historia, ficción y metaficción en la novela latinoamericana contemporánea*, ed. Mignon Domínguez (Buenos Aires: Ediciones Corregidor, 1996), 69–90.
52. For Brailovsky's studies of ecology and the environment, see *Agua y medio ambiente en Buenos Aires* (1992), *El ambiente en la Constitución de la Ciudad de Buenos Aires* (1996), *El ambiente en la sociedad colonial* (1997), *El ambiente en la Constitución de Buenos Aires* (1996), *Buenos Aires, ciudad inundable* (1994), *La ecología en la Biblia: Un análisis del vínculo con la naturaleza en el texto bíblico* (1993), *La ecología y el futuro argentino* (1992), *Ecos del sur: Otra versión de lo ecológico* (1994), *Memoria verde: Historia ecológica de la Argentina* (1991), *Naturaleza y vida: Propuesta de educación ambiental* (1994), *El negocio de envenenar* (1988), *La situación ambiental en la Argentina en la década de 1970* (1982), *¿Qué hacemos con la basura?* (1994), *¿Qué le pasa al agua?* (1994), *¿Se puede respirar el aire?* (1994), and *Verde contra verde: Las difíciles relaciones entre la economía y la ecología* (1993). On the Argentine economy, see *Historia de las crisis argentinas* (1982), revised and updated as *Historia de las crisis argentinas: Un sacrificio inútil* in 1996. For additional biographical information about Brailovsky, see the following articles by Clark M. Zlotchew: "Entrevista con Antonio Brailovsky," *Alba de América: Revista Literaria* 5, nos. 8–9 (1988): 371–83; "Opresión, libertad y la magia: Entrevista con Antonio Elio Brailovsky,"*Hispania* 71 (1988): 595–97; "Problematic Identity in Brailovsky's *Identidad*," *Yiddish* 9, no. 1 (1993): 111–21; and "La segunda Jerusalem de la Nueva Sefarad de las Indias: *Identidad* de A. E. Brailovsky," *Noa h* 7–8 (1992): 96–105.
53. As Fernando Moreno Turner has noted, the myth of La Ciudad de los Césares has been the subject of numerous Latin American narratives: Roberto Payró's *Los tesoros del Rey Blanco, Por qué no fue descubierta la maravillosa Ciudad de los Césares* (1935), Hugo Silva's *Pacha Pulai* (1938), and Manuel Mújica Laínez's short story "La ciudad encantada"

in his *Misteriosa Buenos Aires* (1950). He further argues that such narratives follow the established historiographic model to narrate the founding of Los Césares, which serves as a pretext for elaborating the construction of historical periods. Fernando Moreno Turner, "La ciudad, el mito, la historia: En torno a *Esta maldita lujuria* de Antonio E. Brailovsky," *Licorne* 34 (1995): 280.

54. Antonio Elio Brailovsky, Esta maldita lujuria (Havana: Casa de las Américas, 1990), 11.
55. Sara Almarza, *Pensamiento crítico hispanoamericano: Arbitristas del siglo XVIII* (Madrid: Pliegos, 1990), 17–18.
56. Andrés Avellaneda, "Argentina militar: los discursos del silencio," in *Literatura argentina hoy: De la dictadura a la democracia,* ed. Karl Kohut and Andrea Pagini, 2nd ed. (Frankfurt: Vervuert, 1993), 14–15.
57. Fernando Reati, "Posse, Saer, Di Benedetto y Brailovsky: Deseo y paraíso en la novela argentina sobre la Conquista," *Revista de Estudios Hispánicos* 19, no. 1 (1995): 128.
58. Ibid., 132. Moreno Turner examines the role of the Ciudad de los Césares myth in the novel and interprets the novel as contemporary historiographic metafiction. Moreno Turner, "La ciudad, el mito" (see n. 53), 281.
59. David Rock, *Argentina, 1516–1987: From Spanish Colonization to Alfonsín* (Berkeley and Los Angeles: University of California Press, 1987), 8.
60. Antonio Elio Brailovsky, *Esta maldita lujuria* (Havana: Casa de las Américas, 1990), 106.
61. Ibid., 105–6.
62. Ibid., 15.
63. Ibid., 15–16.
64. Rock, *Argentina* (see n. 59), 10.
65. Brailovsky, *Esta maldita lujuria* (see n. 60), 95.
66. Ibid., 96.
67. Ibid., 93.
68. Ibid., 97.
69. Ibid., 35.
70. Ibid., 34.
71. Ibid., 35.
72. Ibid., 40.
73. Ibid., 64.
74. Ibid., 65.
75. Ibid., 36.
76. Ibid., 36–37.
77. Ibid., 38.
78. Ibid.
79. Ibid.
80. Ibid.
81. Ibid., 17.
82. Ibid.
83. Ibid., 18.
84. Ibid.
85. Ibid., 17.
86. Ibid., 27.
87. Ibid., 66–67.

88. Ibid., 66.
89. Barry Gough, *The Falkland Islands/Malvinas: The Contest for Empire in the South Atlantic* (London: Athlone Press, 1992), 20.
90. Ibid., 20–21.
91. Ibid., 23.
92. Ibid., 26–27.
93. Brailovsky, *Esta maldita lujuria* (see n. 60), 76.
94. Zlotchew, "Entrevista con Antonio Brailovsky" (see n. 52), 382.
95. Luis Fernando Valente, "Fiction as History: The Case of João Ubaldo Ribeiro," *Latin American Research Review* 28, no. 1 (1993): 41.

CHAPTER 3. REWRITING STORIES ABOUT VILIFIED FIGURES

1. Manuel F. Medina, "El pasado en el presente. La historia en la novela mexicana (1980–1993)" (PhD diss., University of Kansas, 1994), 41. Other novels by Aguirre include *Jesucristo Pérez* (1973), *Pajar de imaginación* (1975), *El caballero de las espadas* (1978), *El testamento del diablo* (1982), *En el campo* (1983), *Pájaros de fuego* (1984), *Segunda persona* (1984), *Cadáver exquisito* (1985), *El rumor que llegó del mar* (1986), *La suerte de la fea* (1986), *Amor de mis amores* (1988), *Pasos de sangre* (1988), *El canto de las aguas* (1991), *Los niños de colores* (1993), *Elena, o, el laberinto de la lujuria* (1994), *La fascinación de la bestia* (1994), *Desierto ardiente* (1995), and *El hombre baldío* (1998).

2. For a detailed discussion of the creation and circulation of the Gonzalo Guerrero tale in sixteenth- and seventeenth-century chronicles, see Rolena Adorno, "La estatua de Gonzalo Guerrero en Akumal: Iconos culturales y la reactualización del pasado colonial," *Revista Iberoamericana* 176–77 (1996), especially 912–23; and José Antonio Rico Ferrer, "Gonzalo Guerrero: La frontera del imaginario español," *Cuadernos Americanos* 81 (May–June 2000): 169–92.

3. Guzmán's conflicts with Cortés as well as Cortés's allies among the Franciscan order are legendary. The political rivalry between Guzmán and Cortés began in 1528, when Charles V appointed Guzmán president of the *Primera audiencia* of New Spain. Although the Primera audiencia was publicly charged with promoting stability by arranging the granting of *encomiendas* in perpetuity, Guzmán bungled the opportunity to institute a permanent *encomienda* system and ignored instructions. Though forbidden to hold Indians, he used his official position as an opportunity to appropriate for himself, his friends, and relatives innumerable villages in *encomienda*. Peggy K. Liss, *Mexico under Spain, 1521–1556: Society and the Origins of Nationality,* (Chicago: University of Chicago Press, 1975), 51–52. He also made other grants and revoked them at will, forced Indians to work in labor mines and on private projects, and enslaved large numbers of them. The Primera audiencia, instead of assuming a mediating posture above local interest and of reflecting the royal position, pursued self-interest directly among the Spanish factions in New Spain (52).

As to his clashes with the Franciscans and Zumárraga, such conflicts originated over the question of their respective judicial authority. Zumárraga had been appointed protector of the Indians and inquisitor of New Spain by the crown, and both of these positions carried a judicial function and responsibility. (In Mexico City, Zumárraga initiated court proceedings to hear Amerindian complaints about Spanish atrocities, including those against Guzmán.) These activities, however, overlapped with the civil jurisdiction of the Primera audiencia. The resulting jurisdictional ambiguity was the primary reason for Guzmán's frequent and violent clashes with Zumárraga. Bernardino Verástique, *Michoacán and Eden: Vasco de*

Quiroga and the Evangelization of Western Mexico (Austin: University of Texas Press, 2000), 77.

4. While Guzmán was on this expeditionary campaign, Queen Isabel named him governor of Nueva Galicia (Jalisco) in 1531 and appointed the Segunda audiencia of New Spain, a body that overturned many of Guzmán's decisions. In 1532 the Segunda audiencia reprimanded Guzmán for his conquest of Colima and stripped him of his governorship of Pánuco. In 1536 Guzmán decided to return to Spain, where he would ask the crown for absolution or punishment for his alleged misdeeds. While he was passing through Mexico City en route to Spain, Diego Pérez de la Torre—the judge of the Segunda residencia and Guzmán successor as governor of Nueva Galicia—arrested him for his mismanagement as governor of Pánuco and as president of the Primera Audiencia. José Rogelio Alvarez, "Guzmán, Nuño de," in *Enciclopedia de México* (Mexico City: SEP, 1987). Guzmán lived in the house of Viceroy Antonio de Mendoza until his 1537 arrest and incarceration in the public jail in Mexico City. In 1538 royal authorities recalled him to Spain, where he endured a form of house arrest until his death in the 1550s, somewhere between 1550 and 1558. Nuño de Guzmán spent his final years a bitter and sickly man, one of the great losers in the battles that occurred as the Spaniards fought over their newly seized wealth. James Krippner-Martínez, *Rereading the Conquest: Power, Politics, and the History of Early Colonial Michoacán, Mexico, 1521–1565* (University Park: Pennsylvania State University Press, 2001), 44–45.

5. Krippner-Martínez, *Rereading the Conquest* (see n. 4), 9. The execution of the Cazonci, which has long been considered one of the most infamous events of the conquest of Mexico, culminated a series of encounters between Spanish conquistadors (mainly Cortés and Guzmán) and the Cazonci.

6. The Spaniard Julián Juderías originally coined the term "black legend" in his book *La leyenda negra y la verdad histórica* (1914). William S. Maltby, "Black Legend," in *Encyclopedia of Latin American History and Culture* ed. Barbara A. Tenenbaum (New York: Charles Scribner's Sons, 1996). The author of revisionist works on a variety of topics, Juderías was convinced that Spain and its culture had been systematically vilified by foreign authors who were inspired by Protestantism or the Enlightenment. His book, which was popular in Spain, defends Spanish accomplishments. In 1944 the Argentine scholar Rómulo Carbia applied the concept to the historical treatment of the Spanish conquest of America and linked the black legend specifically to the work of Bartolomé de las Casas, whose *Brevísima relación de la destrucción de las Indias* had been widely circulated in translation since the sixteenth century. Maltby, "Black Legend". For Carbia, Las Casas had exaggerated the brutality of the conquest in an effort to secure improved treatment for the Indians, and in the process, he had provided Spain's political and religious enemies with a source of propaganda. Like Juderías, Carbia was primarily interested in defending the Spanish record. Maltby, "Black Legend."

The black legend as a body of literature that portrays Spain, its history, and its people in a consistently unfavorable light has achieved a measure of acceptance in the non-Hispanic world. It has resulted in a widespread perception that the Spanish people were uniquely cruel, lazy, bigoted and ignorant, and that their culture had contributed little to Western civilization. Maltby, "Black Legend." If few scholars would now argue that Spain's reputation and conduct in the New World were beyond reproach, fewer still would claim that it was uniquely reprehensible, especially in comparison to the behavior of other imperialist powers from the same time period. Nuño de Guzmán shares center stage with another conquistador, Lope de Aguirre (1513?–1561), as human incarnations of the black legend. Lope de Aguirre was the self-proclaimed rebel leader of an ill-fated descent of the Amazon River in search for El Dorado. He was a soldier from Oñate, in the province of Guipuzcoa, Spain, who joined the Pedro de Ursúa expedition to the Amazon. Aguirre was one of the instigators of a plot to assassinate Ursúa, and at first supported Fernando de Guzmán (no relation to Nuño de Guzmán) to replace the slain Ursúa. As the group traveled downstream, discipline disintegrated, Indian carriers were abandoned, and an increasing number of men were killed in brawls. Noble David Cook, "Aguirre, Lope de," in Tenenbaum, ed. *Encyclopedia*. Aguirre captained Fernando de Guzmán's militia, heading fifty Basque harquebusiers. Paranoid and filled with delusions of grandeur, Aguirre cowed followers and massacred Fernando de Guzmán and others suspected of disloyalty. Challenging the authority of king and church, Aguirre argued that the land belonged to the conquerors. His unrealistic goal was to descend the Amazon, sail northwestward until he could attack Spanish authorities in Peru frontally, then assume the land's administration. Shortly after he reached the Venezuelan coast, however, royal supporters surrounded his encampment. Aguirre killed his own daughter to prevent her capture. Cook, "Aguirre, Lope de."

The Lope de Aguirre episode is one of the bloodiest and most controversial expeditions of the Age of Discovery. By the end of the nineteenth century Lope de Aguirre had become the prototype of the Spanish oppressor. For further discussion of the representation of Lope de Aguirre in Latin American literature, see Amaryll Chanady, "Abel Posse and the Rewriting of the Aguirre Myth," in *Latin American Postmodernisms,* ed. Richard A. Young (Amsterdam: Rodopi, 1997), 175–87; Ingrid Galster, "El conquistador Lope de Aguirre en la Nueva Novela Histórica," in *La invención del pasado: La novela histórica en el marco de la posmodernidad,* ed. Karl Kohut (Frankfurt: AEY, 1997), 196–204; Bart Lewis, *The Miraculous Lie: Lope de Aguirre and the Search for El Dorado in the Latin American Historical Novel* (Lanham, MD: Lexington Books, 2003) and Consuelo Ramos-Nadal, "Las crónicas como forjadoras de una tradición literaria en la figura de Lope de Aguirre" (PhD diss., University of Massachusetts, Amherst, 1997). For an analysis of Lope de Aguirre in Werner Herzog's 1972 film *Aguirre, the Wrath of God* (Peru and Germany), see John E. Davidson, "As Others Put Plays Upon the Stage: *Aguirre,* Neocolonialism, and the New German Cinema," *New German Critique* 60 (1993): 101–32; Thomas H. Holloway, "Whose Conquest Is This, Anyway? *Aguirre, the Wrath of God,*" in *Based on a True Story: Latin American History at the Movies,* ed. Donald F. Stevens (Wilmington, DE: Scholarly Resources, 1997), 29–46; and Lutz P. Koepnick, "Colonial Forestry: Sylvan Politics in Werner Herzog's *Aguirre* and *Fitzcarraldo,*" *New German Critique* 60 (1993): 133–60.

7. In a chapter entitled "De la Nueva España, y Pánuco y Jalisco," Las Casas denounces Guzmán for exchanging Indians for cattle while he was resident governor of Pánuco, and for torturing and executing the Cazonci during the conquest of Michoacán.

8. Krippner-Martínez, *Rereading the Conquest* (see n. 4), 39. Generations of Mexican intellectuals have depicted Guzmán as an exceptional figure, sometimes even as a tyrant, deviant, or psychopath. In the nineteenth century, the historian Joaquín García Icazbalceta elaborated on Las Casas's unfavorable image of Guzmán in *Don fray Juan de Zumárraga: Primer obispo y arzobispo de México* (1881). Icazbalceta remarks on Guzmán's:

> índole perversa, desmedida codicia e insaciable sed de mando. [. . .] Guzmán que pudo haber alcanzado alto renombre en la conquista, donde mostró dotes de buen capitán y sobre todo una asombrosa energía, junta con una constancia a toda prueba, no ha dejado memoria sino de tiranía y crueldad. Joaquín García Icazbalceta, *Don fray Juan de Zumárraga, primer obispo y arzobispo de México* (1881; reprint Mexico City: Porrúa, [1947], 39 and 78.)

> [perverse nature, limitless avarice, and insatiable thirst to control. . . . Guzmán could have attained renown in the conquest, for he exhibited the characteristics of an effective captain. Above all, he had

boundless energy and was obstinate in the face of substantial adversity. Instead, he is remembered only for his tyrannical and cruel nature.]

In the twentieth century, José López-Portillo y Weber in *La conquista de la Nueva Galicia* (1935) and Manuel Toussaint in *La conquista de Pánuco* (1948) discussed Guzmán in the context of alleged Spanish excesses during the conquest. López-Portillo wrote that the conquistador was "feroz, codicioso, cruel, impío, lascivo, cínico, avaro y calumniador, [. . .] fue pura sombra [. . .]" José López-Portillo y Weber, *La conquista de la Nueva Galicia* [Mexico City: Talleres Gráficas de la Nación, 1935], 134 [vicious, greedy, cruel, impious, lascivious, cynical, avaricious, slanderous . . . pure darkness. . . .]. Toussaint echoes a similarly negative assessment: "[D]espués de muerto conserva Nuño la execración universal, la memoria de algo funesto, de una pesadilla dantesca [. . .]" [after his death Nuño is remembered with universal abhorrence, as something deplorable, a Dantesque nightmare]. (Manuel Toussaint, *La conquista de Pánuco* [Mexico City: Colegio Nacional, 1948] 134).

These images of Guzmán—while containing elements of truth—inaccurately tend to cast Guzmán's behavior in terms of exceptionality, thus reproducing a bias embedded in the historical record itself. As James Krippner-Martínez has pointed out, one of the primary ways one discredited a rival during the founding of the Spanish colonial order was to accuse him of being exceptionally abusive or violent. Krippner-Martínez, *Rereading the Conquest* (see n. 4), 38–39. When one engaged in similar activities, this had the benefit of establishing moral distance between truly evil excess and one's own behavior. The attack figure provided a symbolic foil, an example of someone whose behavior was truly deviant, thus legitimating less-"excessive" actions (39). For example, Francisco López de Gómara, the personal secretary of Cortés, authored a history of the Spanish conquest extremely favorable to his patron. In it he lamented that Guzmán had burned "King Cazoncin, friend of Cortés, servant of Spaniards and vassal of the Emperor, and who was in peace" (39). In a similar way Zumárraga would write to the king that Guzmán needed to repent to the church for his activities as a slave trader. This was despite the fact that Zumárraga himself possessed both slaves and Indian vassals (39). The written evidence left by such men as Gómara and Zumárraga long served as the basis for the historical understanding of the conquest generation, which explains how the political context of early Spanish colonialism shaped the representation of Guzmán found in the documentation of this period (38–39).

Only recently have North American historians Donald E. Chipman (1967), in a monograph on Guzmán's tenure as governor of Pánuco, and J. Benedict Warren (1985), on the conquest of western Mexico, sought to challenge Guzmán's immutable reputation for excessive cruelty in the New World. Both argue that while Guzmán did engage in brutal activities, his behavior was quite similar to that of other conquistadors. Thus, he did not deserve the particular opprobrium that had been heaped upon his name. Krippner-Martínez, however, criticizes Chipman and Warren for their inability to break out of the either/or dichotomy of "black and white" legends of Spanish colonialism. While both historians show that the historical image of Guzmán is flawed, there is little about his activities that can be described as benign, or even less than brutal. Krippner-Martínez, *Rereading the Conquest* (see n. 4), 41–42.

9. Benjamin Keen, *The Aztec Image in Western Thought* (New Brunswick, NJ: Rutgers University Press, 1971), 528.

10. Desmond Rochfort, *Mexican Muralists: Orozco, Rivera, Siqueiros* (San Francisco: Chronicle Books, 1998), 44.

11. Ibid., 46.

12. Frances Karttunen, "La Malinche and Malinchismo," in *Encyclopedia of Mexico*, vol. 2, ed. Michael S. Weiner (Chicago: Fitzroy Publishers, 1997).

13. Octavio Paz, "Hernán Cortés: Exorcismo y liberación," in *México en la obra de Octavio Paz: El peregrino en su patria; Historia y política de México*, ed. Octavio Paz and Luis Mario Schneider (Mexico City: Fondo de Cultura Económica, 1987), 1:105.

14. Ibid., 106.

15. Rolando J. Romero, "Text, Pre-texts, Con-texts: Gonzalo Guerrero in the Chronicles of the Indies," *Revista de Estudios Hispánicos* 26, no. 3 (1992): 363.

16. Guerrero also has been the subject of two other Mexican novels: Otilia Meza's *Un amor inmortal: Gonzalo Guerrero, Símbolo de origen del mestizaje mexicano; Novela histórica* (1994) and Carlos Villa Roiz's *Gonzalo Guerrero: Memoria olvidada, trauma de México* (1995). Meza, a writer of romantic love stories involving figures from the conquest of Mexico, supports the idea of Guerrero as the father of Mexican *mestizaje*, when she notes in the novel's epilogue that Gonzalo Guerrero is "el origen de nuestro mestizaje, . . . desconocido por muchos mexicanos [. . .]" (*Un amor inmortal* [Mexico City: Alpe, 1994], 140) [the origin of our *mestizaje* . . . unbeknownst to many Mexicans . . .] and substantiates claims about the existence of the so-called *Memorias de Gonzalo de Guerrero* (which I will describe below). Villa Roiz, a Mexican journalist who based his novel on chronicles about Guerrero and the conquest of Yucatán, narrates Guerrero's story from the vantage point of his mestiza daughter and that of Guerrero himself.

Guerrero's story, buried in sixteenth-century Spanish chronicles, resurfaced when the Mexico City newspaper *El Universal* featured a series of articles on secondary figures from the conquest. In 1975 Editorial Jus published two thousand copies of *Gonzalo de Guerrero: Padre del mestizaje iberomexicano* by Mario Aguirre Rosas, editor of *El Universal*. The narrative, drawing on Aguirre Rosas's access to and reading of Gonzalo Guerrero's so-called memoirs (*Memorias de Gonzalo de Guerrero*)—then in the possession of an antiquities collector named José López Pérez—consists of a preface and three parts, which in turn are divided into nineteen chapters.

In the preface, entitled "Reportazgo de Altura," an Alfonso Taracena laments the apathy of Mexican journalists and academic scholars in learning more about Mexican culture in general and the Guerrero story in particular. Taracena regards episodes from Guerrero's *Memorias* as "hazañas" (Mario Aguirre Rosas, *Gonzalo de Guerrero: Padre del mestizaje iberomexicano* [Mexico City: Jus, 1975], 6) [findings] that would shed new light on various aspects of Mayan culture. Part 1 (chapters 1–9) summarizes the content from the first part of the *Memorias*, which consists of thirty sheets *(folios)* bound in deerskin and is characterized by Aguirre Rosas as a "crónica novelesca" (Aguirre Rosas, *Gonzalo Guerrero*, 55) [novelesque chronicle]. In these chapters he dubs Guerrero "el padre del mestizaje" (11) [the father of our *mestizaje*], regards the *Memorias*, second only to Columbus's *Diario de a bordo*, as the first document written in Spanish and from the Americas, and tells Guerrero's life, beginning in 1511. Part 2 (chapters 10–16), written on paper allegedly supplied by a Spaniard named José de Villavicencio, alludes to the presence of Hernán Cortés and his troops after the fall of Tenochtitlán. This part focuses on Guerrero's recollection of the episode in which Cortés's soldiers unsuccessfully attempted to persuade him to rejoin them, his decision to teach the Mayas how to make firearms, his explanation of the Mayans' conception of time and space, including their use of hieroglyphics, and celebrations related to the birth of his fifth child. Part 3 (chapters 17–19), the briefest section of the manuscript and written on six folios that Francisco de Montejo had given him, recapitulates selected events from the conquest of the Aztecs and the arrival of Montejo in the Yucatán Peninsula. Stylistically, in all chapters of *Gonzalo de Guerrero*, Aguirre Rosas's role parallels that of

Bartolomé de las Casas, transcriber and editor of Columbus's *Diario de a bordo*. As Las Casas paraphrases passages from the *Diario,* inserts quotation marks around the words of the Admiral, and comments on the *Diario* in the margins, Aguirre de Rosas inserts editorial comments about the style and history of the *Memorias,* modernizes the orthography of the manuscript, and at others times, maintains the original orthography.

Aguirre Rosas's book provides the earliest available documented evidence of the notion of Gonzalo Guerrero as the father of Mexican *mestizaje*. In 1994, the Universidad Autónoma de Yucatán published Fray Joseph de San Buenaventura's *Historias de la conquista del Mayab, 1511–1697,* written between 1724 and 1725. San Buenaventura was a Franciscan friar based in Mérida, and based on his discovery of so-called writings of Gonzalo Guerrero (purported memoirs written on deerskin and partly on European paper supplied later by conquerors) and other indigenous reports, he composed a narrative about Spanish and Mayan history at the beginning of the seventeenth century. Supposedly, a copy of this account was discovered 269 years later in the Centro de Estudios de Historia de Mexico CONDUMEX in Mexico City. Rose Anna Mueller, "From Cult to Comics: The Representation of Gonzalo Guerrero as a Cultural Hero in Mexican Popular Culture," in *A Twice-Told Tale: Reinventing the Encounter in Iberian/Iberian American Literature and Film,* ed. Santiago Juan-Navarro and Theodore Robert Young (Newark: University of Delaware Press, 2001), 146.

As Meza, Villa Roiz, and Aguirre Rosas correctly assert, the notion of Gonzalo Guerrero as the father of Mexican miscegenation never achieved widespread currency or acceptance among elite audiences. In monographs devoted to miscegenation in Mexico, little, if any, space is devoted to explaining how Guerrero became known as the originator of *mestizaje,* which is seen traditionally as having been originated by Cortés and Malinche. For further discussion of Gonzalo Guerrero in Mexican popular culture (the 1992 comic book *Conquistadores en Yucatán: La descripción de Gonzalo Guerrero,* Guerrero statues in Akumal and Mérida, and murals in Mérida), see Rose Anna Mueller,"From Cult to Comics."

17. Medina, *El pasado en el presente* (see n. 1), 42–43.

18. Ibid., 45. Medina's analysis of *Gonzalo Guerrero* has been published in article form. See his "Buscando el origen del mestizaje en las crónicas: Eugenio Aguirre re-crea a Gonzalo Guerrero," *Confluencia: Revista Hispánica de Cultura y Literatura* 11, no. 1 (1995): 148–62; or Medina, "La revisión de la historia: Re-creando a Gonzalo Guerrero en la novela de Eugenio Aguirre," in *Más de 500 años de cultura en México,* ed. Lilia Granillo Vázquez (Mexico City: Universidad Autónoma Metropolitana Azcapotzalco, 1994), 357–76.

19. Alice Ruth Reckley, "Irony and License in New Memories of the Conquest: Gonzalo Guerrero," *Symposium* 46, no. 2 (1992): 133.

20. Ibid.

21. Monique Sarfati-Arnaud, "Gonzalo Guerrero, de la crónica a la novela," *Texto Crítico* 16 (1990): 97–98. In *Visión de los vencidos* (1957)—a compilation of indigenous narrations of the conquest—Miguel León Portilla coined the expression to refer to indigenous populations that the Spanish conquistadors defeated.

22. Sarfati-Arnaud, "Gonzalo Guerrero" (see n. 21), 104.

23. Jorge Klor de Alva, "The Postcolonialization of the (Latin) American Experience: A Reconsideration of 'Colonialism,' 'Postcolonialism,' and 'Mestizaje,'" in *After Colonialism: Imperial Histories and Postcolonial Displacements,* ed. Gyan Prakash (Princeton, NJ: Princeton University Press, 1995), 250. For further analysis of the conservative elements of *mestizaje,* see especially his 248–54. For further discussion of Latin America's experience of *mestizaje* through literature, the visual and performing arts, social commentary, and music, see Marilyn Grace Miller, *Rise and Fall of the Cosmic Race: The Cult of Mestizaje in Latin America* (Austin: University of Texas Press, 2004).

24. For an in-depth discussion of the ascendancy of the ideology of *mestizaje* after the Mexican Revolution, see Alan Knight, "Racism, Revolution, and Indigenismo: Mexico, 1910–1940," in *The Idea of Race in Latin America, 1870–1940,* ed. Richard Graham (Austin: University of Texas Press, 1990), 71–113.

25. In fact, in the 1990s, the mestizo's sole claim to Mexican national identity has begun to erode, at least rhetorically. In 1992 the administration of former president Carlos Salinas de Gotari, in response to pressures from national and international indigenous groups and human-rights observers, reformed Article 4 of the Constitution of 1917. The first paragraph now reads as follows:

> The Mexican Nation has a pluricultural composition, originally based on its indigenous peoples. The law will protect and promote the development of their languages, cultures, uses, customs, resources and specific forms of social organization and will guarantee their members effective access to the jurisdiction of the State. (Ctd. in Stephen E. Lewis, "Mestizaje," *Encyclopedia of Mexico,* vol. 2 [Chicago: Fitzroy Publishers, 1997].)

Never before had the postrevolutionary state admitted that nonmestizos also have a claim to a Mexican national identity. Yet while this reform appears to represent a major shift away from mestizo revolutionary nationalism, it remains nothing more than a symbolic gesture. The Mexican constitution is more a statement of principles than a binding legal and political document. Until regulatory laws are passed that specify how the article is to be implemented, the reformed article 4 has no force. Lewis, "Mestizaje."

26. Eugenio Aguirre, *Gonzalo Guerrero* (Mexico city: Diana, 1991), 16.
27. Ibid., 24.
28. Ibid., 26.
29. Ibid., 40.
30. Ibid., 61.
31. Ibid., 94.
32. Ibid., 99.
33. Ibid., 71.
34. Ibid., 72.
35. Ibid., 134.
36. Ibid., 147.
37. Ibid., 150–51.
38. Ibid., 178.
39. Ibid., 221.
40. Ibid., 134.
41. Sarfati-Arnaud, "Gonzalo Guerrero," (see n. 21), 103.
42. Aguirre, *Gonzalo Guerrero* (see n. 26), 116–17.
43. Carrie C. Chorba, "Metaphors of Mestizo Mexico: New Narrative Rewritings of the Conquest" (PhD diss., Brown University, 1998), 1.
44. Ibid., 2.
45. Ibid.
46. Seymour Menton, Review of *Diario maldito de Nuño de Guzmán,* by Herminio Martínez, *Hispania* 74, no. 2 (1991): 330.
47. Kimberle S. López, "Eros and Colonization: Homosexual Colonial Desire and the Gendered Rhetoric of Conquest in Herminio Martínez's *Diario maldito de Nuño de Guzmán,*" in *Latin American Novels of the Conquest: Reinventing the New World* (Columbia: University of Missouri Press, 2002), 95.

48. The location in which Guzmán composed his *relación* and its exact date remain unknown. Adrián Blázquez and Thomas Calvo hypothesize, based on internal evidence from the document, that Guzmán wrote the *relación* in Seville between 1538 and 1539. Adrián Blázquez and Thomas Calvo, *Guadalajara y el Nuevo Mundo. Nuño Beltrán de Guzmán: Semblanza de un conquistador* (Guadalajara, Spain: Instituto Provincial de Cultura "Marqués de Santillana," 1992), 52. This memorial, undoubtedly, served as his defense against pending lawsuits for his cruelty in the New World. For an annotated edition of Guzmán's *relación*, see Manuel Carrera Stampa, ed., *Memorias de los servicios que había hecho Nuño de Guzmán desde que fue nombrado gobernador de Pánuco en 1525*, by Nuño de Guzmán (Mexico City: Porrúa, 1955).

49. Blázquez, and Calvo, *Guadalajara y el Nuevo Mundo* (see n. 48), 52.

50. Herminio Martínez, *Diario maldito de Nuño de Guzmán* (Mexico City: Diana, 1990), 68.

51. Ibid., 117–18.

52. Ibid., 156.

53. Ibid., 162.

54. Kimberle López has noted that, although "Guzmania" is a fictionalized dystopian projection in the *Diario maldito*, a number of historians have argued that the historical Nuño de Guzmán intended to establish a utopian or dystopian kingdom. López, *Latin American Novels of the Conquest* (see n. 47), 208, n. 22. Donald Chipman attributes to the historical Nuño de Guzmán a "grand design" of extending his power westward from the gulf coast of Pánuco all the way to the Pacific Ocean. Donald E. Chipman, *Nuño de Guzmán and Pánuco in New Spain (1518–1523)*, (Glendale, CA: Arthur H. Clark Company, 1967), 232. He also had the utopian dream of conquering north to the fortieth parallel, where in 1530 and 1531 letters to the crown he claimed would be found a race of Amazon women who lived without men most of the year. Blázquez and Calvo, *Guadalajara y el Nuevo Mundo* (see n. 48), 197.

55. Martínez, *Diario maldito de Nuño de Guzmán* (see n. 50), 65.

56. Ibid., 18.

57. Ibid.

58. For more information about utopian discourses circulating during the conquest of the New World, see Beatriz Pastor, "Utopía y conquista," *Nuevo Texto Crítico* 5, nos. 9–10 (1992): 33–45.

59. Martínez, *Diario maldito de Nuño de Guzmán* (see n. 50), 76.

60. Ibid., 169.

61. Ibid., 222–23.

62. Ibid., 26.

63. Ibid., 27.

64. Ibid., 28.

65. Ibid., 74.

66. Ibid., 42. Kimberle López views the reference to London hooligans as highlighting the Amerindians' autonomy and their ability to use their bodies in an act of defiance against the conquistadors. López, *Latin American Novels of the Conquest* (see n. 54), 101.

67. Martínez, *Diario maldito de Nuño de Guzmán* (see n. 50), 42.

68. Ibid., 62.

69. Ibid., 199.

70. Ibid., 33.

71. Ibid., 89.

72. Ibid., 228.

73. Ibid., 41.

74. Ibid., 222.

75. Alfredo Corona Ibarra, ed., *Memorias de los servicios que había hecho Nuño de Guzmán desde que fue nombrado gobernador de Pánuco en 1525,* by Nuño de Guzmán (Jalisco, Mexico: Instituto Jalisciense de Antropología e Historia, 1992), 12.

76. Krippner-Martínez, *Rereading the Conquest* (see n. 4), 43–44.

77. Chorba, "Metaphors of Mestizo Mexico" (see n. 43), 65.

Chapter 4. Restaging Columbus

1. For additional biographical information on Roa Bastos, see Angel Flores, "Augusto Roa Bastos," in *Spanish American Authors: The Twentieth Century* (New York: H.W. Wilson Company, 1992), 736–40; and Jelena Kristovic, "Augusto Roa Bastos," in *Hispanic Literature Criticism,* vol. 2: *Lorca to Zamora* (Detroit: Gale Research, 1994), 1100–117.

2. Ilán Stavans, *Imagining Columbus: The Literary Voyage* (Boston: Twayne Publishers, 1993), 8.

3. Ibid., 8–9. In 1992, the governments and cultural institutions of the Southern Hemisphere supported the encounter thesis when it came to celebrating the quincentennial. In Madrid, Rome, Hollywood, London, and Washington, DC, however, there was a readiness to celebrate and there was money to spend. The supporters of the discovery thesis planned innumerable galas full of color and fireworks, museum exhibits, operas, film, public television programs, outer-space projects, diplomatic gatherings, and the publication of some thirty-five commemorative books. With as much energy, the opponents—among the most important was the Alliance for Cultural Democracy in Minneapolis—sabotaged the occasion; they claimed their campaign reached back to Fray Bartolomé de las Casas and his accusation of European atrocities (9). For further discussion about the debates and controversies surrounding the Columbian quincentenary in Italy, Latin America, Spain and the United States, see Stephen J. Summerhill and John Alexander Williams, *Sinking Columbus: Contested History, Cultural Politics, and Mythmaking during the Quincentenary* (Gainesville: University of Florida Press, 2000).

4. The above section draws on Ilan Stavans's excellent summary in *Imagining Columbus,* (see n. 7), 26–28. For information about earlier Columbus biographies see Stavans, *Imagining Columbus,* 15–30.

5. Ibid., 79. For other studies on *El arpa y la sombra* see Leonardo Acosta, "El almirante según Don Alejo," *Casa de las Américas* 21 (1980): 26–40; Barbara Bockus Aponte, "*El arpa y la sombra*: The Novel as Portrait," *Hispanic Journal* 3, no. 1 (1981): 93–105; Juan José Barrientos, "América, ese paraíso perdido," *Omnia* (Universidad Nacional Autónoma de México) 2, no. 3 (1986): 69–75; Víctor Bravo, "*El arpa y la sombra:* La urdimbre de la mentira," *Escritura* 9, nos. 17–18 (1984): 117–25; Carmen Bustillo, "Imágenes de América en *El arpa y la sombra,*" in *Crítica y descolonización: El sujeto colonial en la cultura latinoamericana,* ed. Beatriz González Stephan and Lúcia Helena Costigan (Caracas: Ediciones de la Universidad de Simón Bolívar and the Ohio State University, 1992): 647–63; Alicia Chibán, "*El arpa y la sombra:* Desocultamiento y visión integradora de la historia," in *La historia en la literatura iberoamericana: Textos del XXVI Congreso del Instituto Internacional de Literatura Iberoamericana,* ed. Raquel Chang-Rodríguez and Gabriella de Beer (New York: Ediciones del Norte and City University of New York, 1989), 117–28; Antonio Fama, "Historia y narración en *El arpa y la sombra,*" *Revista Iberoamericana* 52, nos. 135–36 (1986): 547–57; Sandra H. Ferdman, "The Dis-Orientation of Christopher Columbus: A Reading of the Discoverer's Writing" (PhD diss., Yale University, 1992);

Argelia Fernández-Carracedo, "El 'contrapunto' en *El arpa y la sombra* de Alejo Carpentier," *Escritura: Revista de Teoría y Crítica Literarias* 12, nos. 23–24 (1987): 73–88; Roland Forgues, "*El arpa y la sombra* de Alejo Carpentier: ¿Desmitificación o mixtificación?" *Revista de Crítica Literaria Latinoamericana* 7, no. 13 (1981): 87–102; Roberto González Echevarría, "Colón, Carpentier y los orígenes de la ficción latinoamericana," *La Torre: Revista de la Universidad de Puerto Rico* 7 (1988): 439–52; Aníbal González Pérez, "Ética y teatralidad: *El retablo de las maravillas* de Cervantes y *El arpa y la sombra* de Alejo Carpentier," *La Torre: Revista de la Universidad de Puerto Rico* 7, nos. 27–28 (1993): 485–502; Margarita Graetzer, "'Crónicas de Indias' y narrativa hispanoamericana: Espacio de encuentros" (PhD diss., University of Texas at Austin, 1994); Amelia Mondragón, "Colón desde el Nuevo Mundo," *Inti* 39 (1994): 59–71; Klaus Müller-Bergh, "The Perception of the Marvelous: Paul Claudel and Carpentier's *El arpa y la sombra*," *Comparative Literature Studies* 24, no. 2 (1987): 165–91; Max Parra, "La parodia histórica en *El arpa y la sombra* de Alejo Carpentier," *Discurso Literario* 23, no. 1 (1994–95): 65–74; Viviana P. Plotnik, "La reescritura del descubrimiento de América en cuatro novelas hispanoamericanas contemporáneas: Intertextualidad, carnaval y espectáculo" (PhD diss., New York University, 1993); Francisco Eduardo Porrata, "Relectura del discurso novomundista de Alejo Carpentier y Abel Posse en el contexto de la nueva novela histórica" (PhD diss., Florida International University, 2002); Eva Toth, "*El arpa y la sombra:* Variación sobre el tema del descubrimiento,*" *Escritura* 9, nos. 17–18 (1984): 21–26; and Alicia Valero Covarrubias, "*El arpa y la sombra* de Alejo Carpentier: Una confesión a tres voces," *Cuadernos Americanos* 14, no. 2 (1989): 140–46.

On *Los perros del paraíso,* see José Barrientos, "Colón, personaje novelesco," *Cuadernos Hispanoamericanos* 437 (1986): 45–62; Ahna Bishop-Jara, "Metahistories: Constructions of Memory in Contemporary Latin American Fiction" (PhD diss., University of Minnesota, 2001); Blanca De Arancibia, "Identity and Narrative Fiction in Argentina: The Novels of Abel Posse," in *Latin American Identity and Constructions of Difference,* ed. Amaryll Chanady (Minneapolis: University of Minnesota Press, 1994), 67–85; Malva Filer, "La visión de América en la obra de Abel Posse," in *La novela argentina de los años 80,* ed. Roland Spiller, 2nd ed., (Frankfurt: Vervuert, 1993), 99–118; Seymour Menton, "Christopher Columbus and the New Historical Novel," *Hispania* 75, no. 4 (1992): 930–40; Graciela Michelotti-Cristóbal, "Abel Posse y la nueva novela histórica: *Daimón* y *Los perros del paraíso*"(PhD diss., University of Pennsylvania, 1992); Plotnik, "La reescritura del descubrimiento de América"; Porrata, "Relectura"; Amalia Pulgarin-Cuadrado, *Metaficción historiográfica: La novela histórica en la narrativa hispánica posmodernista* (Madrid: Editorial Fundamentos, 1995); Fernando Reati, "Posse, Saer, Di Benedetto y Brailovsky: Deseo y paraíso en la novela argentina sobre la Conquista," *Revista de Estudios Hispánicos* 19, no. 1 (1995): 121–36; Sonia Rose de Fuggle, "La impugnación de la historia: Dos obras de Abel Posse," in *La nueva novela histórica hispanoamericana,* ed. Hub Hermans and Maarten Steenmeijer (Amsterdam: Rodopi, 1991), 9–20; Donald L. Shaw, "Columbus and the Discovery in Carpentier and Posse," *Romance Quarterly* 40, no. 3 (1993): 181–89; Elzbieta Sklodowska, "El (re)descubrimiento de América: La parodia en la novela histórica," *Romance Quarterly* 37, no. 3 (1990): 345–52; Raymond D. Souza, "Columbus in the Novel of the Americas: Alejo Carpentier, Abel Posse, and Stephen Marlowe," in *The Novel in the Americas,* ed. Raymond Leslie Williams (Boulder: University Press of Colorado, 1992), 40–55; Karen Stolley, "Death by Attrition: The Confessions of Christopher Columbus in Carpentier's *El arpa y la sombra*," *Revista de Estudios Hispánicos* 31 (1997): 505–31; Gabriela Tineo, "Resonancias y claroscuridades en *El arpa y la sombra,*" in *La reinvención de la memoria: Gestos, textos, imágenes en la cultura latinoamericana,* ed. Mónica

Scarano, Mónica Marinone, and Gabriela Tineo (Buenos Aires: Beatriz Viterbo Editora, 1997), 73–114.

6. Sandra H. Ferdman, "The Dis-Orientation of Christopher Columbus: A Reading of the Discoverer's Writing" (PhD diss., Yale University, 1992), 198.

7. Columbus was a prolific writer about his voyages. The longest and most important of his writings are his reports on three of his voyages to the New World. These are Columbus's diary (*Diario de a bordo*) of his first voyage (1492–93) and a long letter (*Primera carta de América*) to King Ferdinand and Queen Isabella written during the return passage. He left no report of his second voyage (1493–96). Columbus also wrote a report on his third voyage (1498–1500), and a letter to the monarchs reporting on his fourth voyage (1502–04). None of Columbus's writings about his voyages and exploration survives in his own handwriting or in notarized copies. Bartolomé de las Casas included large parts of them in his *Historia de las Indias*. Most of Columbus's other writings that have survived were not made by Columbus himself and, therefore, raise questions of authenticity, completeness, and accuracy. These are summarized in Helen Nader, "Writings: An Overview," in *The Christopher Columbus Encyclopedia*, ed. Silvio A. Bedini 2 vols. (New York: Simon and Schuster, 1992), 737–38. For an authoritative analysis of Columbus's writings about the voyages in relation to their sociohistorical context, see Margarita Zamora, *Reading Columbus* (Berkeley and Los Angeles: University of California Press, 1993).

8. Rosalía Cornejo-Parriego, "De escribas y palimpsestos: *Vigilia del Almirante*, de Augusto Roa Bastos," *Revista Canadiense de Estudios Hispánicos* 30, no. 3 (1996): 45.

9. Robin Lefere, "Sentidos y alcance de *Vigilia del Almirante* de A. Roa Bastos," *Bulletin of Hispanic Studies*, 76, no. 4 (1999): 536, 552.

10. José Ortega, "Verdad poética e histórica en *Vigilia del Almirante*," *Cuadernos Hispanoamericanos* 513 (March 1993): 108–11.

11. Milagros Ezquerro, "Don Quijote de la Mar Océana," *Cuadernos Hispanoamericanos* 522 (1993): 128–32.

12. Ibid., 129.

13. Seymour Menton, Review of "Vigilia del Almirante," by Augusto Roa Bastos, *World Literature Today* (Spring 1992): 346. For a reading of *Vigilia* as a kaleidoscopic novel, see Mónica Marinone, "*Vigilia del Almirante:* Una variante de la narración de la historia," in *La reinvención de la memoria: Gestos, textos, imágenes en la cultura latinoamericana*, ed. Mónica Scarano, Mónica Marinone, and Gabriela Tineo (Buenos Aires: Beatriz Viterbo Editora, 1997), especially 119–20.

14. Alejo Carpentier, *El arpa y la sombra* (Mexico City: Siglo XXI, 1979), 202.

15. Thomas Christensen and Carol Christensen, trans., *The Harp and the Shadow*, by Alejo Carpentier (San Francisco: Mercury House, 1990), 157.

16. Cornejo-Parriego, "De escribas y palimpsestos" (see n. 8), 454–56.

17. Augusto Roa Bastos, *Vigilia del Almirante* (Buenos Aires: Editorial Sudamericana, 1992), 205.

18. Ibid., 5.

19. Helene Carol Weldt-Basson, *Augusto Roa Bastos's "I the Supreme": A Dialogic Perspective* (Columbia: University of Missouri Press, 1993), 171–80.

20. Cited in Consuelo Varela, *Cristóbal Colón: Retrato de un hombre* (Madrid: Alianza, 1992), 184.

21. Roa Bastos, *Vigilia del Almirante* (see n. 17), 380–81.

22. Ibid., 383.

23. This section about the legend of *Piloto Desconocido* draws heavily on the excellent

summary by Hortensia Calvo-Stevenson, "Sinking Being: Shipwrecks and Colonial Spanish American Writings" (PhD diss., Yale University, 1990), 164–66.
 24. Ibid., 164.
 25. Ctd. in ibid., 165–66.
 26. Ibid., 166.
 27. Roa Bastos, *Vigilia del Almirante* (see n. 17), 65.
 28. Ibid., 66.
 29. Ibid.
 30. Ibid., 68.
 31. Ibid., 71.
 32. Ibid., 72–79.
 33. Ibid., 80–81.
 34. Ibid., 11.
 35. Ibid., 379.
 36. Iibd., 380–81.
 37. Ibid., 382.
 38. Ibid., 383.
 39. Delno C. West and August Kling, eds., *The "Libro de las profecías" of Christopher Columbus: An "En face" Edition* (Gainesville: University of Florida Press, 1991), 226.
 40. Ibid., 227.
 41. Herminio Martínez, *Las puertas del mundo: Una autobiografía hipócrita del Almirante* (Mexico City: Diana, 1992), epigraph to the novel.
 42. Miguel León Portilla, "Word and Mirror: Presages of the Encounter," trans. Jennifer M. Lang, in *Amerindian Images and the Legacy of Columbus,* ed. René Jara and Nicholas Spadaccini (Minneapolis: University of Minnesota Press, 1992), 99.
 43. E. Michael Gerli, "Columbus and the Shape of the Word: Authority and Experience in the *Relación* of the Third Voyage," *Journal of Hispanic Philology* 16 (1992): 218.
 44. Ibid., 219.
 45. Martínez, *Las puertas del mundo* (see n. 41), 75.
 46. Zamora, *Reading Columbus* (see n. 7), 121–22.
 47. Martíncz, *Las puertas del mundo* (see n. 41), 12.
 48. Ibid., 10.
 49. Ibid., 15.
 50. Ibid., 25.
 51. Ibid., 129.
 52. Ibid., 33.
 53. Valerie I. J. Flint, *The Imaginative Landscape of Christopher Columbus* (Princeton, NJ: Princeton University Press, 1992), xvii. The *Libro copiador* is a sixteenth-century copybook of letters by Columbus, Italian in origin, and found in a private collection from the island of Mallorca. It contains nine letters in all: five *cartas-relaciones,* two short personal letters written by Columbus to his sovereigns (previously unknown), and additional texts of the third and fourth voyages. Flint, *Imaginative Landscape,* xv n. 4. For an in-depth discussion of the *Libro copiador* see Antonio Rumeu de Armas, *Libro copiador de Cristóbal Colón: Correspondencia inédita con los Reyes Católicos sobre los viajes a América,* 2 vols. (Madrid: Testimonio, 1989).
 54. Zamora, *Reading Columbus* (see n. 7), 128.
 55. Martínez, *Las puertas del mundo* (see n. 41), 118–21.
 56. Ibid., 150–51.

57. Ibid., 110.
58. Ibid., 126.
59. Zamora, *Reading Columbus,* (see n. 7), 128.
60. Ibid., 129.
61. Ibid.
62. Michel de Certeau,*The Writing of History,* trans. Tom Conley (New York: Columbia University Press, 1988), xv.
63. Zamora, *Reading Columbus* (see n. 7), 152. For further discussion of the gendering of the New World, see especially her pages 152–79.
64. Consuelo Varela, *Cristóbal Colón: Textos y documentos completos,* (Madrid: Alianza, 1984), 216.
65. Zamora, *Reading Columbus* (see n. 7), 143.
66. Martínez, *Las puertas del mundo* (see n. 41), 159.

Afterword

1. Cited in Amaryll Chanady, "Saer's Fictional Representation of the Amerindian in the Context of Modern Historiography," in *Amerindian Images and the Legacy of Columbus,* ed. René Jara and Nicholas Spadaccini (Minneapolis: University of Minnesota Press, 1992), 679–80.
2. Cited in ibid., 680.
3. For a further discussion of these issues see ibid., 680–81.
4. Amaryll Chanady, "Latin American Imagined Communities and the Postmodern Challenge," in *Latin American Identity and Constructions of Difference* (Minneapolis: University of Minnesota Press, 1994), xii.
5. The following summary draws heavily on the discussion of the quincentenary in Ella Shohat and Robert Stam, *Unthinking Eurocentrism: Multiculturalism and the Media* (New York: Routledge, 1994), 71. For further discussion of the debates surrounding the quincentennial, see Stephen J. Summerhill and John Alexander Williams, *Sinking Columbus: Contested History, Cultural Politics, and Mythmaking during the Quincentenary* (Gainesville: University of Florida Press, 2000).
6. For more information about reflections by Fusco and Gómez Peña on their experiences as undiscovered Amerindians based on their performance piece *Two Undiscovered Amerindians Visit* (1992), which became the video documentary *The Couple in the Cage* (1993), see Coco Fusco, "The Other History of Intercultural Performance," in *English Is Broken Here: Notes on Cultural Fusion in the Americas* (New York: New Press, 1995), 37–63. For an analysis of the performance piece and the video documentary, see JuanVelasco, "Performing Multiple Identities: Guillermo Gómez Peña and His *Dangerous Border Crossings,*" in *Latino/a Popular Culture,* ed. Michelle Habell-Pallán and Mary Romero (New York: New York University Press, 2002), especially 209–13; and Diana Taylor, *The Archive and the Repertoire: Performing Cultural Memory in the Americas* (Durham, NC: Duke University Press, 2003), especially chapter 2 .
7. For a comprehensive discussion of U.S. and Latin American films related to the quincentenary, see Shohat and Stam, *Unthinking Eurocentrism,* especially chapter 2.
8. Representative Latin American plays include Carlos Tulio Altan and the Teatro de los Andes's *Colón* (1992) and Enrique Buenaventura's *Crónica* (1988) about Gonzalo Guerrero. Years before the quincentenninal, Amerindian and Spanish figures from the conquest of Mexico were the subject of numerous Mexican plays, including Sergio Magaña's

Moctezuma II (1953) and *Cortés y la Malinche* (1967), Rodolfo Usigli's *Corona de fuego* (1960), Salvador Novo's *Cuauhtémoc* (1962), and Carlos Fuentes's *Todos los gatos son pardos* (1970). For a discussion of contemporary Mexican plays that engage the discourse of the conquest, see Anne Lombardi Cantú, "La destabilización del discurso de la conquista en el teatro contemporáneo mexicano: Poder, mito e identidad nacional en obras de Sergio Magaña, Sabina Berman y Hugo Argüelles" (PhD diss., Boston College, 2003). For an excellent analysis of the role of La Malinche in Mexican theater, see Sandra Messinger Cypess, *La Malinche in Mexican Literature: From History to Myth* (Austin: University of Texas Press, 1991), especially chapter 6.

9. Juan Villegas, "El teatro histórico latinoamericano como discurso e instrumento de apropiación de la historia," in *Teatro histórico (1975–1998): Textos y representaciones,* ed. José Romera Castillo and Francisco Gutiérrez Cabajo (Madrid: Visor, 1999), 240.

10. For further discussion of *Aguila o sol* see Jacqueline Bixler, "The Postmodernization of History in the Theatre of Sabina Berman," *Latin American Theatre Review* 30, no. 2 (1997): 45–60; Priscilla Meléndez, "Co(s)mic Conquest in Sabina Berman's *Aguila o sol,*" in *Perspectives on Contemporary Spanish American Theatre,* ed. Frank N. Dauster (Lewisburg, PA: Bucknell University Press, 1996), 19–36; and Laurietz Seda, "De Cortés al mago de Oz: Estrategias posmodernas en el teatro latinoamericano (1980–1992)" (PhD diss., University of Kansas, 1994), especially 24–47. On *La noche de Hernán Cortés,* see Kirsten Nigro, "Un revuelto de la historia, la memoria y el género: Expresiones de la posmodernidad sobre las tables mexicanas," *Gestos* 17 (1994): 29–41. On *La Malinche,* see Stuart Alexander Day, *Staging Politics in Mexico: The Road to Neoliberalism* (Lewisburg, PA: Bucknell University Press, 2004), especially chapter 5. While the forementioned plays focus on figures and episodes related to the conquest of Mexico (i.e., the fall of Tenochtitlán), Víctor Castillo Bautista's *Nuño de Guzmán o la espada de Dios: Una obra en un acto* (1994) centers on Guzmán and the conquest of Michoacán. For a detailed analysis of this play, see my "Restaging the Conquest of Michoacán: Víctor Castillo Bautista's *Nuño de Guzmán o la espada de Dios,*" *Latin American Theatre Review* 37, no. 1 (Fall 2003): 25–42. On the performance piece *La representación de la salida de 400 familias* (a historical reenactment that celebrates the 1591 colonization of northern New Spain by Christianized Tlaxcaltecan Indians) as part of a campaign to disseminate Tlaxcalan history in Tlaxcala, see Patricia Ybarra, "Re-imagining Identity and Re-centering History in Tlaxcalan Performance," *Theatre Journal* 55 (2003): 633–55.

11. Richard Allen Gordon, "Reviewing the Colony/Revising the Nation: Mexican and Brazilian Cinematic Dialogue with Colonial Texts" (PhD diss., Brown University, 2002), 1–2. Other published articles on *Cabeza de Vaca* include Wilfried Floeck, "El conquistador como transfuga cultural en la película *Cabeza de Vaca* de Nicolás Echevarría," *Anales de Literatura Española Contemporánea* 26, no. 1 (2001): 357–81; Santiago Juan-Navarro, "Constructing Cultural Myths: Cabeza de Vaca in Contemporary Hispanic Criticism, Theater and Film," in *A Twice-Told Tale: Reinventing the Encounter in Iberian/Iberian American Literature and Film,* ed. Santiago Juan-Navarro and Theodore Robert Young (Newark: University of Delaware Press, 2001), 67–79; Luis Fernando Restrepo, "Primitive Bodies in Latin American Cinema: Nicolás Echeverría's *Cabeza de Vaca,*" in *Primitivism and Identity in Latin America: Essays on Art, Literature and Culture,* ed. Erik Camayd-Freixas and José Eduardo González (Tucson: University of Arizona Press, 2000), 189–208; and Richard A. Young, "Cabeza de Vaca en la literatura y el cine: Lectura y representación de un relato histórico," *Anclajes* 4, no. 4 (2000): 177–206.

Bibliography

Acevedo, Rubén. "'Maluco': Crónica de las desesperanzas y locuras de un bufón." Review of *Maluco: La novela de los descubridores,* by Napoleón Baccino Ponce de León. *Revista Iberoamericana* 160–61 (1992): 1187–90.

Acosta, Leonardo. "El almirante según Don Alejo." *Casa de las Américas* 21 (1980): 26–40.

Adorno, Rolena. "Colonial Spanish American Literary Studies: 1982–1992." *Revista Interamericana de Bibliografía/Inter-American Review of Bibliography* 38, no. 2 (1988): 167–76.

———. "La estatua de Gonzalo Guerrero en Akumal: Iconos culturales y la reactualización del pasado colonial." *Revista Iberoamericana* 176–77 (1996): 905–23.

———. *Guamán Poma: Writing and Resistance in Colonial Peru.* Austin: University of Texas Press, 1986.

———. "The Negotiation of Fear in Cabeza de Vaca's *Naufragios. Representations* 33 (1991): 163–99.

Adorno, Rolena, and Patrick Charles Pautz, eds. *Alvar Núñez Cabeza de Vaca: His Account, His Life, and the Expedition of Pánfilo de Narváez.* 3 vols. Lincoln: University of Nebraska Press, 1999.

Aguirre, Eugenio. *Gonzalo Guerrero.* 1980. Primera Edición Conmemorativa, 1492–1992. Mexico City: Diana, 1991.

Aguirre Rosas, Mario. *Gonzalo de Guerrero: Padre del mestizaje iberomexicano.* Mexico City: Jus, 1975.

Aínsa, Fernando. "La reescritura de la historia en la nueva narrativa latinoamericana." *Cuadernos Americanos,* (nueva época), 28 (1991): 13–31.

Albornoz, María Victoria. "Caníbales a la carta: Mecanismos de incorporación y digestión del 'otro' en *El entenado* de Juan José Saer." *Chasqui: Revista de Literatura Latinoamericana* 32, no. 1 (2003): 56–73.

Alcalá, Jerónomo de. *La relación de Michoacán.* Edited by Francisco Miranda. Morelia, Michoacán: Fimax Publicistas, 1980.

Almarza, Sara. *Pensamiento crítico hispanoamericano: Arbitristas del siglo XVIII.* Madrid: Pliegos, 1990.

Alvarez, José Rogelio. "Guzmán, Nuño de." *Enciclopedia de México.* Mexico City: SEP, 1987.

Anderson-Imbert, Enrique. *Historia de la literatura hispanoamericana.* vol. 1, *La Colonia: Cien años de República.* Sixth ed. Mexico City: Fondo de Cultura Económica, 1967.

Aponte, Barbara Bockus "'El arpa y la sombra': The Novel as Portrait." *Hispanic Journal* 3, no. 1 (1981): 93–105.

Arciniégas, Germán. "Don Quijote, un demócrata de izquierda." In *Don Quijote: Medita-*

ciones hispanoamericanas, edited by Frederick Viña, 1:1–16. Lanham: University Press of America, 1988.

Arias, Santa, and Mariselle Meléndez, eds. *Mapping Colonial Spanish America: Places and Commonplaces of Identity, Culture, and Experience.* Lewisburg, PA: Bucknell University Press, 2002.

Avelar, Idelber. "De Macondo al Huarochirí: El canon literario latinoamericano ante prácticas discursivas emergentes." *Dispositio* 18, no. 44 (1993): 193–214.

Avellaneda, Andrés. "Argentina militar: Los discursos del silencio." In *Literatura argentina hoy: De la dictadura a la democracia,* edited by Karl Kohut and Andrea Pagini, 2nd ed. 13–30. Frankfurt: Vervuert, 1993.

———. *Censura, autoritarismo y cultura: Argentina, 1960–1983.* Buenos Aires: Centro Editor de América Latina, 1986.

Ayala Anguiano, Armando. *Cómo conquisté a los aztecas.* Mexico City: Diana, 1990.

Baccino Ponce de León, Napoleón. *Maluco: La novela de los descubridores.* Barcelona: Seix Barral, 1990.

Baker, Daniel B. *Explorers and Discoverers of the World.* Detroit: Gale Research, 1994.

Barrientos, Juan José. "América, ese paraíso perdido." *Omnia* (Universidad Nacional Autónoma de México) 2, no. 3 (1986): 69–75.

———. "Colón, personaje novelesco." *Cuadernos Hispanoamericanos* 437 (1986): 45–62.

———. *Ficción-Historia: La nueva novela histórica hispanoamericana.* Mexico City: UNAM, 2001.

Bastos, María Luisa. "Eficacias del verosímil no realista: Dos novelas recientes de Juan José Saer." *La Torre: Revista de la Universidad de Puerto Rico* 4, no. 13 (1990): 1–20.

Beardsell, Peter. *Europe and Latin America: Returning the Gaze.* Manchester: Manchester University Press, 2000.

Beverly, John. *Against Literature.* Minneapolis: University of Minnesota Press, 1993.

Bilello, Suzanne. "Massacre at Tlatelolco." In vol. 2 of *Encyclopedia of Mexico,* edited by Michael Werner. Chicago: Fitzroy Publishers, 1997.

Bishop-Jara, Ahna. "Metahistories: Constructions of Memory in Contemporary Latin American Fiction." PhD diss., University of Minnesota, 2001.

Bixler, Jacqueline E. "The Postmodernization of History in the Theatre of Sabina Berman." *Latin American Theatre Review* 30, no. 2 (1997): 45–60.

———. "Re-Membering the Past: Memory-Theatre and Tlatelolco." *Latin American Research Review* 37, no. 2 (2002): 119–35.

Blázquez, Adrián, and Thomas Calvo. *Guadalajara y el Nuevo Mundo. Nuño Beltrán de Guzmán, Semblanza de un conquistador.* Guadalajara: Instituto Provincial de Cultura "Marqués de Santillana," 1992.

Bolaños, Alvaro Félix, and Gustavo Verdesio, eds. *Colonialism Past and Present: Reading and Writing about Colonial Latin America Today.* Albany: SUNY Press, 2002.

Bost, David. "Reassessing the Past: Abel Posse and the New Historical Novel." In *La Chispa '95: Selected Proceedings,* edited by Gilbert Paolini, 39–47. New Orleans: Tulane University Press, 1995.

Bouza, Fernando. *Locos, enanos y hombres de placer en la corte de los austrias: Oficio de burlas.* Madrid: Ediciones Temas de Hoy, 1991.

Bowsher, Kerstin. "Shipwrecks of Modernity: Abel Posse's *El largo atardecer del caminante*." *Forum for Modern Language Studies* 38, no. 1 (2002): 88–98.

Brailovsky, Antonio Elio. *Esta maldita lujuria*. Havana: Casa de las Américas, 1990.

Bravo, Víctor. "'El arpa y la sombra': La urdimbre de la mentira." *Escritura* 9, nos. 17–18 (1984): 117–25.

Bustillo, Carmen. "Imágenes de América en 'El arpa y la sombra.'" In *Crítica y descolonización: El sujeto colonial en la cultura latinoamericana*, edited by Beatriz González Stephan and Lúcia Helena Costigan, 647–63. Caracas: Ediciones de la Universidad de Simón Bolívar and the Ohio State University, 1992.

Caballero, José, ed. "Presentación." In *Nuño de Guzmán o la espada de Dios (Obra en un acto)*, by Víctor M. Castillo Bautista, 5–6. Guadalajara: Universidad de Guadalajara, 1994.

Cabrero, Leoncio, ed. *Primer viaje alrededor del mundo*. By Antonio de Pigafetta. Madrid: Historia 16, 1985.

Caistor, Nick, trans. *Five Black Ships: A Novel of the Discoverers*. By Napoleón Baccino Ponce de León. New York: Harcourt Brace and Company, 1994.

Calvo-Stevenson, Hortensia. "Sinking Being: Shipwrecks and Colonial Spanish American Writings (Christopher Columbus, Sor Juana Inés de la Cruz, Alvar Núñez Cabeza de Vaca)." PhD diss., Yale University, 1990.

Campos, Jorge. "Nueva relación entre la novela y la historia: Abel Posse y Denzil Romero." *Insula* 38, nos. 440–41 (1983): 19.

Campos, María Luisa del Luján. "*Maluco:* La pendularidad de sus opuestos." In *Historia, ficción y metaficción en la novela latinoamericana contemporánea*, edited by Mignon Domínguez, 70–89. Buenos Aires: Corregidor, 1996.

Campos, Victoria Eugenia. "Twentieth-Century Debates on Mexican History and the Juan Cabezón Novels of Homero Aridjis." PhD diss., Princeton University, 1996.

Cantú, Anne Lombardi. "La destabilización del discurso de la conquista en el teatro contemporáneo mexicano: Poder, mito e identidad nacional en obras de Sergio Magaña, Sabina Berman y Hugo Argüelles." PhD diss., Boston College, 2003.

Carpentier, Alejo. *El arpa y la sombra*. Mexico City: Siglo XX, 1979.

Carrera Stampa, Manuel, ed. *Memorias de los servicios que había hecho Nuño de Guzmán desde que fue nombrado gobernador de Pánuco en 1525*. By Nuño de Guzmán. Mexico City: Porrúa, 1955.

Casas, Bartolomé de las. *Brevísima relación de la destrucción de las Indias*. Edited by André Saint-Lu. Madrid: Cátedra, 1987.

Castillo Bautista, Víctor M. *Nuño de Guzmán o la espada de Dios (obra en un acto)*. Guadalajara: Universidad de Guadalajara, 1994.

Ceballos y Borjas, José Armando. *Gonzalo Guerrero (Apuntes para su biografía)*. Chetumal, Mexico: Fondo de Fomento Editorial del Gobierno del Estado de Quintana Roo, n.d.

Cella, Susana Beatriz. "Una heterología por plenitud. Acerca de 'El entenado' de Juan José Saer y '1492: Vida y tiempos de Juan Cabezón de Castilla' de Homero Aridjis." *Literatura Mexicana* 2 (1991): 455–61.

Certeau, Michel de. *The Writing of History*. Translated by Tom Conley. New York: Columbia University Press, 1988. (Originally published in 1975.)

Chanady, Amaryll. "Abel Posse and the Rewriting of the Aguirre Myth." In *Latin American Postmodernisms,* edited by Richard A. Young, 175–87. Amsterdam: Rodopi, 1997.

———. "Latin American Imagined Communities and the Postmodern Challenge." In *Latin American Identity and Constructions of Difference,* edited by Amaryll Chanady, ix–xlv. Minneapolis: University of Minnesota Press, 1994.

———. "Saer's Fictional Representation of the Amerindian in the Context of Modern Historiography." In *Amerindian Images and the Legacy of Columbus,* edited by René Jara and Nicholas Spadaccini, 678–708. Minneapolis: University of Minnesota Press, 1992.

Chase, Victoria. "Re-Discovering the New World: Columbus and Carpentier." *Comparative Civilizations Review* 12 (1985): 28–43.

Chejfec, Sergio. "La organización de las apariencias." *Hispamérica: Revista de Literatura* 23, no. 67 (1994): 109–16.

Chibán, Alicia. "'El arpa y la sombra': Desocultamiento y visión integradora de la historia." In *La historia en la literatura iberoamericana: Textos del XXVI Congreso del Instituto Internacional de Literatura Iberoamericana,* edited by Raquel Chang-Rodríguez and Gabriella de Beer, 117–28. New York: Ediciones del Norte and City University of New York, 1989.

Chipman, Donald E. *Nuño de Guzmán and Pánuco in New Spain (1518–1523).* Glendale, CA: Arthur H. Clark Company, 1967.

Chorba, Carrie C. "Metaphors of Mestizo Mexico: New Narrative Rewritings of the Conquest." PhD diss., Brown University, 1998.

Christensen, Thomas, and Carol Christensen, trans., *The Harp and the Shadow.* By Alejo Carpentier. San Francisco: Mercury House, 1990.

Colomina-Garrigós, Lola. "La reescritura de la Historia y el peso de la conciencia histórica en *El largo atardecer del caminante.*" *Tropos* 27 (2001): 7–20.

Cook, Noble David. "Aguirre, Lope de." In *Encyclopedia of Latin American History and Culture,* edited by Barbara Tenenbaum. New York: Charles Scribner's Sons, 1996.

Cordones-Cook, Juana María. "Contexto y proceso creador de *Maluco: La novela de los conquistadores.*" *Chasqui* 22, no. 2 (1993): 103–8.

Cornejo-Parriego, Rosalía. "De escribas y palimpsestos: *Vigilia del Almirante,* de Augusto Roa Bastos." *Revista Canadiense de Estudios Hispánicos* 30, no. 3 (1996): 449–62.

Corona Ibarra, Alfredo, ed. *Memorias de los servicios que había hecho Nuño de Guzmán desde que fue nombrado gobernador de Pánuco en 1525.* By Nuño de Guzmán. Jalisco, Mexico: Instituto Jalisciense de Antropología e Historia, 1992.

Cypess, Sandra Messinger. *La Malinche in Mexican Literature: From History to Myth.* Austin: University of Texas Press, 1991.

Davidson, John E. "As Others Put Plays upon the Stage: *Aguirre,* Neocolonialism, and the New German Cinema." *New German Critique* 60 (1993): 101–32.

Day, Stuart Alexander. *Staging Politics in Mexico: The Road to Neoliberalism.* Lewisburg, PA: Bucknell University Press, 2004.

De Arancibia, Blanca. "Identity and Narrative Fiction in Argentina: The Novels of Abel Posse." In Chanady, *Latin America, Identity and Constructions of Difference,* 67–85.

De Grandis, Rita. "*El entenado* de Juan José Saer y la idea de historia." *Revista Canadiense de Estudios Hispánicos* 18, no. 3 (1994): 417–26.

———. "*The Witness* by Juan José Saer: Paratextuality and Post-Modernism." *Latin American Literary Review* 41 (1993): 30–40.
Del Arenal Fenochio, Jaime. "La desmitificación de la historia en México." *Istmo* 204 (1993): 4–8.
Delgado Gómez, Angel, ed. *Cartas de relación.* By Hernán Cortés. Madrid: Clásicos Castalia, 1993.
Díaz-Quiñones, Arcadio. "*El entenado:* Las palabras de la tribu." *Hispamérica* 21, no. 63 (1992): 3–14.
Emery, Amy Fass. *The Anthropological Imagination in Latin American Literature.* Columbia: University of Missouri Press, 1996.
Ezquerro, Milagros. "Don Quijote de la Mar Océana." *Cuadernos Hispanoamericanos* 522 (1993): 128–34.
Fama, Antonio. "Historia y narración en *El arpa y la sombra.*" *Revista Iberoamericana* 52, nos. 135–36 (1986): 547–57.
Ferdman, Sandra H. "The Dis-Orientation of Christopher Columbus: A Reading of the Discoverer's Writing." PhD diss., Yale University, 1992.
Fernández-Carracedo, Argelia. "El 'contrapunto' en *El arpa y la sombra* de Alejo Carpentier." *Escritura: Revista de Teoría y Crítica Literarias* 12, nos. 23–24 (1987): 73–88.
Filer, Malva E. "La historia apócrifa en las novelas de los postmodernistas rioplatenses." *Alba de América: Revista Literaria* 12, nos. 22–23 (1994): 193–99.
———. "*Maluco:* Re-escritura de los relatos de la expedición de Magallanes." In *Actas Irvine-92: Encuentros y desencuentros de culturas; siglos XIX y XX,* edited by Juan Villegas, 4:293–301. Irvine, CA: Regents of the University of California, 1994.
———. "La visión de América en la obra de Abel Posse." In Spiller, 99–118.
Flint, Valerie I. J. *The Imaginative Landscape of Christopher Columbus.* Princeton, NJ: Princeton University Press, 1992.
Floeck, Wilfried. "El conquistador como transfuga cultural en la película *Cabeza de Vaca* de Nicolás Echevarría." *Anales de Literatura Española Contemporánea* 26, no. 1 (2001): 357–81.
Flores, Angel. "Augusto Roa Bastos." In *Spanish American Authors: The Twentieth Century,* 736–40. New York: H.W. Wilson Company, 1992.
Forgues, Roland. "*El arpa y la sombra* de Alejo Carpentier: ¿Desmitificación o mixtificación?" *Revista de Crítica Literaria Latinoamericana* 7, no. 13 (1981): 87–102.
Franco, Jean. "The Nation as Imagined Community." In *The New Historicism,* edited by Aram Veeser, 204–12. New York: Routledge, 1989.
Frisch, Mark. "Armando Ayala Anguiano." In *Dictionary of Mexican Literature,* edited by Eladio Cortés, 57–58. Westport, CT: Greenwood Press, 1992.
Fuentes, Carlos. *La nueva novela hispanoamericana.* Mexico City: Cuadernos de Joaquín Mortíz, 1969.
Fusco, Coco. "The Other History of Intercultural Performance." In *English Is Broken Here: Notes on Cultural Fusion in the Americas,* 37–63. New York: New Press, 1995.
Galster, Ingrid. "El conquistador Lope de Aguirre en la Nueva Novela Histórica." In Kohut, *La invención del pasado,* 196–204.
García Icazbalceta, Joaquín. 1981. *Don Fray Juan de Zumárraga, primer obispo y arzobispo de México.* Mexico City: Porrúa, 1947.

García Márquez, Gabriel. "Fantasía y creación artística en América Latina y el Caribe." *Texto Crítico* 14 (1979): 3–8.

———. "La soledad de América Latina." *Anthropos* 187 (1999) [1982]: 46–48. (Text of his Nobel Lecture of 1982).

———. "The Solitude of Latin America (Nobel Lecture, 1982)." Trans Marina Castañeda. In *Gabriel García Márquez and the Powers of Fiction,* edited by Julio Ortega, 87–92. Austin: University of Texas Press, 1988.

García Ronda, Angel. "La melancolía del caminante." Review of *El largo atardecer del caminante,* by Abel Posse. *Quimera* 86–87 (1993): 54–55.

Garramuño, Florencia. *Genealogías culturales: Argentina, Brasil y Uruguay en la novela contemporánea (1981–1991).* Rosario: Viterbo, 1997.

Gerbi, Antonello. *Nature in the New World: From Christopher Columbus to Gonzalo Fernández de Oviedo.* Translated by Jeremy Moyle. Pittsburgh: University of Pittsburgh Press, 1985.

Gerli, E. Michael. "Columbus and the Shape of the Word: Authority and Experience in the *Relación* of the Third Voyage." *Journal of Hispanic Philology* 16 (1992): 209–22.

Gnutzmann, Rita. "*El entenado* o la respuesta de Saer a las crónicas." *Iris* (1992): 23–36.

Gollnick, Brian. "'El color justo de la patria': Agencia discursiva en *El entenado* de Juan José Saer." *Revista de Crítica Literaria Latinoamericana* 39, no. 57 (2003): 107–24.

González Echevarría, Roberto. "Colón, Carpentier y los orígenes de la ficción latinoamericana." *La Torre: Revista de la Universidad de Puerto Rico* 7 (1988): 439–52.

———. "Humanismo, retórica y las crónicas de la Conquista." In *Historia y ficción en la narrativa hispanoamericana. Coloquio de Yale,* edited by Roberto González Echevarría, 149–68. Caracas: Monte Avila, 1984.

———. "José Arrom, autor de la *Relación acerca de las antigüedades de los indios* (picaresca e historia)." In *Relecturas,* 17–35. Caracas: Monte Avila, 1976.

González Echevarría, Roberto, and Enrique Pupo-Walker, eds. *The Cambridge History of Latin American Literature.* Vol. 1: *Discovery to Modernism.* Cambridge: Cambridge University Press, 1996.

González Pérez, Aníbal. "Ética y teatralidad: *El retablo de las maravillas* de Cervantes y *El arpa y la sombra* de Alejo Carpentier." *La Torre: Revista de la Universidad de Puerto Rico* 7, nos. 27–28 (1993): 485–502.

———. "Imágenes de la conquista y la colonia en la novelística hispanoamericana contemporánea: Notas para una interpretación." *Revista de Estudios Hispánicos* (San Juan, Puerto Rico) 19 (1992): 431–48.

Gordon, Richard Allen. "Reviewing the Colony/Revising the Nation: Mexican and Brazilian Cinematic Dialogue with Colonial Texts." PhD diss., Brown University, 2002.

Gough, Barry. *The Falkland Islands/Malvinas: The Contest for Empire in the South Atlantic.* London: Athlone Press, 1992.

Graetzer, Margarita. "'Crónicas de Indias' y narrativa hispanoamericana: Espacio de encuentros." PhD diss., University of Texas at Austin, 1994.

Hamed, Amir. "Lope de Aguirre: Autógrafo y novela (1947–1987)." PhD diss., Northwestern University, 1991.

Hernández, Mark A. "Restaging the Conquest of Michoacán: Victor Castillo Bautista's *Nuño de Guzmán o la espada de Dios.*" *Latin American Theatre Review* 37, no. 1 (Fall 2003): 25–42.

Holloway, Thomas H. "Whose Conquest Is This, Anyway? *Aguirre, the Wrath of God*." In *Based on a True Story: Latin American History at the Movies,* edited by Donald F. Stevens, 29–46. Wilmington, DE: Scholarly Resources, 1997.

Housková, Anna, and Martin Prochazka, eds. *Utopías del Nuevo Mundo.* Prague: Instituto de Literatura Checa y Universal de la Academia Checa de Ciencias y Departamento de Estudios Iberoamericanos de la Universidad Carolina, 1993.

Ibsen, Kristine. *Women's Spiritual Autobiography in Colonial Spanish America.* Gainesville: University of Florida Press, 1999.

Jara, René. "Crítica de una crisis: Los estudios literarios hispanoamericanos." *Ideologies & Literature* 4, no. 16 (1983): 330–52.

Jitrik, Noé. *Los dos ejes de la cruz: La escritura de la apropiación en el Diario, el Memorial, las Cartas y el Testamento del enviado real Cristóbal Colón.* Puebla, Mexico: Editorial Universidad Autónoma de Puebla, 1983.

Juan-Navarro, Santiago. "Constructing Cultural Myths: Cabeza de Vaca in Contemporary Hispanic Criticism, Theater and Film." In Juan-Navarro and Young, *Twice-Told Tale,* 67–79.

Juan-Navarro, Santiago, and Theodore Robert Young, eds. *A Twice-Told Tale: Reinventing the Encounter in Iberian/Iberian American Literature and Film.* Newark, DE: University of Delaware Press, 2001.

Karttunen, Frances. "La Malinche and Malinchismo." In vol. 2 of *Encyclopedia of Mexico,* edited by Michael S. Werner. Chicago: Fitzroy Publishers, 1997.

Keen, Benjamin. *The Aztec Image in Western Thought.* New Brunswick, NJ: Rutgers University Press, 1971.

Klor de Alva, Jorge. "The Postcolonialization of the (Latin) American Experience: A Reconsideration of 'Colonialism,' 'Postcolonialism,' and 'Mestizaje.'" In *After Colonialism: Imperial Histories and Postcolonial Displacements,* edited by Gyan Prakash, 241–78. Princeton, NJ: Princeton University Press, 1995.

Knight, Alan. "Racism, Revolution, and Indigenismo: Mexico, 1910–1940." In *The Idea of Race in Latin America, 1870–1940,* edited by Richard Graham, 71–113. Austin: University of Texas Press, 1990.

Koepnick, Lutz P. "Colonial Forestry: Sylvan Politics in Werner Herzog's *Aguirre* and *Fitzcarraldo.*" *New German Critique* 60 (1993): 133–60.

Kohut, Karl. *De Conquistadores y conquistados: Realidad, justificación, representación.* Frankfurt: Vervuert Verlag, 1992.

———. *La invención del pasado: La novela histórica en el marco de la posmodernidad.* Frankfurt: AEY, 1997.

Krafft-Ebing, Richard von. *Psychopathia Sexualis: A Medico-Forensic Study.* 1881. New York: Pioneer Publications, 1947.

Krippner-Martínez, James. *Rereading the Conquest: Power, Politics, and the History of Early Colonial Michoacán, Mexico, 1521–1565.* University Park: Pennsylvania State University Press, 2001.

Kristovic, Jelena. "Augusto Roa Bastos." In *Hispanic Literature Criticism,* vol. 2, *Lorca to Zamora,* 1100–17. Detroit: Gale Research, 1994.

Lafaye, Jacques. *Quetzalcóatl and Guadalupe: The Formation of Mexican National Con-*

sciousness, 1531–1813. Translated by Benjamin Keen. Chicago: University of Chicago Press, 1976.

Lefere, Robin. "Sentidos y alcance de *Vigilia del Almirante* de A. Roa Bastos." *Bulletin of Hispanic Studies* 76, no. 4 (1999): 535–55.

León Portilla, Miguel. "Word and Mirror: Presages of the Encounter." Translated by Jennifer M. Lang. In *Amerindian Images and the Legacy of Columbus,* edited by René Jara and Nicholas Spadaccini, 96–102. Minneapolis: University of Minnesota Press, 1992.

Lewis, Bart L. *The Miraculous Lie: Lope de Aguirre and the Search for El Dorado in the Latin American Historical Novel.* Lanham, MD: Lexington Books, 2003.

Lewis, Stephen E. "Mestizaje." In vol. 2 of *Encyclopedia of Mexico,* edited by Michael S. Werner. Chicago: Fitzroy Publishers, 1997.

Liss, Peggy K. *Mexico under Spain, 1521–1556: Society and the Origins of Nationality.* Chicago: University of Chicago Press, 1975.

López, Kimberle S. *Latin American Novels of the Conquest: Reinventing the New World.* Columbia: University of Missouri Press, 2002.

López-Portillo y Weber, José. *La conquista de la Nueva Galicia.* Mexico City: Talleres Gráficas de la Nación, 1935.

Luján Campos, María Luisa. "*Maluco* y la pendularidad de sus opuestos." In *Historia, ficción y metaficción en la novela latinoamericana contemporánea,* edited by Mignon Domínguez, 69–90. Buenos Aires: Ediciones Corregidor, 1996.

Maltby, William S. "Black Legend." In *Encyclopedia of Latin American History and Culture,* edited by Barbara Tenenbaum. New York: Charles Scribner's Sons, 1996.

Marinone, Mónica. "*Vigilia del Almirante:* Una variante de la narración de la historia." In Scarano, Marinone, and Tineo, *Reinvención de la memoria,* 115–38.

Mariscal, George. "A Clown at Court: Francesillo de Zúñiga's *Crónica burlesca.*" In *Autobiography in Early Modern Spain,* edited by Nicholas Spadaccini and Jenaro Taléns, 59–77. Minneapolis: Prisma Institute, 1988.

Márquez Villanueva, Francisco. "Literatura bufonesca o del loco." *Nueva Revista de Filología Hispánica* 24 (1985–86): 501–28.

Martínez, Herminio. *Diario maldito de Nuño de Guzmán.* Mexico City: Diana, 1990.

———. *Las puertas del mundo: Una autobiografía hipócrita del Almirante.* Mexico City: Diana, 1992.

Martínez, José Luis. *Hernán Cortés.* Mexico City: Fondo de Cultura Económica, 1990.

McKnight, Kathryn Joy. *The Mystic of Tunja: The Writings of Madre Castillo, 1671–1742.* Amherst: University of Massachusetts Press, 1997.

Medina, Manuel F. "Buscando el origen del mestizaje en las crónicas: Eugenio Aguirre re-crea a Gonzalo Guerrero." *Confluencia: Revista Hispánica de Cultura y Literatura* 11, no. 1 (1995): 148–62.

———. "El pasado en el presente: La historia en la novela mexicana (1980–1993)." PhD diss., University of Kansas, 1994.

———. "La revisión de la historia: Re-creando a Gonzalo Guerrero en la novela de Eugenio Aguirre." In *Más de 500 años de cultura en México,* edited by Lilia Granillo Vázquez, 357–76. Mexico City: Universidad Autónoma Metropolitana Azcapotzalco, 1994.

Meléndez, Priscilla. "Co(s)mic Conquest in Sabina Berman's *Aguila o sol.*" In *Perspectives* on Contemporary Spanish American Theatre, edited by Frank N. Dauster, 19–36. Lewisburg, PA: Bucknell University Press, 1996.

Menton, Seymour. "Christopher Columbus and the New Historical Novel." *Hispania* 75, no. 4 (1992): 930–40.

———. "La historia verdadera de Álvar Núñez Cabeza de Vaca en la última novela de Abel Posse, *El largo atardecer del caminante*." *Revista Iberoamericana* 52, no. 175 (1996): 421–26.

———. *Latin America's New Historical Novel*. Austin: University of Texas Press, 1993.

———. Review of "Diario maldito de Nuño de Guzmán," by Herminio Martínez. *Hispania* 74, no. 2 (1991): 330.

———. Review of "Vigilia del Almirante," by Augusto Roa Bastos *World Literature Today*, Spring 1992, 346.

Merrim, Stephanie. "Ariadne's Thread: Auto-bio-graphy, History and Cortés's *Segunda Carta de Relación*." *Dispositio* 2 (1986): 57–83.

Meuser-Blincow, Frances. "Rereading the New World Chronicles." *MIFLC Review* 1 (1991): 129–38.

Meza, Otilia. *Un amor inmortal: Gonzalo Guerrero, Símbolo del orígen del mestizaje mexicano (novela histórica)*. Mexico City: Alpe, 1994.

Michelotti-Cristóbal, Graciela. "Abel Posse y la nueva novela histórica: *Daimón* y *Los perros del paraíso*." PhD diss., University of Pennsylvania, 1992.

Mignolo, Walter D. "Cartas, crónicas y relaciones del descubrimiento y la conquista." In *Historia de la literatura hispanoamericana: Epoca colonial*, edited by Luis Iñigo Madrigal, 56–125. Madrid: Cátedra, 1982.

———. "The Darker Side of the Renaissance: Colonization and the Discontinuity of the Classical Tradition." *Renaissance Quarterly* 14, no. 4 (1992): 808–28.

———. "La lengua, el territorio (o la crisis de los estudios literarios coloniales)." *Dispositio* 11, nos. 28–29 (1986): 137–60.

———. "El metatexto historiográfico y la historiografía indiana." *MLN* 96 (1981): 358–402.

———. "Second Thoughts on Canon and Corpus." *Latin American Literary Review* 20, no. 40 (1992): 66–69.

Miller, Marilyn Grace. *Rise and Fall of the Cosmic Race: The Cult of Mestizaje in Latin America*. Austin: University of Texas Press, 2004.

Miranda, Alvaro. "Apuntes a propósito de *Don Quixote*." *Foro Literario* 2, no. 2 (1978): 48–51.

Molloy, Sylvia. *At Face Value: Autobiography in Spanish America*. Cambridge: Cambridge University Press, 1991.

Mondragón, Amelia. "Colón desde el Nuevo Mundo." *Inti* 39 (1994): 59–71.

Monteleone, Jorge. "Eclipse del sentido: De *Nadie nada nunca* a *El entenado* de Juan José Saer." In Spiller, *Novela argentina de los años 80*, 153–76.

Moreno Turner, Fernando. "La ciudad, el mito, la historia: En torno a *Esta maldita lujuria* de Antonio E. Brailovsky." *Licorne* 34 (1995): 279–85.

———. "Parodia, metahistoria y metaliteratura (En torno a *Maluco* de Napoleón Baccino Ponce de León)." *Hispamérica* 28, no. 82 (1999): 3–20.

Moretti, Gabriela. "Nec sit terris ultima Thule (La profezia di Seneca sulla scoperta del Nuovo Mondo)." *Columbeis* 1 (1986): 95–106.

Mueller, Rose Anna. "From Cult to Comics: The Representation of Gonzalo Guerrero as a Cultural Hero in Mexican Popular Culture." In Juan-Navarro and Young, *Twice-Told Tale,* 137–48.

Müller-Bergh, Klaus. "The Perception of the Marvelous: Paul Claudel and Carpentier's *El arpa y la sombra.*" *Comparative Literature Studies* 24, no. 2 (1987): 165–91.

Murray, James C. *Spanish Chronicles of the Indies: Sixteenth Century.* New York: Twayne, 1994.

Myers, Kathleen Ann. "Bibliographical Essay: Autobiographical Writing in Spanish-American Convents, 1650–1800." In *Word from New Spain: The Spiritual Autobiography of Madre María de San José (1656–1719),* 209–15. Liverpool: Liverpool University Press, 1993.

———. *Neither Saints nor Sinners: Writing the Lives of Women in Spanish America.* New York: Oxford University Press, 2003.

Nader, Helen. "Writings: An Overview." In *The Christopher Columbus Encyclopedia,* with continuous punctuation, edited by Silvio A. Bedini. 737–38. 2 vols., New York: Simon & Schuster, 1992.

Nigro, Kirsten. "Un revuelto de la historia, la memoria y el género: Expresiones de la posmodernidad sobre las tables mexicanas." *Gestos* 17 (1994): 29–41.

O'Gorman, Edmundo. *Cuatro historiadores de Indias, siglo XVI: Pedro Mártir de Anglería, Gonzalo Fernández de Oviedo y Valdés, Fray Bartolomé de las Casas, Joseph de Acosta.* Mexico City: Alianza Editorial Mexicana, 1989.

Orozco y Berra, Manuel. *Historia antigua de las culturas aborígines de México.* 2 vols. 1880. Mexico City: Porrúa, 1954.

Ortega, José. "Verdad poética e histórica en *Vigilia del Almirante.*" *Cuadernos Hispanoamericanos* 513 (March 1993): 108–11.

Ortega, Julio, and José Amor y Vásquez, eds. *Conquista y contraconquista: La escritura del Nuevo Mundo.* Mexico City and Providence, RI: Colegio de México and Brown University Press, 1994.

Oviedo, José Miguel. *Historia de la literatura hispanoamericana.* vol. 1. *De los orígenes a la Emancipación.* Madrid: Alianza, 1995.

Pamp de Avalle Arce, Diane, ed. *Crónica burlesca del emperador Carlos V.* By Francesillo de Zúñiga. Barcelona: Edición Crítica, 1981.

Parra, Max. "La parodia histórica en *El arpa y la sombra* de Alejo Carpentier." *Discurso Literario* 23, no. 1 (1994–95): 65–74.

Pastor, Beatriz. "Utopía y conquista." *Nuevo Texto Crítico* 5, nos. 9–10 (1992): 33–45.

Pastor Bodmer, Beatriz. *The Armature of Conquest: Spanish Accounts of the Discovery of America, 1492–1589.* Translated by Lydia Longstreth Hunt. Stanford, CA: Stanford University Press, 1992.

———. *Discursos narrativos de la conquista: mitificación y emergencia.* Hanover, NH: Ediciones del Norte, 1988.

Paz, Octavio. "Hernán Cortés: Exorcismo y liberación." In *México en la obra de Octavio Paz: El peregrino en su patria; Historia y política de México,* edited by Octavio Paz and Luis Mario Schneider, 1:101–6. Mexico City: Fondo de Cultura Económica, 1987.

Perkowska-Alvarez, Magdalena. "Historias híbridas: El posmodernismo y la novela histórica latinoamericana, 1985–1995." PhD diss., Rutgers University, 1997.

Pites, Silvia. "Entrevista con Abel Posse." *Chasqui* 22, no. 2 (1993): 120–28.

Pizarro, Ana, ed. *America Latina: Palavra, literatura, cultura*. Vol. 1. *A Situação Colonial*. Campinas, São Paulo: Editora da Unicamp, 1993.

Plotnik, Viviana P. "La reescritura del descubrimiento de América en cuatro novelas hispanoamericanas contemporáneas: Intertextualidad, carnaval y espectáculo." PhD diss., New York University, 1993.

Pons, María Cristina. *La novela histórica de fines del siglo XX*. Mexico City: Siglo XXI, 1996.

Poole, Stafford. *Our Lady of Guadalupe: The Origins and Sources of a Mexican National Symbol, 1531–1797*. Tucson: University of Arizona Press, 1995.

Porrata, Francisco Eduardo. "Relectura del discurso novomundista de Alejo Carpentier y Abel Posse en el contexto de la nueva novela histórica." PhD diss., Florida International University, 2002.

Posse, Abel. *El largo atardecer del caminante*. Buenos Aires: Emecé Editores, 1992.

———. "La novela como nueva crónica de América: Historia y mito." In Kohut, *De conquistadores y conquistados*, 249–55.

Premat, Julio. "El eslabón perdido: *El entenado* en la obra de Juan José Saer." *Cahiers du Monde Hispanique et Luso Bresilien/Caravelle* 66 (1996): 75–93.

Pulgarin-Cuadrado, Amalia. *Metaficción historiográfica: La novela histórica en la narrativa hispánica posmodernista*. Madrid: Editorial Fundamentos, 1995.

Pupo-Walker, Enrique. *Historia, creación y profecía en los textos del Inca Garcilaso de la Vega*. Madrid: José Porrúa Turanzas, 1982.

———, ed. *Los naufragios*. By Alvar Núñez Cabeza de Vaca. Madrid: Castalia, 1993.

———. "Notas para la caracterización de un texto seminal: *Los naufragios* de Alvar Núñez Cabeza de Vaca." *Nueva Revista de Filología Hispánica* 28, no. 1 (1990): 163–96.

———. *La vocación literaria del pensamiento histórico en América: Desarrollo de la prosa de ficción; Siglos XVI, XVII, XVIII y XIX*. Madrid: Gredos, 1982.

Quintana Esther. "El bufón como narrador: *Maluco: La novela de los descubridores*." In *Pensamiento y crítica : Los discursos de la cultura hoy*, edited by Manuel F. Medina, 123–38. East Lansing: Michigan State University Press, 2000.

———. "Los pícaros, bufones y cronistas de *Maluco, la novela de los descubridores*." PhD diss., University of California at Berkeley, 1998.

Rabasa, José. "Allegory and Ethnography in Cabeza de Vaca's *Naufragios* and *Comentarios*." In *Violence, Resistance and Survival in the Americas: The Legacy of Conquest*, edited by William B. Taylor and Franklin Pease, 40–66. Washington, DC: Smithsonian Institute Press, 1993.

———. *Inventing A-M-E-R-I-C-A: Spanish Historiography and the Formation of Eurocentrism*. Norman: University of Oklahoma Press, 1993.

Ramírez, Alejandro. *Epistolario de Justo Lipsio y los españoles (1577–1606)*. Madrid: Editorial Castalia, 1966.

Ramos-Nadal, Consuelo. "Las crónicas como forjadoras de una tradición literaria en la figura de Lope de Aguirre." PhD diss., University of Massachusetts at Amherst, 1997.

Reati, Fernando. "Posse, Saer, Di Benedetto y Brailovsky: Deseo y paraíso en la novela argentina sobre la Conquista." *Revista de Estudios Hispánicos* 19, no. 1 (1995): 121–36.

Reckley, Alice Ruth. "Irony and License in New Memories of the Conquest: Gonzalo Guerrero." *Symposium* 46, no. 2 (1992): 133–46.

Restrepo, Luis Fernando. "Primitive Bodies in Latin American Cinema: Nicolás Echeverría's

Cabeza de Vaca." In *Primitivism and Identity in Latin America: Essays on Art, Literature and Culture,* edited by Erik Camayd-Freixas and José Eduardo González, 189–208. Tucson: University of Arizona Press, 2000.

Reyes, Alfonso. *Letras de la Nueva España.* Mexico City: Fondo de Cultura Ecónomica, 1948.

Rico Ferrer, José Antonio. "Gonzalo Guerrero: La frontera del imaginario español." *Cuadernos Americanos* 81 (May–June 2000): 169–92.

Riera, Gabriel. "La ficción de Saer: ¿Una 'antropología especulativa'? (Una lectura de 'El entenado.'" *MLN* 111 (1996): 368–90.

Roa Bastos, Augusto. *Vigilia del Almirante.* Buenos Aires: Editorial Sudamericana, 1992.

Robles, Humberto E. "The First Voyage Around the World: From Pigafetta to García Márquez." *History of European Ideas* 6, no. 4 (1985): 385–404.

Rochfort, Desmond. *Mexican Muralists: Orozco, Rivera, Siquieros.* San Francisco: Chronicle Books, 1998.

Rock, David. *Argentina, 1516–1987: From Spanish Colonization to Alfonsín.* Berkeley and Los Angeles: University of California Press, 1987.

Romano Thuesen, Evelia. "'El entenado': Relación contemporánea de las memorias de Francisco del Puerto." *Latin American Literary Review* 23, no. 4 (January–June 1995): 43–63.

———. "La ocasión para narrar: Historia, realidad y alegoría en un texto de Juan José Saer." *Nueva Revista de Filología Hispánica* 47, no. 1 (1999): 99–119.

Romero, Rolando J. "Text, Pre-texts, Con-texts: Gonzalo Guerrero in the Chronicles of the Indies." *Revista de Estudios Hispánicos* 26, no. 3 (1992): 345–67.

Rose de Fuggle, Sonia. "La impugnación de la historia: Dos obras de Abel Posse." In *La Nueva novela histórica hispanoamericana,* edited by Hub Hermans and Maarten Steenmeijer, 9–20. Amsterdam: Rodopi, 1991.

Ross, Kathleen. *The Baroque Narrative of Carlos de Sigüenza y Góngora: A New World Paradise.* Cambridge: Cambridge University Press, 1994.

Rumeu de Armas, Antonio. *Libro copiador de Cristóbal Colón: Correspondencia inédita con los Reyes Católicos sobre los viajes a América.* 2 vols. Madrid: Testimonio, 1989.

Salcedo, Hugo. *Los endemoniados.* Mexico City: Tablado IberoAmericano, 1996.

Sánchez Paso, José Antonio, ed. *Crónica burlesca del emperador Carlos V.* By Francesillo de Zúñiga. Salamanca: Europa Artes Gráficas, 1989.

———. "La sociología literaria de don Francés de Zúñiga." *Nueva Revista de Filología Hispánica* 24 (1985–86): 848–65.

Sarfati-Arnaud, Monique. "Gonzalo Guerrero, de la crónica a la novela." *Texto Crítico* 16 (1990): 97–104.

Scarano, Mónica E. "*Los perros del paraíso* de Abel Posse: La trama oculta de la escritura." In Scarano, Marinone, and Tineo, *Reinvención de la memoria,* 73–114.

Scarano, Mónica, Mónica Marinone, and Gabriela Tineo, eds. *La reinvención de la memoria: Gestos, textos, imágenes en la cultura latinoamericana.* Buenos Aires: Beatriz Viterbo Editora, 1997.

Scharlau, Birgit. "Nuevas tendencias en los estudios de crónicas y documentos del período colonial latinoamericano." *Revista de Crítica Literaria Latinoamericana* 16, nos. 32–33 (1990): 365–75.

Scheines, Graciela. "La última generación del ochenta: La peculiaridad del fracaso en la novela argentina actual." In Spiller, *Novela argentina de los años 80,* 271–82.

Schlau, Stacey. "Wanted, Dead (to the World): Autobiographical Narratives by Colonial Nun Authors Gerónima Nava y Saavedra and Ursula Suárez." In *Spanish American Women's Use of the Word: Colonial through Contemporary Narratives,* 3–26. Tucson: University of Arizona Press, 2001.

Scholes, France V., and Eleanor B. Adams, eds. *Proceso contra Tzintzincha Tangaxoan el Caltzontzin, formado por Nuño de Guzmán, año de 1530.* Mexico City: Porrúa y Obregón, 1952.

Schumm, Petra. "La 'cultura' en la crítica sobre los siglos coloniales en Hispanoamérica y el Brasil." *Dispositio* 18, no. 44 (1993): 79–98.

Seda, Laurietz. "De Cortés al mago de Oz: Estrategias posmodernas en el teatro latinoamericano (1980–1992)." PhD diss., University of Kansas, 1994.

Shaw, Donald L. "Columbus and the Discovery in Carpentier and Posse." *Romance Quarterly* 40, no. 3 (1993): 181–89.

Shohat, Ella, and Robert Stam. *Unthinking Eurocentrism: Multiculturalism and the Media.* New York: Routledge, 1994.

Simson, Ingrid. "Apuntes para una nueva orientación en los estudios de la literatura colonial hispanoamericana." *Revista de Crítica Literaria Latinoamericana* 15 (1989): 183–208.

Sklodowska, Elzbieta. "El (re)descubrimiento de América: La parodia en la novela histórica." *Romance Quarterly* 37, no. 3 (1990): 345–52.

Smith, Sara Ann. "Lost-Body Writing in Latin America's Contemporary Historical Novel." PhD diss., Michigan State University, 2001.

Sommer, Doris. *Foundational Fictions: The National Romances of Latin America.* Berkeley and Los Angeles: University of California Press, 1991.

Souza, Raymond D. "Columbus in the Novel of the Americas: Alejo Carpentier, Abel Posse, and Stephen Marlowe." In *The Novel in the Americas,* edited by Raymond Leslie Williams, 40–55. Boulder: University Press of Colorado, 1992.

Spiller, Roland, ed. *La novela argentina de los años 80.* 2nd ed. Frankfurt: Vervuert, 1993.

Stavans, Ilán. *Imagining Columbus: The Literary Voyage.* Boston: Twayne Publishers, 1993.

Stolley, Karen. "Death by Attrition: The Confessions of Christopher Columbus in Carpentier's *El arpa y la sombra.*" *Revista de Estudios Hispánicos* 31 (1997): 505–31.

Summerhill, Stephen J., and John Alexander Williams. *Sinking Columbus: Contested History, Cultural Politics, and Mythmaking during the Quincentenary.* Gainesville: University of Florida Press, 2000.

Taylor, Diana. *The Archive and the Repertoire: Performing Cultural Memory in the Americas.* Durham, NC: Duke University Press, 2003.

Tineo, Gabriela. "Resonancias y claroscuridades en *El arpa y la sombra.*" In Scarano, Marinone, and Tineo, *Reinvención de la memoria,* 73–114.

Torodash, Martin. "Magellan's Historiography." *Hispanic American Historical Review* 51 (1971): 313–15.

Toth, Eva. "*El arpa y la sombra:* Variación sobre el tema del descubrimiento." *Escritura* 9, nos. 17–18 (1984): 21–26.

Toussaint, Manuel. *La conquista de Pánuco.* Mexico City: Colegio Nacional, 1948.

Urbina, José Leandro. "La nueva novela histórica latinoamericana: El descubrimiento revisitado en Roa Bastos, Carpentier y Posse." PhD diss., Catholic University of America, 1994.

Usable González, Antonio. *La novela histórica hispanoamericana: Desde 1931 hasta nuestros días.* Madrid: Ediciones de la Universidad Autónoma de Madrid, 2000.

Valdés, Mario, and Djelal Kadir, eds. *Literary Cultures of Latin America: A Comparative History.* 3 vols. Cambridge: Oxford University Press. 2004.

Valente, Luis Fernando. "Fiction as History: The Case of João Ubaldo Ribeiro." *Latin American Research Review* 28, no. 1 (1993): 41–60.

Valero Covarrubias, Alicia. "*El arpa y la sombra* de Alejo Carpentier: Una confesión a tres voces." *Cuadernos Americanos* 14, no. 2 (1989): 140–46.

Varela, Consuelo. *Cristóbal Colón: Retrato de un hombre.* Madrid: Alianza, 1992.

———. *Cristóbal Colón: Textos y documentos completos.* Madrid: Alianza, 1984.

Velasco, Juan. "Performing Multiple Identities: Guillermo Gómez Peña and His *Dangerous Border Crossings.*" In *Latino/a Popular Culture,* edited by Michelle Habell-Pallán and Mary Romero, 208–24. New York: New York University Press, 2002.

Verani, Hugo. "Napoleón Baccino Ponce de León: La imaginación del Nuevo Mundo; La ficcionalización de la historia." In *De la vanguardia a la posmodernidad: Narrativa uruguaya (1925–1995),* 207–22. Montevideo: Ediciones Trilce, 1996.

Verástique, Bernardino. *Michoacán and Eden: Vasco de Quiroga and the Evangelization of Western Mexico.* Austin: University of Texas Press, 2000.

Verdesio, Gustavo. "Colonialism Now and Then: Colonial Latin American Studies in the Light of the Predicament of Latin Americanism." In Bolaños and Verdesio, *Colonialism Past and Present,* 1–17.

———. *Forgotten Conquests: Rereading New World History from the Margins.* Philadelphia: Temple University Press, 2001.

———. "The Literary Appropriation of the American Landscape: The Historical Novels of Abel Posse and Juan José Saer and Their Critics." In Bolaños and Verdesio, *Colonialism Past and Present,* 239–60.

Vich, Cynthia. "El diálogo intertextual en *Maluco.*" *Revista Iberoamericana* 63, no. 180 (1997): 405–18.

Villegas, Juan. "El teatro histórico latinoamericano como discurso e instrumento de apropiación de la historia." In *Teatro histórico (1975–1998): Textos y representaciones,* edited by José Romera Castillo and Francisco Gutiérrez Cabajo, 233–49. Madrid: Visor, 1999.

Warren, J. Benedict. *The Conquest of Michoacán: The Spanish Domination of the Tarascan Kingdom in Western Mexico, 1521–1530.* Norman: University of Oklahoma Press, 1985.

Wasserman, Jacob. *Columbus: Don Quixote of the Seas.* Translated by Eric Sutton. Boston: Little, Brown and Company, 1930.

Weldt-Basson, Helene Carol. *Augusto Roa Bastos's 'I the Supreme': A Dialogic Perspective.* Columbia: University of Missouri Press, 1993.

West, Delno C., and August Kling, eds. *The "Libro de las profecías" of Christopher Columbus: An "En face" Edition.* Gainesville: University of Florida Press, 1991.

Ybarra, Patricia. "Re-imagining Identity and Re-centering History in Tlaxcalan Performance." *Theatre Journal* 55 (2003): 633–55.

Young, Richard A. "Cabeza de Vaca en la literatura y el cine: Lectura y representación de un relato histórico." *Anclajes* 4, no. 4 (2000): 177–206.

Zamora, Margarita. "Historicity and Literariness: Problems in the Literary Criticism of Spanish American Colonial Texts." *MLN* 102 (1987): 334–46.

———. *Language, Authority and Indigenous History in the "Comentarios reales."* Cambridge: Cambridge University Press, 1988.

———. *Reading Columbus.* Berkeley and Los Angeles: University of California Press, 1993.

Zlotchew, Clark M. "Entrevista con Antonio Brailovsky." *Alba de América: Revista Literaria* 5, nos. 8–9 (1988): 371–83.

———. "Opresión, libertad y la magia: Entrevista con Antonio Elio Brailovsky." *Hispania* 71 (1988): 595–97.

———. "Problematic Identity in Brailovsky's 'Identidad.'" *Yiddish* 9, no. 1 (1993): 111–21.

———. "La segunda Jerusalem de la Nueva Sefarad de las Indias: *Identidad* de A. E. Brailovsky." *Noa h* 7–8 (1992): 96–105.

Index

Page numbers in italics refer to illustrations.

Acosta, José de: *Historia natural y moral de las Indias,* 145n. 17
Acosta, Leonardo, 164n. 5
Adorno, Rolena, 16, 143n. 2, 144–45n. 16, 150–51n. 43, 151n. 45, 156n. 2
Africa, 77–78
Aguilar, Jerónimo de, 88, 89, 91
Aguilar, Rosario: *La niña blanca y los pájaros sin pies,* 146n. 24
Aguirre, Eugenio, career of, 84; and rewriting of Mexican cultural identity/mestizaje, 21, 84, 86–91, 93–95, 107–9
—Works: *Amor de mis amores,* 156n. 1; *El caballero de las espadas,* 156n. 1; *Cadáver exquisito,* 156n. 1; *El canto de las aguas,* 156n. 1; *Desierto ardiente,* 156n. 1; *Elena, o, el laberinto de la lujuria,* 156n. 1; *En el campo,* 156n. 1; *La fascinación de la bestia,* 156n. 1; *Gonzalo Guerrero,* 19, 21, 84–95, 107–9, 146n. 24, 161n. 18; *El hombre baldío,* 156n. 1; *Jesucristo Pérez,* 156n. 1; *Los niños de colores,* 156n. 1; *Pajar de imaginación,* 156n. 1; *Pájaros de fuego,* 156n. 1; *Pasos de sangre,* 156n. 1; *El rumor que llegó del mar,* 156n. 1; *Segunda persona,* 156n. 1; *La suerte de la fea,* 156n. 1; *El testamento del diablo,* 156n. 1
Aguirre, Lope de, 18, 61, 89, 147n. 29, 157–58n. 6
Aguirre Rosas, Mario, 160–61n. 16
Aínsa, Fernando, 147n. 25
Albornoz, María Victoria, 148n. 31
Alemán, Lucas, 150n. 28
Alemán, Mateo de: *Guzmán de Alfarache,* 153n. 15

allegory, 18
Almagro, Diego de, 48
Almarza, Sara, 73
Alvarado, Pedro de, 48
Álvarez Saenz, Félix: *Crónica de blasfemos,* 146n. 24, 147n. 25
Amazon River, 157–58n. 6
Amor y Vásquez, José, 148n. 29
Anderson Imbert, Enrique, 14
anticlericalism, 13
Aparicio Quintana, José: *Retrato de Hernán Cortés,* 32, *33,* 150n. 25
Aponte, Barbara Bockus, 164n. 5
arbitrista writing, 20, 73
Arciniegas, Germán, 116–17
Arenas, Reinaldo: *El mundo alucinante,* 18
Argentina, 19, 20, 21, 47, 48, 57, 60, 72, 73, 74, 79, 80–82, 84, 139, 146n. 24. *See also* Dirty War; Falkland Islands; Proceso de reorganización nacional
Arias, Santa, 17, 145n. 16
Aridjis, Homero: *1492, Vida y tiempos de Juan Cabezón de Castilla,* 146n. 24, 147n. 28; *Memorias del Nuevo Mundo,* 146n. 24, 147n. 28
Artaud, Antonin, 46
Asturias, Miguel Angel: *Maládrón,* 144n. 11
Atahualpa, 49
autobiography, 19, 20, 24–25, 26–27, 28, 30–32, 35, 37, 38, 41, 42, 43, 44, 46, 47, 48, 49–51, 53–55, 56, 84, 98, 113, 114, 140, 149n. 12
Avelar, Idelber, 143n. 2
Avellaneda, Andrés, 73
Ayala Anguiano, Armando: career of, 23–24, 149n. 1; and challenge to

Ayala Anguiano, Armando (*continued*)
Cortés's image and authority, 20, 24, 25, 28, 30–33, 34–39, 54, 56, 84, 140.
—Works: *La aventura de México,* 24; *Cómo conquisté a los aztecas,* 20, 23, 24, 25, 27, 28–33, 35–39, 41, 44, 54, 56, 84, 98, 140, 141, 146n. 24, 150n. 25; *Conquistados y conquistadores,* 24; *El día que perdió el PRI: Ficción política,* 24; *La ganas de creer,* 23; *JLP: Secretos de un sexenio,* 24; *El paso de la nada,* 23–24; *Juárez: Biografía novelada,* 24; *México antes de los aztecas,* 24; *México de carne y hueso,* 24; *México en crisis: El fin del sistema,* 24; *Salinas y su México,* 24; *Unos cuantos dias,* 24; *Zapata y las grandes mentiras de la Revolución Mexicana,* 24
Aztecs, 28–29, 32, 33, 35, 36, 38–39, 49, 105, 107, 139, 160n. 16

Baccino Ponce de León, Napoleón: career of, 59; and parallels of colonial and recent history, 57, 62, 71, 82, 154n. 50; and use of buffoon to contest official history, 20, 57, 59–71, 82, 152n. 12, 152–53n. 14.
—Works: *Aaron de Anchorena: Una vida priviligiada,* 59; *Un amor en Bangkok,* 59; *El arte de perder,* 59; *Maluco: La novela de los descubridores,* 19, 20–21, 56–57, 59–72, 75, 82, 139, 146n. 24, 152nn. 12 and 13, 152–53n. 14, 154nn. 45, 49, 50, and 51
Bakhtin, M. M., 147n. 25
baroque, 62
Barrientos, Juan José, 147n. 25, 148n. 29, 164n. 5, 165n. 5
Bastos, María Luisa, 148n. 31
Béjar, Duque de, 63
Bello, Andrés, 144n. 10
Benítez Rojo, Antonio: *El mar de las lentejas,* 18, 146n. 24, 147n. 25
Berman, Sabina: *Aguila o sol,* 141, 169n. 10
Beverly, John, 44
Bilbao, Manuel: *El inquisador mayor: Historia de unos amores,* 143n. 7
biography, 112, 113, 114, 116, 119, 125, 164n. 4

Bishop-Jara, Ahna, 148n. 29, 152n. 12, 165n. 5
Bixler, Jacqueline, 169n. 10
black legend, 82, 84, 85, 86, 87, 97, 101, 104, 106, 108, 157–58n. 6, 159n. 8
Blázquez, Adrián, 97, 163n. 48
Bloom, Harold, 19
Bobabilla, 125
Bolaños, Alvaro Félix, 17, 145n. 16
Boom writers, Spanish American, 15, 16, 17, 58, 96, 144n. 16
Borges, Jorge Luis, 147n. 25; "Pierre Menard, autor del Quijote," 138
Bost, David, 26, 151n. 58
Boullosa, Carmen: *Cielos de la tierra,* 146n. 24; *Duerme,* 146n. 24; *Llanto: Novelas imposibles,* 95, 146n. 24
Bouza, Fernando, 153n. 15
Bowsher, Kersten, 25–26
Brailovsky, Antonio Elio: career of, 72, 154n. 52; and parallels of colonial and recent history, 21, 57, 72–74, 80–82, 139.
—Works: *El asalto al cielo,* 72; *Esta maldita lujuria,* 20, 21, 56, 57, 72–82, 139, 146n. 24, 155n. 58; *Identidad* (or *Isaac Halevy, rey de los judíos*), 72; *Libro de desmesuras,* 72; *Me gustan sus cuernos,* 72; *No abrirás esta puerta,* 72; *Tiempo de opresión,* 72
Bravo, Victor, 164n. 5
Brazil, 82, 141
Bucareli, Don Francisco, 80
Buenaventura, Enrique: *Crónica,* 168n. 8
Buenos Aires, 57, 72, 73, 76, 80
Bustillo, Carmen, 164n. 5

Cabeza de Vaca, Alvar Núñez, 12, 18, 20, 21, 25, 26–28, 41–55, 56, 78, 98, 141, 150–51n. 43, 151n. 45; *Los naufragios,* 11, 13, 20, 24, 26, 27, 28, 41–43, 44, 50, 53–54, 65, 84, 147n. 27, 150n. 39
Cabrero, Leoncio, 152n. 5
Cahonaboa, 133
Calvo, Thomas, 163n. 28
Calvo-Stevenson, Hortensia, 120, 166–67n. 23
Campos, Victoria Eugenia, 148n. 29
canonicity: of colonial writings, 11, 12, 14, 139, 145n. 16

Cantú, Anne Lombardi, 169n. 8
Capitulaciones de Santa Fe, 113
Carbia, Rómulo, 157n. 6
Carlos I, King. *See* Charles I, King
Carmen de Patagones, 57, 72, 74, 75, 76, 79
carnivalesque, 64, 74, 147n. 25
Carpentier, Alejo: *El arpa y la sombra,* 20, 23, 112, 114, 115–16, 119, 123, 124–25, 138, 146n. 24, 147n. 25, 148n. 34, 164–65n. 5; *Los pasos perdidos,* 147n. 27
Carrera-Stampa, Manuel, 163n. 48
Carrión, Benjamin: *Atahualpa,* 147n. 27
Casas, Bartolomé de las, 12, 43, 53, 122, 124, 129, 161n. 16; *Brevísima relación de la destrucción de las Indias,* 13, 85–86, 157n. 6, 158nn. 7 and 8, 164n. 3; *Historias de las Indias,* 13, 118, 121, 134, 166n. 7
Castile, 42, 74
Castillo Bautista, Victor: *Nuño de Guzmán o la espada de Dios: Una obra en un acto,* 169n. 10
Castillo Maldonado, Alonso del, 42
Cazonci, 107, 157n. 5, 158n. 7, 159n. 8
Catholic Church, 25, 73, 74, 80, 81, 82, 91, 93, 130. *See also* Christianity
Cella, Susana Beatriz, 148n. 31
Cempoala, 39, *40*
censorship, 45, 47–48, 57, 73, 82, 154n. 50
Cervantes, Miguel de: *Don Quixote,* 46–47, 61, 69, 114–18, 121, 123–25, 138; *Los trabajos de Persiles y Sigismunda,* 113
Champotón, 89
Chanady, Amaryll, 148n. 31, 158n. 6
Charles I, King (Charles V of Germany), 28, 31, 38, 42, 48, 49, 57, 58, 59, 61, 63, 64, 67, 71, 85, 97, 101, 107, 152n. 12, 156n. 3
Chibán, Alicia, 164n. 5
Chipman, Donald E., 159n. 8, 163n. 54
Chorba, Carrie, 95, 108, 148n. 29
Christianity, 12, 22, 32, 35, 37, 47, 73, 74, 80, 91, 93, 100–101, 106, 111, 130, 133, 150n. 28, 169n. 10. *See also* Catholic Church

chronicles: of the Indies, Spanish, 12–18, 22, 24, 27, 42, 55, 58, 60, 61, 62, 63, 69, 71, 88, 90, 95, 96, 97, 98, 99, 103, 138–40, 142, 143n. 2, 147n. 27
Cieza, Pedro de, 52
Ciudad de los Césares, 21, 57, 72, 73, 75, 76, 154–55n. 53
class, social, 63–64, 71, 85, 88–89, 93
Colombia, 146n. 24
Colomina-Garrigós, Lola, 26
colonialism/colonization, 12, 19, 20, 21, 26, 44, 45, 46, 47, 52, 53–54, 56, 57, 72, 73, 76, 77, 81–82, 85–87, 107, 112, 115, 133, 144n. 11, 159n. 8. *See also* imperialism
Columbus, Christopher, 11, 12, 16, 18, 19, 21–22, 43, 57, 71, 96, 99–100, 103–4, 106, 109, 111–37, 139, 140, 144n. 16, 147n. 25, 164n. 4, 166n. 7; *Diario de a bordo,* 13, 16, 42, 68–69, 77, 113, 115, 128–31, 133, 144n. 10, 147n. 27, 160–61n. 16, 166n. 7; *Libro copiador,* 133, 167n. 53; *Libro de las profecías,* 127–28; *Prima carta de América,* 166n. 7; *Relación del tercer viaje,* 134, 135; Torres Memorandum, 133
Columbus, Ferdinand: *Vida del Almirante,* 118
Conquistadores en Yucatán: La descripción de Gonzalo Guerrero, 161n. 16
conquistadors, 13, 57, 72, 84, 98–99, 101, 139, 140, 157n. 5, 159n. 8; canonical writings and hegemonic voices of, 11, 12, 13, 22; recent revisionings and deconstruction of, 19–22, 24, 84; within a hierarchy of power, 48–49. *See also* individual names
convent literature, 27, 149n. 12
conversos/Jews, 25, 61, 63, 124, 126
Cook, Noble David, 158n. 6
Cordones-Cook, Juana María, 62, 153n. 14
Cornejo-Parriego, Rosalía, 114, 116
Corona Ibarra, Alfredo, 107
Cortés, Hernán, 12, 20, 21, 24, 25–33, *33, 34,* 35–39, 41, 48, 49, 52, 54, 56, 85–88, 90, 94, 96, 97, 98, 103–8, 139, 140, 141, 150n. 28, 156–57n. 3, 157n. 5, 159n. 8, 160–61n. 16; *Cartas de relación,* 11, 13, 20, 24–32, 37, 38, 39, 41, 42, 43, 54, 84,

Cortés, Hernán (*continued*)
  95, 103, 150nn. 16 and 22; *Primera relación (Carta de Vera Cruz)*, 28, 30; *Segunda relación*, 27, 28, 30, 104; *Tercera relación*, 29, 30; *Cuarta relación*, 29, 30; *Quinta relación*, 29, 30
Cortés, Martín, 86
Coyoacán, 29
Crosthwaite, Luis Humberto: *La luna siempre será un amor difícil*, 146n. 24
Cruz, Sor Juana Inés de la, 141
Cuauhtémoc, 29, 141
Cuba, 28, 29, 42, 104, 146n. 24
Cypess, Sandra Messinger, 169n. 8

da Gama, Vasco, 21, 57, 77–78
Dante Alighieri: *Divine Comedy*, 79
Darío, Rubén: "Marcha triunfal," 101
Davidson, John E., 158n. 6
Dávila, Alonso, 89
Day, Stuart Alexander, 169n. 10
de Arancibia, Blanca, 165n. 5
Debroise, Olivier: *Crónica de las destrucciones*, 146n. 24
de Certeau, Michel, 135
de Fuggle, Sonia Rose, 165n. 5
De Grandis, Rita, 148n. 31
Delgado Gómez, Angel, 29, 30, 150nn. 16 and 22
del Paso, Fernando: *Noticias del Imperio*, 138, 147n. 25
Díaz del Castillo, Bernal, 27, 62, 144n. 10; *Historia verdadera de la conquista de la Nueva España*, 13, 24, 30, 35, 42, 64, 65, 67, 68, 72–73, 89, 95
Díaz de Solís, Juan, 74–75, 77, 144n. 11
Díaz-Quiñones, Arcadio, 148n. 31
Di Benedetto, Antonio: *Zama*, 74, 144n. 11
dictatorship, 20, 45, 47, 48, 54, 71, 82, 117, 154n. 50
Dirty War, 20, 47, 82, 84, 139
Don Juan, 48
Dorado, El, 21, 57, 72, 144n. 11, 158n. 6
Dorantes, Andrés, 42
dos Santos, Pereira: *Como era gostoso o meu frances*, 141

Echevarría, Nicolás: *Cabeza de Vaca*, 141, 169n. 11

Emery, Amy Fass, 148n. 31
epistolary writing, 21, 29, 57, 72, 73, 134
Erauso, Catalina de, 141
Espinosa, Germán: *La tejedora de coronas*, 147n. 25
Estevanico, 42
ethnography, 132
Ezquerro, Milagros, 114

Falkland Islands, 80–81
Fama, Antonio, 164n. 5
Ferdinand, King, 77, 124, 125, 133, 134, 166n. 7
Fernández-Carracedo, Argelia, 165n. 5
Fernández de Lizardi, Joaquín: *El periquillo sarniento*, 62
Fernández de Oviedo, Gonzalo, 12, 122, 151n. 58; *Historia general y natural de las Indias*, 13, 24, 42, 50, 54
Filer, Malva, 60, 61, 69, 152–53n. 14, 165n. 5
film, 140, 141, 148n. 29, 158n. 6, 164n. 3, 168n. 7, 169n. 11
Flint, Valerie I. J., 167n. 53
Floeck, Wilfried, 169n. 11
Florida, 42, 49
Forgues, Roland, 165n. 5
Franciscans, 156n. 3, 161n. 16
Franco, Jean, 62
Frisch, Mark, 149n. 1
Fuentes, Carlos, 144–45n. 16; *Cristóbal Nonato*, 146n. 24; *El naranjo, o los círculos del tiempo*, 95; *Terra Nostra*, 138; *Todos los gatos son pardos*, 169n. 8
Funes, Jorge Ernesto: *Una lanza por Lope de Aguirre*, 147n. 29
Fusco, Coco, 140, 168n. 6

Galeano, Eduardo: *Memorias del fuego*, 60
Galster, Ingrid, 158n. 6
Galván, Manuel de Jesús: *Enriquillo*, 89, 143n. 7
Gamboa, Pedro de, 76, 77
García Icazbalceta, Joaquín, 158–59n. 8
García Márquez, Gabriel, 58–59; *Cien años de soledad*, 154n. 49; "Fantasía y creación artística en América Latina y el Caribe," 15; *El general en su laberinto*, 138

García Ronda, Angel, 26
Garcilaso de la Vega, El Inca, 16, 122; *Cometarios reales,* 16, 41, 42, 43, 61, 103, 147n. 27
Garibay K., Angel María, 36
Garramuño, Florencia, 148n. 31, 152n. 13
Genette, Gérard, 117
genocide, 22, 33, 35, 37, 39, 87, 111–12, 119
Gerbi, Antonello, 152n. 5
Gerli, E. Michael, 128
Gnutzmann, Rita, 148n. 31
gold, 96, 100, 101, 125, 129, 131, 133, 134, 140
Golden Age, 20, 153n. 14
Gollnick, Brian, 148n. 31
Gómez de Avellaneda, Gertrudis: *Guatimozín,* 143n. 7
Gómez Muriel, Emilio: *La monja alférez,* 141
Gómez Peña, Guillermo, 140, 168n. 6
González Barcia, Andres, 30
González Echeverría, Roberto, 27, 146n. 22, 148n. 29, 165n. 5
González Pérez, Aníbal, 12, 18, 19, 143n. 7, 147n. 27, 165n. 5
Gordon, Richard Allen, 141, 169n. 11
Goya, Francisco, 147n. 25
Graetzer, Margarita, 147n. 27, 165n. 5
Great Britain, 80, 81
Guadalupe, Virgin of, 106
Guamán Poma de Ayala, Felipe: *Nueva corónica y buen gobierno,* 11, 16
Guatemala, 29
Guerrero, Gonzalo, 21, 84, 85, 86–95, 108–9, 140, 156n. 2, 160–61n. 16, 168n. 8; *Memorias,* 160–61n. 16
Guzmán, Fernando de, 158n. 6
Guzmán, Nuño de, 21, 84, 85, 86, 96–109, 156–57n. 3, 157nn. 4, 5, and 6, 158–59n. 8, 169n. 10; *Memorias,* 97, 163n. 48

hagiography, 42, 123
Hamed, Amir, 147n. 29
Henderson, Walter Brooks Drayton: *The New Argonautica,* 151n. 45
Herzog, Warner: *Aguirre, the Wrath of God,* 158n. 6

Hispaniola, 42, 85, 88, 96, 120, 133
history/historiography, 12–14, 16–21, 22, 24, 25, 26, 30, 31, 32, 35, 38, 39, 41, 43, 45–47, 49–54, 56, 60, 61, 62, 63, 64, 67–68, 71, 72–73, 74, 75, 76, 77, 79, 81, 82, 84, 87, 90, 96–97, 99, 104, 107, 108, 138–42, 143n. 2, 143–44n. 10, 145nn. 16 and 17, 145–46n. 19, 147n. 25, 153n. 14, 155nn. 53 and 58, 159n. 8; and interpretations of Columbus, 21–22, 112–37, 139, 140
Holloway, Thomas H., 158n. 6
Honduras (Hibueras), 29, 85
homosexuality, 97
honor, 13
Housková, Anna, 148n. 29
Huacuja, Mario: *El viaje más largo,* 59, 146n. 24
humanism, 13
Hutcheon, Linda, 62

Ibsen, Kristine, 149n. 12
Iglesia, Ramón, 30
Inquisition, 44, 47, 48, 71, 85, 154n. 50
imperialism, 18, 19, 46, 48, 49, 51, 52, 53, 54, 61, 62, 157n. 6. *See also* colonialism/colonization
Indies. *See* West Indies
Isabella, Queen, 77, 123, 125, 126, 133, 134, 157n. 4, 166n. 7
Islas Malvinas. *See* Falkland Islands
Ix Chel Can, 21, 86, 89, 90, 108
Ix Mo, 86, 89
Ixtlixóchitl, 35

Jabes, Edmond: *El libro de las preguntas,* 113
Jamaica, 85, 88
Jara, René, 14–15
Jerez de la Frontera, 43
Jitrik, Noé, 16
Juan-Navarro, Santiago, 148n. 29, 169n. 11
Juana, Queen, 38
Juderías, Julián, 157n. 6

Kadir, Djelal, 146n. 22
Keen, Benjamin, 87
Klor de Alva, Jorge, 91, 161n. 23
Knight, Alan, 162n. 24

Koepnick, Lutz P., 158n. 6
Kohut, Karl, 148n. 29
Krippner-Martínez, James, 107, 157nn. 4 and 5, 158–59n. 8

language, 15, 19, 47–48, 64, 126, 129, 132, 133
Lazarillo de Tormes, 60, 152n. 13
Lefere, Robin, 114
Leñero, Vicente: *La noche de Hernán Cortes*, 24, 141, 169n. 10
León Portilla, Miguel de: *Vision de los venicidos*, 36
Lewis, Bart L., 147n. 29, 158n. 6
Lezama Lima, José, 144n. 11
Libertella, Héctor: "La historia de historias de Antonio Pigafetta," 59
Lima, 80
Liss, Peggy K., 156n. 3
Loca, Juana la, 123, 133
López, Kimberle S., 19, 25, 97, 144n. 11, 146n. 24, 147n. 28, 148n. 31, 163nn. 54 and 66
López, Vicente Fidel: *La novia del hereje*, 143n. 7
López de Gómara, Francisco, 12, 36, 62, 122; *Historia de la conquista de México*, 13, 24, 31, 159n. 8
López Pérez, José, 160n. 16
López-Portillo y Weber, José, 159n. 8
Luján Campos, María Luisa, 154n. 51

MacNutt, F. A., 30
Magaña, Sergio: *Moctezuma II*, 168–69n. 8
Magellan, Ferdinand, 20, 56, 57–58, 59, 60, 61, 62, 64, 66, 69, 70, 71, 72, 75, 77, 139, 147n. 25, 152n. 12, 153n. 14
Malinche, La, 21, 49, 86–88, 90, 94, 108, 140, 161n. 16, 169n. 8
Maltby, William S., 157n. 6
Manrique, Jorge: *Coplas*, 131
Manzano Manzano, Juan Francisco, 116
Mariátegui, José Carlos, 144n. 11
Marinone, Mónica, 166n. 13
Mariscal, George, 63
Márquez Villanueva, Francisco, 61
Martín del Campo, Marisol: *Amor y conquista: La novela de Malinalli mal llamada la Malinche*, 146n. 24

Martínez, Herminio: career of, 84, 111; and examination of ideological shaping of history, 21, 86, 87, 97, 107–9; and parody of Columbus's writings that contrasts with official historiography, 22, 112, 113, 125–37.
—Works: *Diario maldito de Nuño de Guzmán*, 21, 84, 86, 87, 95–109, 146n. 24, 147n. 28, 163n. 54; *La eternidad no tiene mirasoles*, 84; *Hombres de temporal*, 84; *Invasores del paraíso*, 84, 146n. 24; *La jaula del tordo*, 84; *Las puertas del mundo: Una autobiografía hipócrita del Almirante*, 21–22, 84, 109, 111, 112, 125–37, 140, 146n. 24; *El regreso*, 59, 84, 146n. 24; *Ruido de hombres*, 84
Martínez, José Luis, 24, 150n. 28
Martyr of Anglería, Peter, 62, 122; *Decades*, 58, 59, 66, 67, 152n. 5
Mauro, Humberto: *Descobrimento do Brasil*, 141
Maya, 85, 88, 89, 91, 92, 94, 95, 108, 160–61n. 16
May Revolution of 1810, 72
McKnight, Kathryn Joy, 27, 149n. 12
Medina, Manuel F., 25, 90, 161n. 18
Meléndez, Mariselle, 17, 145n. 16
Meléndez, Priscilla, 169n. 10
Mendoza, Antonio, 157n. 4
Mendoza, Pedro de, 41, 76
Menéndez y Pelayo, Marcelino, 30
Menton, Seymour, 26, 89, 96, 114, 146–47n. 25, 148n. 29, 165n. 5
Merrim, Stephanie, 27, 30
mestizaje, 17, 19, 21, 82, 84, 86–87, 88, 90–91, 93, 95, 108–9, 160–61n. 16, 161n. 23, 162nn. 24 and 25
metafiction, 62, 71, 142, 147n. 25, 155n. 58
Meuser-Blincow, Frances, 11, 22
Mexican Revolution, 91, 162n. 24
Mexico, 18, 25, 35, 38, 39, 42, 48, 49, 72, 96, 100, 138, 146n. 24, 157nn. 4 and 5, 159n. 8, 168–69n. 8, 169n. 10; contemporary identity and reality of, 20, 24, 90–91, 95, 106–9, 141, 142, 162nn. 24 and 25; foundational myths and *mestizaje* of, 19, 21, 24, 25, 28–29, 30, 32, 37–39, 41, 54, 82, 84–95, 104, 107–9,

139, 141, 142, 160–61n. 16, 162nn. 24 and 25
Mexico City, 32, 39, 87, 96, 97, 98, 102, 105, 106, 108, 156n. 3, 157n. 4, 160n. 16
Meza, Otilia: *Gonzalo Guerrero,* 146n. 24, 160–61n. 16
Michelotti-Cristóbal, Graciela, 147n. 29, 165n. 5
Michoacán, 107, 158n. 7, 169n. 10
Mignolo, Walter, 12, 16, 143n. 2, 145n. 16
Miller, Marilyn Grace, 161n. 23
Miranda, Francisco de, 147n. 25
missions, Jesuit, 78
Moctezuma, 28, 35, *36,* 38, 49, 141
modernity, 26
Molloy, Sylvia, 26–27
Moluccas Islands, 57, 64
Mondragón, Amelia, 165n. 5
Montejo, Francisco de, 89, 160n. 16
Monteleone, Jorge, 148n. 31
Mora Catlett, Juan: *Retorno a Aztlán,* 141
Moreno Turner, Fernando, 152n. 12, 153n. 14, 154n. 45, 154–55n. 53, 155n. 58
Moretti, Gabriella, 127
Morison, Samuel Eliot, 111–12
Morla, Francisco de, 105
Morley, William F. E., 57
Mújica Laínez, Manuel: *Misterioso Buenos Aires,* 154–55n. 53
Müller-Bergh, Klaus, 165n. 5
Myers, Kathleen Ann, 27, 149n. 12

Na Chan Can, 89
Nader, Helen, 166n. 7
Narváez, Pánfilo de, 28, 41, 42, 49
national identity, 11, 13, 24, 25, 37, 54, 91, 95, 104, 107, 108, 109, 139, 141, 162n. 25
New Historicism, 145–46n. 19
New World: gendering of, 135–36; representation of through language, 15, 126, 129, 132, 133; varying representations of discovery and conquest of, 11–13, 16–21, 23, 25, 36–37, 56, 138–42, 146n. 24; as utopia/dystopia, 22, 57, 72, 76–79, 81–83, 100, 101, 135–36, 163nn. 54 and 58. *See also* colonialism/colonization; imperialism
Nicaragua, 146n. 24
Nigro, Kirsten, 169n. 10
Nolla, Olga: *El castillo de la memoria,* 146n. 24
novel: historical, 18–19, 22, 25, 90, 112, 116, 122, 125, 146–47n. 25, 148n. 29; New Historical, 25, 62, 89, 114, 146n. 24, 147n. 25
Novo, Salvador: *Cuauhtémoc,* 169n. 8

O'Gorman, Edmundo, 120, 145n. 17, 152n. 5
Olid, Cristóbal de, 29
Orellana, Francisco de, 48
Orozco, José Clemente: *Cortés and Malinche,* 87
Ortega, José, 114
Ortega, Julio, 148n. 29
Otero Silva, Miguel: *Lope de Aguirre, príncipe de la libertad,* 146n. 24, 147n. 29
otherness, 16, 88, 135, 140
Oviedo, José Miguel, 146n. 22

Pamp de Valle Arce, Diane, 153n. 18
Panama (Darién), 85
Panger, Daniel: *Black Ulysses,* 151n. 45
Pánuco, 85, 96, 97, 98, 101, 102, 158n. 7, 159n. 8, 163n. 54
Paraguay, 18, 19, 46, 53, 78, 146n. 24
Parish, Helen Rand: *Estebanico,* 151n. 45
Parra, Max, 165n. 5
Partida, Eugenio: *La ballesta de Dios,* 146n. 24
Pastor, Beatriz, 16, 55, 163n. 58
Patagonia, 20, 21, 57, 58, 79, 139
Paternain, Alejandro: *Crónica del descubrimiento,* 146n. 24
Pautz, Patrick Charles, 150–51n. 43
Payró, Roberto J.: *El mar dulce,* 144n. 11; *Los teseros del Rey Blanco, Por qué no fue descubierta la maravillosa Ciudad de los Césares,* 154–55n. 53
Paz, Octavio, 87, 88; *El laberinto de la soledad,* 109
Pérez de la Torre, Diego, 157n. 4
performativity. *See* theatricality

Perkowska-Alvarez, Magdalena, 152–53n. 14
Peru, 18, 146n. 24, 158n. 6
Philippines, 57, 75
Phillip II, King, 20, 59, 61, 64, 71, 147n. 25
picaresque, 31, 42, 60–62, 64–65, 66, 71, 152nn. 12 and 14, 153n. 15
Picón Salas, Mariano, 144n. 11
Pigafetta, Antonio, 152n. 5; *Relación del primer viaje en torno del mundo,* 58–59, 60, 66, 67
Piloto Desconocido, 114, 115, 116, 119–21, 123, 125, 166–67n. 23
Pites, Silvia, 149n. 1
Pius IX, Pope (Giovanni Mastei), 115
Pizarro, Ana, 17
Pizarro, Francisco, 48
Plotnik, Viviana, 60, 62, 69, 147n. 29, 148n. 31, 153n. 14, 165n. 5
Ponce de León, Juan, 48–48
Pons, María Cristina, 147n. 25, 148n. 31
Porrata, Francisco Eduardo, 148n. 29, 165n. 5
Portilla, Miguel León, 161n. 21
positivism, 14, 145n. 17
Posse, Abel, career of, 24, 149n. 1; and historical parallels to twentieth-century Latin America, 18, 20, 26, 41, 45–48, 54, 55, 84, 139; and importance of challenging official history, 17–18, 25–26, 43, 45–46, 49–54, 56, 84, 139.
—Works: *La boca del tigre,* 24; *Los bogavantes,* 24; *Los cuadernos de Praga,* 24; *Daimón,* 18, 24, 74, 89–90, 146n. 24, 147n. 29; *Los demonios ocultos,* 24; *El inquietante día de la vida,* 24; *El largo atardecer del caminante,* 18, 19, 20, 23, 24, 25–27, 28, 41, 43–55, 56, 84, 98, 139, 141, 146n. 24, 147n. 28; *Momento de morir,* 24; *La pasión según Eva,* 24; *Los perros del paraíso,* 18, 20, 24, 60, 112, 114, 146n. 24, 147nn. 25 and 27, 148n. 31, 165n. 5; *La reina del Plata,* 24; *El viajero del Agartha,* 24
postcolonialism, 18
postmodernism, 19, 20, 62, 71, 114, 139, 141, 142
Premat, Julio, 148n. 31

Proceso de reorganización nacional, 21, 57, 73, 81, 82
Prochazka, Martin, 148n. 29
providence, 13, 14
Ptolemy, 135
Puerto Rico, 146n. 24
Pulgarin-Cuadrado, Amalia, 165n. 5
Pupo-Walker, Enrique, 16, 42, 55, 146n. 22, 150nn. 39 and 43, 151n. 45
Purhépecha Indians, 85

Querandí Indians, 75, 76
Quincentennial, Columbian, 11, 12, 21, 22, 71, 111, 112, 126, 130, 140, 144n. 16, 147n. 25, 164n. 3, 168 nn. 5–8
Quintana, María Esther, 148n. 29, 154nn. 45 and 58

Rabasa, José, 53, 145n. 17
Ramos Nadal, Consuelo, 147n. 29, 158n. 6
Rascón Banda, Hugo: *La Malinche,* 141, 169n. 10
rationalism, 14, 16
Reati, Fernando, 74, 148n. 29, 165n. 5
Reckley, Alice, 90
refranes, 98, 127, 131–32
relación de servicio, 13, 19, 20, 24, 27, 29–30, 31, 41, 43, 44, 56, 57, 60, 61, 62, 65–67, 71, 82, 84, 87, 97–98, 101
Renaissance, 13, 14, 60, 61, 62, 63, 82, 119
Representación de la salida de 400 familias, 169n. 10
Restrepo, Luis Fernando, 169n. 11
Retrato de Hernán Cortés, 32, 34
Reyes, Alfonso, 14, 144n. 11
rhetoric, 16, 19, 22, 38, 42, 52, 61, 65, 67, 95, 96–97, 128, 130, 137
Rico Ferrer, José Antonio, 156n. 2
Riera, Gabriel, 148n. 31
River Plate, 19, 20, 21, 41, 53, 56, 57, 60, 72–79, 81, 82, 84, 110, 138, 139, 142, 151n. 1
Roa Bastos, Augusto: career of, 111, 164n. 1; and revision of conventional images of Columbus, 21–22, 112–25, 136–37, 139.
—Works: *Antología personal,* 111; *El baldío,* 111; *Contar un cuento, y otros*

relatos, 111; *Contravida,* 111; *Cuerpo presente, y otros textos,* 111; *El fiscal,* 111; *Hijo de hombre,* 111; *Madama Sui,* 111; *Madera quemada,* 111; *El naranjal ardiente, nocturno paraguayo, 1947-1949,* 111; *Los pies sobre el agua,* 111; *El ruiseñor de la aurora y otras poemas,* 111; *El trueno entre las hojas,* 111; *Vigilia del Almirante,* 19, 21–22, 109, 111, 112–25, 136–37, 139, 146n. 24, 166n. 13; *Yo el supremo,* 111, 117, 138
Robles, Humberto E., 152n. 5
Rodríguez Juliá, Edgardo: *La noche oscura del Niño Avilés,* 18, 146n. 24
Rogelio Alvarez, José, 157n. 4
romances, 98
Romero, Flor: *Malintizín: La princesa regalada,* 146n. 24
Romero, Rolando, 88
Rosoff, Eduardo: *Ave María,* 141
Ross, Kathleen, 16
Rumeu de Armas, Antonio, 167n. 53

Sad Night, 29, 38, 105
Saer, Juan José: *El entenado,* 20, 60, 74, 147n. 28, 148n. 31
Sahagún, Bernardino de, 35
Sale, Kirkpatrick, 112
Salinas de Gotari, Carlos, 162n. 25
San Buenaventura, Fray Joseph de: *Historias de la conquista del Mayab, 1511–1697,* 161n. 16
Sánchez Alonso, B., 27
Sánchez Paso, José, 153n. 18
San Salvador, 130
Santángel, Luis de, 126
Santángel, Raquel de, 130, 131
Santiago, 105
Santiago, Silviano, 82
Sarfati-Arnaud, Monique, 90, 94, 95
Scharlau, Birgit, 16
Schimdel, Ulrich, 76
Schlau, Stacey, 149n. 12
Schumm, Petra, 145n. 16
Seda, Laurietz, 169n. 10
Segura, Manuel Ascencio: *Gonzalo Pizarro,* 143n. 7
Segura de la Frontera, 29
Seneca: *Medea,* 125, 127

Seville, 43, 57
sexuality, 21, 32, 57, 70, 72–80, 81, 87, 97, 130–36, 139
Shaw, Donald L., 148n. 29, 165n. 5
Shohat, Ella, 168n. 5, 168n. 7
Sigüenza y Góngora, Carlos de, 17; *Los infortunios de Alonso Ramírez,* 42
Silva, Hugo: *Pacha Pulai,* 154–55n. 53
Sklodowska, Elzbieta, 148n. 29, 165n. 5
Smith, Sara Ann, 148nn. 29 and 31
Solares, Ignacio: *Nen, la inútil,* 95, 146n. 24
Sommer, Doris, 143–44n. 10
Souza, Raymond, 148n. 29, 165n. 5
Spain: and the Falkland Islands, 80–81; Latin American independence from, 13, 79, 87. *See also* black legend; colonialism/colonization; imperialism
Staden, Hans, 141
Stam, Robert, 168nn. 5 and 7
Stavans, Ilan, 164n. 4
Stolley, Karen, 165n. 5
Summerhill, Stephen J., 164n. 3, 168n. 5

Tarahumara Indians, 46
Taxmal, 89
Taylor, Diana, 168n. 6
Teatro de los Andes, 168n. 8
Tenochtitlán, 28, 29, 104, 160n. 16, 169n. 10
Tenuxtitán, 29
Terrell, John Upton: *Journey into Darkness,* 151n. 45
testimonial narrative, 19, 44–45, 84, 129, 140
Texcoco, 35
Texmixtitán, 29
theater, 14, 140–41, 168–69n. 8, 169n. 10
theatricality, 46, 48–49, 51–52, 67, 70, 71, 141
Thuesen, Evelina Romano, 148n. 31
Tierra del Fuego, 76
time, 18, 160n. 16
Tineo, Gabriela, 165n. 5
Tlatelolco, massacre at, 108
Tlaxcala, 29, 169n. 10
Todorov, Tzvetan, 144n. 16
Toth, Eva, 165n. 5
Totonaca Indians, 39

Toussaint, Manuel, 159n. 8
transculturation, 19
travel writing, 42, 86, 87, 96, 97, 98, 107, 109
Tulio Altan, Carlos: *Colón,* 168n. 8

United Kingdom. *See* Great Britian
United States, 18, 41, 42, 140
Urbina, José Leandro, 114, 147n. 29
Ureña, Pedro Henríquez, 144n. 11
Ursúa, Pedro de, 158n. 6
Uruguay, 19, 20, 57, 60, 71, 84, 146n. 24, 154n. 50
Usable González, Antonio, 148n. 29
Usigli, Rodolfo: *Corona de fuego,* 169n. 8
Uslar Pietri, Arturo: *El camino de El Dorado,* 144n. 11, 147n. 29

Valdés, Mario J., 146n. 22
Valdivia, Pedro de, 144n. 10
Valero Covarrubias, Alicia, 165n. 5
Valladolid, 22, 41
Valle Inclan, Ramón, 46–48; *Luces de bohemia,* 78; *Sonatas,* 47–48; *Tirano banderas,* 48
van der Straet, Jan: *America,* 135
Vargas Llosa, Mario: *La guerra del fin del mundo,* 147n. 25
Vaz de Caminha, Pero, 141
Vega, Lope de: *El mundo nuevo,* 113
Velasco, Juan, 168n. 6
Velázquez, Diego, 28, 29, 104
Venezuela, 135, 146n. 24, 158n. 6
Vera Cruz, 28, 102
Verani, Hugo, 62, 153n. 14
Verástique, Bernardino, 156–57n. 3

Verdesio, Gustavo, 17, 145n. 16, 148–49n. 31, 151n. 1
Vespucci, Amerigo, 135
Vich, Cynthia, 154nn. 45 and 49
Villa Roiz, Carlos: *Gonzalo Guerrero,* 146n. 24, 160–61n. 16
Villegas, Jaun, 141

Warren, J. Benedict, 159n. 8
Wasserman, Jacob, 114
Weldt-Basson, Helene Carol, 117
West Indies, 99, 103, 113, 117, 120, 121, 124, 127, 129, 130, 133, 137
White, Hayden, 25
Williams, John Alexander, 164n. 3, 168n. 5
women, 27, 68, 75, 77–78, 98, 126, 133–36, 146n. 24

Xicoténcatl, 143n. 7
Ximena, José: *La muerte de Moctezuma,* 35, *36*

Young, Richard A., 25, 169n. 11
Young, Robert, 19
Young, Theodore Robert, 148n. 29
Yucatán Peninsula, 28, 85, 88–89, 90, 92, 96, 160n. 16

Zamora, Margarita, 16, 129, 134, 135, 166n. 7
Zlotchew, Clark, 82, 154n. 52
Zumárraga, Juan de, 85, 86, 106, 156n. 3, 159n. 8
Zúñiga, Francesillo de, 61, 63; *Crónica burlesca del emperador Carlos V,* 61, 63, 64, 82, 153n. 18